Angels In My Life

A biographical narrative of an ordinary man's spiritual and angel communications.

By Victor K. Hosler
With Claricé, Archie, and others!

© 2002 by Victor K. Hosler. All rights reserved.

No part of this book may be reproduced, stored in a retrieval system, or transmitted by any means, electronic, mechanical, photocopying, recording, or otherwise, without written permission from the author.

ISBN: 1-4033-5512-6 (e-book)
ISBN: 1-4033-5513-4 (Paperback)
ISBN: 1-4033-5514-2 (Dustjacket)

Library of Congress Control Number: 2002095172

This book is printed on acid free paper.

Printed in the United States of America
Bloomington, IN

1stBooks - rev. 12/12/02

As you will read, Claricé was a fine artist and each of her paintings had a story about them and often within them. This painting was completed before we met, and she did have a story about it that she often told as we toured the Art Show circuit from early 1996 through the spring of 1998. As I study my wife's painting now and think about this biographical narrative detailing my experiences since her death, I wonder now if the painting was a premonition of what was to come in our lives.

Note the solitary figure under the tree of life, contemplating what is before him. This was my immediate reaction following the loss of her. I thought, "What am I going to do with the rest of my life?"

At the focal point above is the "Angel of the Night." With the fingertip moon in one hand and the stars in her other hand and trailing behind her, she's bringing in the heavens of God's universe. In her first spiritual communication with me she said I was to develop my spirituality and that she would now be my Guardian Angel. In closing one of her visits she said, "I will guide you, guide you… guide you…" and when the angel communications began a little later, I found that I have two angel guides, Archie, and Jules who are always with me. On the left side of the painting, sliding down the ribbon of musical notes there are two cherub angels coming into my life.

Was this a premonition, a coincident or one of life's synchronicities that are only discovered long after the experience has come about?

Dedicated to the memory of Claricé's life on earth and celebrating her spiritual afterlife.

Table of Contents

Introduction: Claricé 1
Part One: How An Ordinary Man Began To Receive Spiritual And Angelic
Communications 7
    Chapter One: How I Came To Believe 9
    Chapter Two: More About My Angels 27
    Chapter Three: Spiritual Communications With Claricé, The First Three Visits 37
    Chapter Four: A Spiritual Communication With Dick, My Teen Age Friend and
    Buddy 55
    Chapter Five: Auto Writing Awareness 65
    Chapter Six: Claricé's Return 67
    Chapter Seven: A Spiritual Communication With Sally 77
    Chapter Eight: Spiritual Communications With Barry and John. 95
    Epilogue Part One: Questioning Myself and My Motives 105
Part Two: The Angels Begin To Speak 109
    Chapter Nine: Archie Arrives To Take My Pain Away 111
    Chapter Ten: Archie Defines The Truth 121
    Chapter Eleven: Archie's Insight on Prosperity vs. Abundance 133
    Chapter Twelve: Archie Talks About God 143
    Chapter Thirteen: Angels, God and the Ordinary Man 155
    Chapter Fourteen: More About Angels 167
    Chapter Fifteen: How The World Works, According To Archie 175
    Chapter Sixteen: Changing Your Perception Can Change Your Life 189
    Chapter Seventeen: Reincarnation vs. Only Living Once 203
    Chapter Eighteen: Bits and Pieces 215
        Dancing Candles or Dance of Love 215
        Communicating With The Other Side 219
        Responsibility for Grief, Loss And Evil 224
        Writing It Down 228
        How to Communicate With Your Angels 232
    Epilogue Part Two: The Acceptance of Angels in My Life 237
Part Three: "Conversations with God," Spiritual and Angel Communications - How
They Have Enhanced My Life 241
    Chapter Nineteen: "Conversations with God", *It's Impact On My Life* 243
    Chapter Twenty: Sammy and Synchronicities 261
    Chapter Twenty-one: My Purpose For Being 271
    Chapter Twenty-Two: After-Death Experiences 279
    Chapter Twenty-Three: Archie's Answers To Friend's Questions 293
    Chapter Twenty-Four: Healing And A Return to Joy 303
    Epilogue: Final Thoughts And Clarification 323
Appendix: Author's Note and Bibliography 329

Author's Note:

This manuscript shows examples of spiritual communications between myself, Victor the writer with my late-wife Claricé and others. Several months later, communications with angels began, with Archie, my dominant angel guide, Jules my mentoring angel, and other walk-in angels. These experiences began happening for me on the night of 5 January 2000. Much of the content is "auto writing" which just flows in and out of my mind and will be of a somewhat personal nature. It is presented in a dialogue format and will show examples of what it can be for a reader's communication with his or her own angels and possibly spiritual communications with loved ones who have crossed over.

The communications take place in the "higher self" of my mind and I believe the process is available to all who acknowledge our God, as a supreme being. It is only necessary for you to ask for them, have faith, believe and listen.

In all cases, the content is strictly of my mind and/or resulting from my communications of a spiritual nature and not intended to portray a "universal truth" regarding any of the subjects discussed. As to the truth, it is mine, and my truth and belief system alone. It is being presented so that you, the reader may be able to relate the content to your own personal experiences and belief system and thereby aid you in discovering your own truth if it has not already been realized.

Acknowledgements, Thanks and Appreciation

First to God and His angel messengers and my lovely wife Claricé who never met anyone she didn't love and was such a strong spirit she found the way to contact me spiritually, put me on this wonderful journey and created me to have a personal relationship with God, the Creator of all that is.

Secondly, none of this would have happened without Shirley Anderson in my life for the past 38 years as an associate and loving friend. Shirley, a *Life Coach,* and my editor, has been "coaching" and encouraging my writing for about 25 years. She has edited my work and kept me honest.

To my four children: Kim, Ron, David and Vicki-jean, their mates and grandchildren who have always put up with their dad's adventures and misadventures, and to their mother Jean Miller, my first wife who remains a good friend and had become a dear friend of Claricé's. To Samuel Villegas, his wife Erika, son Henry and daughter Caika-Claricé who brought joy into my home and my life, and named they're baby daughter in my wife's memory and honor.

To the readers of both the *Angels In My Life* and *LifeClouds* manuscripts who have found my errors and given me guidance in their responses: Shirley, Bob Silverstein, Kathy Hosler, Cathy Hamel, Kim Lauer, Colette Jaccard, Rev. Alan Rowbotham, of the First Unity Church of St. Petersburg, Rich Corson, Will Shephard, Jean Williams and Martin, and Rev. Donald Richards.

I would also like to thank Neale Donald Walsch, Author of *Conversations with God.* His book made it all happen for me. To Jane Friend, facilitator of the Tampa CWG discussion group and my friends who have inspired me and given encouragement.

To authors Trudy Griswold and Barbara Marks of the *Angelspeake* series that brought me to *my angels* and all the authors in the bibliography who have shown me that my experiences have been shared by others, which strengthened my belief in my work.

Lastly my thanks also to Sande Gaston, Angie and Loren Hutchinson, of the web site http://Spirit-Works.net who added the Angels Communications section for me and encouraged my writing by accepting chapters of *Angels In My* life for short stories.

And, all the others who have accepted my experiences and encouraged me onward; as well, to those who have doubted my experiences — which encouraged me to persevere even more – in my research to find and discover my own truth.

Introduction

Claricé

My wife, Claricé, (pronounced Clar-i-cee) was a Brazilian native, of Kamaiura Indian heritage from the rain forest in the northeast quadrant of Brazil. She lived in the rainforest village for much of the first six years of her life, and following her mother's death, was raised in a Catholic orphanage in Rio de Janeiro until she was 16, became pregnant with her son, Marcel.

Following this, she and her son's father, Tanaka who was of Japanese heritage married. During her pregnancy and following Claricé finished high-school and began her career in art by becoming a helper in various local art studios... a cartographer, the studio of a political cartoon satirist and eventually the graphics department of TV Globo, Brazil's National Television Network. At TV Globo she entered a company sponsored college program. She first received a degree in Fine Art, and then her employer encouraged her to continue school for another year and to get a degree in journalism. Shortly after finishing school, Claricé and Marcel was involved in an automobile accident with a large truck. Her son was killed and Claricé received a life troubling back injury.

The devastating loss ended a marriage that had become troubled and to assist her personal healing she accepted an offer to become a Foreign Correspondent covering the Arts and Humanities for TV Globo. She moved to London where she lived for about 12 years. Her territory was North Africa, Western Europe and the British Isles. In the late 1970's walking the streets of London with her arms loaded with packages, Claricé bumped into a gentleman from New York City. They laughed over the encounter, had coffee together and the man gave her his business card and asked her to call him if she ever got to New York. Surprisingly, about eight months following, Claricé was transferred to New York City. Once there, she thought about Roger, the man she met in London and contacted him. Roger was an engineer for Eastern Airlines. They became reacquainted, developed a relationship and were married, and soon after, her husband was transferred to Miami, Florida. Their marriage was brief; her husband was diagnosed with liver cancer and during his five-year battle with the disease, she went back to her first love, which was painting and went on to become a very fine artist.

Victor K. Hosler

As for me, after a 35-year career in advertising, I was at a crossroads in my life when I had to close my business due to the failure of my primary client, Eastern Air Lines, Inc. Claricé and I met in January of 1990 after I had ended a love relationship and ran a personals' advertisement in the Miami Herald.

Upon meeting her, I quickly became enamored by her fine talent as a watercolor painter and illustrator. In a sense, she was everything I had wanted to be when I had my youthful dreams of becoming an artist. We married in February of 1992 following our courtship and I became her mentor, guiding her and encouraging her to pursue her dream of becoming a notable Fine Artist rather than continuing a career in graphic art and advertising.

With her encouragement, I retired and we sold both our homes in Miami and moved to St. Petersburg, Florida where she began to follow her dream. Off and on, we each took on consulting assignments or free-lance artwork while Claricé further developed her unique style of painting and began to create new works. Our intent was to have enough original artwork for a gallery show and to produce a broad enough volume of "Artist Proof" reproductions to join the national Art Show Circuit.

By early 1996, we were ready to go. There are thousands of shows around the country, so we bought a used motor home and hit the art show circuit. We toured for 2 ½ years, throughout Florida and up the East coast, down through the Mid-West and out to Texas, Oklahoma and Kansas. We sold pricey original watercolors and mixed media originals, and the less costly lithographs and computerized digital reproductions. Sadly, we found out that even though we sold over 1,600 pieces, the competition was too keen and that the words "starving artist" were a truism rather than a cliché.

The highlight of our touring on the art show circuit came on our last trip out West. In the spring of 1998 Claricé was accepted to be in the Oklahoma City Art Show and she said she had, "achieved her dream." At that time, I believe Oklahoma City was the number two art show in the country. They received thousands of applications for the 650 available spaces. When the show was over her work had sold so well that we received our show fees back and were invited to return for the 1999 show without applying or being juried. Having achieved her dream of acceptance, when we returned home, she was very, very happy.

Unfortunately, we were not able to return to Oklahoma City. In late October of 1997, Claricé discovered a small lump in her right breast. She immediately had the prescribed tests and had a lumpectomy before the end of November. It wasn't cancer, we were told then. A short time later when her pain recurred along with what we thought was another mass, her doctors told her not to worry. Before we left for Oklahoma in mid-April of 1998, her doctor again told her not to worry about it. The doctor had said it was scar tissue and that the residual pain was normal. Upon our return she was told the same thing and, unfortunately, we believed her doctors, and she lived with what they *guessed* was scar tissue or a fibrosis and the uncomfortable, ongoing tenderness.

By spring of 1999 her pain increased and I finally had to take her to the emergency room when we could not get an appointment with her new primary doctor. Two months and eight doctors later after receiving several opinions, each with a different diagnosis, with a new primary doctor, on her third visit to him I insisted that they do a CT scan of her entire torso. Following that, on July 10th, 1999 I received a phone call and was told to take her again to emergency and that she was terminal.

Claricé died 40 days later on August 19, 1999.

After my wife's death, and prior to the spiritual communications I had with her, to appease the anger that had been building within me. I began researching her medical history. I was looking for the *"why"* of her death, as I'm sure many do when faced with the questionable loss of a loved one. Like many others, when her illness was suddenly attributed to breast cancer, which by then had metastasized and spread throughout her system, with her death following in only forty-days, I was in shock.

We had done "everything right" and for 20 months were continually told by about a dozen doctors that she did not have breast cancer. Instead, we were spoon-fed false information and hope that came with an array of different, and less life-threatening, medical diagnosis.

As I accumulated all of the medical records from each of her doctors, the hospital medical reports, radiology reports and pathology report and began to read them I finally discovered the truth. *The truth was we were never told the truth*. When I checked the medical terminology at the library and searched the Internet for information, what I found, would certainly have led us in another direction and my wife well may have survived.

I immediately wanted to cry out and tell the world. I wanted to become an advocate for "breast cancer awareness." That is still a goal

I have today. Our doctors, relied too heavily on mammograms when they know that as high as 15% or more, breast cancers are not detected by them; and, the number is even higher when there is thick glandular tissue or fibrosis. These warnings were on the original mammogram reports that we were not privileged to see. We received only the typical post card notice, which stated the report was negative.

In the early tests and stage of her disease, we were only told, "it was suspicious;" Throughout, we were lied to by omission, by not being given copies of the various reports or not sharing with us *exactly* what the reports said. With copies of the actual reports, we could have asked the right questions and had the opportunity to make intelligent decisions. When symptoms returned within three months her physicians would not give her an appointment even though a "close follow-up" I found out, was strongly suggested on her lumpectomy pathology report.

Her next mammogram in September of 1998 and the one eight weeks before her death *were both* reported to be negative when we now know her cancer was spreading. In the later stage with a new primary doctor, *a psychiatrist was suggested*; after a half dozen or more other doctors continued to misdiagnose her, the last doctor's dictation, on the day I *insisted* they do a CT scan of her torso, stated, *"both the husband and wife should seek education and counseling because they are overly concerned about the wife's health."* This is direct quote from the records just 42 days before her death.

In pursuit of answers to the *why* question and after accumulating all of her medical records I came to the ripe conclusion I had to tell "her story." I was ready, but I didn't know where to begin. I wondered how I could write a story of a tragic string of medical errors; of the mistakes and misjudgments, and the problems of the *bottom line* oriented medical groups, insurance companies and the HMO dominated medical community and have it become a story that would make a difference for other women. I was still struggling with how to begin, when the first communication with my late wife came through to me. It was on the 5th of January 2000.

It was after this I realized that "her story" should not just be about her illness, death, and my subsequent grief. But it was also about her unique life, my own struggle with the acceptance of the reality of her death, the aftermath, and the miracle of the spiritual communications that led my own healing, awakening and recovery through developing a relationship with God.

With this in mind, I began my first manuscript titled *"LifeClouds."* Upon completing the early drafts, a couple of close friends who were reading the story for me suggested that I was really telling three different stories in one. They said that the segment about my spiritual and angel communications could stand alone. At the same time, Archie, my dominant angel guide had made him self known to me and told me the same thing. Because the angels were with me daily, I took the advice and began this manuscript with the working title of *"Angels In My Life."*

True clarity of the God Force within began to come through with Claricé's communications to me, and the angel communications that had followed. I began to truly understand that there is a divine order in the universes created by God and that everything has a purpose and meaning. I now believe Claricé's death, was ordained by God, as a part of her life plan to focus attention on "breast cancer awareness" and our medical community problems. Perhaps also, it was for me to find a greater purpose and meaning in my life when we were both at another crossroads in our lives. The more time that passes, the more truth I see in the lessons of life and how the divine order of the universe comes about.

Victor K. Hosler

PART ONE

How An Ordinary Man Began To Receive Spiritual And Angelic Communications

Victor K. Hosler

Chapter One

How I Came To Believe

The direction of this story had its beginning on a pad of lined 8 1/2" x 11" paper. So much was happening so fast that I had to make notes to remind myself of what was taking place in my life. First, the spiritual communications with my late wife, which began on January 5th, 2000 while I was still trying to sort through her medical records and when my intense grief had moved me to the brink of suicide. Then came other spiritual communications to validate the reality of Claricé coming through to me. And then the following August the visits from the angels began.

I now keep a small pad by my side on the night table to make notes of the thoughts and words that come to me in the twilight time before sleep or when I am awakened during the night. If you find this story that will unfold hard to believe, I want to assure you that before it all began, I would have questioned it myself. I have since found that my personal experience of God is the only truth, which would bring me an understanding of the oneness of God.

I was quite the skeptic for most of my life. I have always been very doubtful about those who communicate with the spiritual realm, such as psychics or those who are intuitive and talk of angels. Even in my youth with my strict Christian upbringing, my head was filled with doubts. I could not comprehend how the God — who we were taught was a forgiving God, the Supreme Being that created all that is, who created mankind, the beautiful world we live in and the universe — would want His children to fear Him. Often we were told we would go to hell for eternity for the slightest indiscretion or sin, while at the same time we were also taught He was a loving God. I found organized religion very confusing, beginning in my earliest years. My logical mind developed early and I began to question all things spiritual.

Today, I do not completely understand all that has been happening with me since my wife crossed over, but I have discovered a faith, truth and relationship with God which was previously unknown to me. I accept that I'm sailing through uncharted waters, learning from each wave of doubt that I still encounter.

In December of 1999, at the close of the 20th century as the world was entering the new millennium I was truly "on the edge." My wife Claricé had passed away the preceding August and facing the newyear without her was something I dreaded. I was going through my first traumatic experience of the Holiday season without my wife and didn't feel I had much to live for in the coming year.

It is true that I still have my four children, their spouses and eight grandchildren. We are a tightly knit family who live fairly close to one another, but my intense grief almost outweighed the benefit of their presence in my life. With little more than loneliness and a large empty house to look forward to, I had serious suicidal thoughts. I am sure many do who have lost a loving spouse, a child, a very close relative or friend. I am certain that I survived only because I could not intentionally expose my family to the emotional trauma of another loved one's untimely death, and the extreme pain I was still feeling. It was my newfound faith, through the spiritual experiences, that gave me strength to face a new day and to find a purpose in life for my remaining years.

I had pent up anger over my wife Claricé's death. It was a premature and an *all too common*, unnecessary death from breast cancer due to medical error, mistakes and/or misjudgments.

My spiritual revelations began on the night of the 5th of January 2000. Unable to sleep due to my deep grief, a heavy heart and with tears flowing, I cried out aloud in the quiet of the night, "Oh, how I wish I could talk to you one more time, Claricé."

She answered me. Loud and clear, in my head I heard her speak to me.

"You can, my love; just talk to me."

With that, for reasons unknown to me at the time, a series of spiritual communications with Claricé began. There were five of them in total. They all took place between the 5th and the 17th of January and are in part, detailed in following chapters. The first two spiritual contacts are summarized in the chapter titled "A Communication With Claricé" and the balance follows a little later.

Some of what she related to me from and about the "other side," or what she spoke of relative to the spiritual realm was — and probably here too — will be met with skepticism. In the beginning, I too was in doubt. Initially I believed I was hallucinating or that it was an overactive imagination brought on by my grief and deep-seated desire to hold onto her in whatever way I could. When talking of the experiences to others, I faced doubt and denial by non-believers and devout fundamentalist Christians. I was even specifically told that it could not be, because some of what my late wife said and implied in her communications to me does not agree with "the word" in the "Bible." In some conversations I've had, a few with opposing strict religious disciplines or doctrines, it was even suggested to me that the communications were coming from "evil spirits masquerading" as my late wife. Then I was presented with *out of context* Biblical verses to support their strict Christian doctrine. Thank God I didn't listen. I might have missed this entire experience.

About this, all I can say is, what about God? Is God not omnipotent? Could God *not* create an experience of this nature to bring one of his children closer to him? Each of us is a child of God. If God, our Creator wanted to get the attention of the skeptic I had been, He certainly could not have found a better way to do it. The communications I had made me a believer, and I firmly accept they were in answer to my anguish and prayers. They were to help me find my way and a new purpose for being.

> Archie, my dominant angel guide whom you will later meet, says this, *"All of mankind is entitled to their own belief and you should not let yourself be troubled by differences. For yourself, however, I would say that for any man to disbelieve your experience and suggest that it was evil spirits masquerading as Claricé, let it pass through your mind. For you to accept this you would then have to forego God's miracle of your experience, and in doing so, you would have to give the evil spirits, Satan or the Devil, more power than God. This cannot be so, for God is omnipotent and your God that lives within you would choose to dispel all evil unless you were previously disposed to evil intentions. And there was nothing of evil intent in your spiritual communications with Claricé. Remember, for most of human kind, like you were before her coming, will disbelieve and doubt what they have not personally experienced themselves. For you Victor, the experience is your truth; never question your experience.*

Prior to the first communication and acceptance of the reality of it, I was what may be referred to as a "convenient Christian." Like many... perhaps even most part-time Christians, I accepted as much as I felt *was necessary* for me to believe and get me through the "pearly gates" to heaven, *just in case* it was all true. Upon becoming an adult, I attended religious services mostly on Christmas, Easter and whenever my Mother or someone else could drag me or coax me into going. Although I had tried a dozen or more denominations throughout my life and studied the life of Christ in college, I was never able to accept much of the strict or questionable prevalent dogma and "give my life to God or Christ."

My later, more mature thinking, even when I may have been of a doubtful mind, was that God was to be loved. Why I wondered would a loving God create mankind and then want His children to fear him or the "wrath of God?" Perhaps the fearful stories in the Old Testament had purpose for early mankind, but it just never made sense to me.

Because of my doubts, I grew to believe I had to maintain control of my own life and believed in God in my own way throughout the years. In doing so, I never doubted Christ or the basis for his teaching as the Son of God and His purpose for being. I accepted it as a truth from my early Sunday school learning and never found a reason to question it.

At the same time, however, I could not intellectually accept every word of the Bible as truth. They are 2,000 year-old words, verbally passed on and on, then written and translated over and over in a hundred or more different languages, *from an archaic and limited vocabulary*. Logically, I could not see how they could have been translated as a clear "truth" with the intent of their original meanings as has been attributed to them in the 20th century or today as we are entering the new millennium. Surely the expanded vocabulary in all languages throughout the years has given translators different choices of words. Often translations from language to language, and new editions within a language have been made by groups of historians and theologians for the purpose of maintaining the integrity of Christ's teaching. The choice of a specific word translation, being done *by committee,* would certainly meet with debate and discussion many times over until a *consensus* of agreement in meaning was reached. When you have a committee made up of independent intellectual thinkers, each with different frames of reference and levels of understanding and expression of thought, you would never have 100% consensus of interpretation.

Who has not played the *Whisper Game* in their youth, where a phrase of about a dozen words is passed along from one to another, in

Angels in My Life

a line of eight or ten people? It was always amusing and interesting how the context of the original words changed.

God's children, *human beings* throughout the world, since the beginning of verbal and written communications have been subject to filtering all data received through their own personal intellect, frames of reference and external influences in making translations as mankind is today. Would a *Whisper Game* or the act of passing the words along, be any different in the time of Christ, than it is today? I think not. This is not intended to cast negativity on the overall truth and intent of the Bible and Christ's teaching, more-so to encourage independent thinking and openness in their thinking and acceptance that God speaks to all who will listen. He will come to you in whatever way you will believe in Him and accept His guidance and direction in your everyday lives.

The belief I have today, based on my recent spiritual and angelic contacts, did not come easy. Although I previously had some doubts as stated above, I cannot say I fully disbelieved in spiritual connections or that there was more to life and our world and universe than we are consciously aware of. I really just didn't give it much thought, one way or the other. I have always been intrigued by the probable untapped power of the mind, which many say that we only use about 10% of the brain's capability, and by unexplainable, miracles and the mysteries of the universe. I think I had an "anything is possible" mind-set, but also it was an "I'll believe it when I see it," or a "wait and see" attitude.

Therefore the initial communications I experienced with my late wife were at first met with my own curiosity and self-doubt. As you will read, I responded facetiously to some of her early comments with questions, such as: "How can you be in Heaven and still be talking to me?" and, "Have you met God yet?" Although she answered me, at the beginning, I still thought the communications were a result of a grief-caused hallucination, or my own creative and active imagination due to a lonely, empty heart. Belief only really came when different communications began to come through to me.

The next spiritual visit and communications was from a teenage friend of mine who had committed suicide in 1963, when he was only about 30 years old. When he came through to me, after my wife's second communication, he said, *"Claricé showed me the way so that you would believe in the reality of her communications with you."* He then gave me information to be passed on to his daughters, some of which was later confirmed, yet contained details I had no way of knowing prior to having had the spiritual experience of him. Soon following, there were three other spiritual visits and communications, beyond those of my teenage friend and my late wife.

Over the next several months, as I began the writing of the first manuscript, my fingers at the computer keyboard seemed to take on a life of their own. First came the transcriptions of the communications I had with Claricé, and the others that followed her.

As I began writing the initial draft of the *LifeClouds* manuscript, I was still questioning the spiritual communications I had with Claricé. It had been one of the most beautiful, and yet heart wrenching, experiences of my life. To be able to talk with her again put me on a "real high." Then almost as quickly, with the realization that I could not touch her, I began sliding backward. This was followed by depression and grief when the spiritual visits and communications came to an abrupt end.

Claricé had related to me that anyone could communicate with the spiritual world by using the sixth sense. That is the untapped resource we all have within our minds. However, when I continued to try and stay in touch with her, after the communication on the January 17th, I couldn't do it. Conversations I tried to have, I quickly realized were being created within the consciousness of my own mind. They were quite different from those of her earlier, direct communications to me.

I soon understood that by doing so, I was only trying to keep her with me and quickly realized it couldn't be so. No matter how much I wanted to, or how hard I tried to keep her with me, I had to let her go. Emotionally, I knew it did not make sense to try to continue. I accepted that spiritual communications with her were possible, but for myself, I needed time to heal.

During this time, the other spiritual visits continued. There were several from my teenage friend, then several from my first mother-in-law, who crossed over in 1967. Next was the husband of a long-time friend, who passed in 1974 and finally one from a friend of Claricé's prior to our marriage who came to her memorial service to do her eulogy. He had a massive coronary the April following Claricé's crossing over and came through to me the following July with a brief and humorous message for his wife.

A final good-bye seemed to come to me a few weeks later. It was at the end of a meditation session, where I had been looking for peace of mind. I was quite relaxed and I opened my eyes to begin to reorient myself to the room. As I did this, the words, *"Reach up and touch me,"* suddenly entered my mind. At the same time, fixed objects across the room in my line of vision, took on a moving, wavy distortion. It was like looking at seashells in the sand, through crystal clear, rippling water.

I reached my right hand palm upwards and immediately felt a warm tingling flow throughout my outstretched fingers to my elbow. I immediately reacted as if it were an electric shock and began to pull my hand back; but I stopped as new words again came into my mind. *"Both hands, my love."* "My love," were Claricé's pet words she always used when speaking to me.

As I raised both hands, palms up, fingers outstretched, the warm, tingling glow returned in a flush of emotion that came through the fingers of both hands, down my arms to the point of the elbow's contact with my sides, crossing and meeting in the middle of my chest. In metaphysics, I've read that this is where the "heart chakra" resides. Tears began to trickle down my face and the objects across the room became clear again as the wavy distortion dissipated. I sensed it was her final goodbye and I didn't believe I would hear from her again. The flush of emotion receded with my awareness and recognition of purpose.

To understand the experiences I'd had, what was happening to me and going on in my mind, I had become a voracious reader. I was always a reader, but in the months following Claricé's first visit, I read over thirty books relating to spirituality, psychics and intuitives, communicating with loved ones who have crossed over, reincarnation, getting in touch with our sixth sense and finally books on angelic communications. The more I read, the more I believed and the more interested I became in the realm of spiritual communications. The reading was an affirmation. It strengthened my own belief in what had happened in my experiences with my late wife.

I am still left with many unanswered questions — questions, which linger — and I'm sure not all will be answered on the following pages. A lot of what I have read and what I have witnessed, watching psychics and others on cable and network television is so different from my own experience that a complete understanding eludes me. As well, I am sure many readers may question my experiences. They were as unique as are the various descriptions of the spiritual world, in the many books I've read and the communications I've received.

One conclusion I have arrived at, however, is that I personally do not want to attempt to do "readings" for others, such as with those on television or in the business, even if I do one day discover I have the capability of doing so. I've been to readings in past and in recent months, and I've watched the nationally known psychics on television. Probing into the lives and minds of others and communicating to them and what I may come to believe about them or loved ones who have crossed over, is not a responsibility I want to undertake. For me, it is a personal issue and I can only accept the truth of the experience as it relates to my own being. However, if something comes to me in the privacy of my home or mind and I believe it is appropriate, beneficial and acceptable for the intended recipient, I will decide then whether to pass it along. I have done this with a few spiritual communications, which were spontaneously received, and I have written about, in the later pages of this biographical essay.

In late August, a year following my wife's death, when I was once again experiencing a deep and heavy grief, I began suffering from sleep deprivation. While in this state of mind, I began hearing voices in my head. They prevented me from sleeping and I wondered if I was in fact if I was starting to "lose it?" There was a myriad of voices and fragments of words and phrases that flowed around and around in my mind; it seemed to be nothing that made sense. Because of the different spiritual communications I previously had received, I thought that there might be others trying to come through to me but there was no clarity.

At this particular time, I had just completed reading four of the books on speaking with and asking angels for guidance; how angels relate to prayer, healing and other angel stories. A friend had given me a book titled *Ask Your Angels* and another *The Angels Within*. Another recommended the "Angelspeake" series (a complete list of helpful books is listed in the bibliography). The Angelspeake books give a simple seven-step process for communicating with your angels. For me, the books about angels brought affirmation and clarity in the possibility of spiritual communications with angels or other entities. All of the books I've now read on angels have stated that they are there and waiting to assist us. All we have to do is ask, and then listen with an open, and trusting mindset and heart.

On the night of the 19th of August, a year following my wife's death, I was tossing and turning in my bed for what seemed to be several hours. I was desperately trying to sleep and becoming very frustrated over my grief, pain and inability to get a good night's rest for several months. I finally decided to give the angels a try. The books said you had to ask; and I thought, so does the Bible: "Ask and you shall receive." As the thought passed through my troubled and noisy mind, I cried out aloud, "All right you guys, if you are my angels, who are you?" And then I asked, "When is this pain going to end?" There was nothing but the ongoing cacophony of voices, words and partial phrases running through the pathways of my mind. The angels didn't answer my plea! Nor did they answer the next night, or during the next two nights as I continued to repeat my questions and utter my plea for them to hear me.

Suddenly, on the fifth night of the 24th I did get an answer. One of the voices in my mind clearly came through to me and said, *"All right Victor, I think now you are ready to listen. My name is Archie and I have been with you throughout your life. I am your angel guide."* An angel had answered me! Archie, my angel guide, had begun to speak to me, and many of his communications that have since followed, are transcribed in the following pages.

The number of angels present I've learned will vary from one person to another and from time to time depending upon the activities in your life. Early on, I understood that I presently have four who are with me at all times. "Archie," who declares male gender, is my dominant Angel Guide who I communicate with most often. Another, going only by the initials "ML" is of female gender and said she is my "Relationship Angel." Ali, another of female gender says she is my "Angel of Good Health," and Miriam, a third female is my "Angel of Miracles." I don't know why he wasn't mentioned in the beginning, but six months later "Jules," who said he is another life-long angel guide, surfaced. He informed me he has worked with me primarily in my mentoring activities throughout my life. Mental/verbal messages are not always clear, so I would assume the omission was some form of misunderstanding on my part within the context and newness of the experiences.

Since Archie first came through to me, he has been the primary source of my angelic communications and I have spent many hours with him. In the beginning it was often on a nightly basis whenever he chose to. He comes to me in the twilight time just prior to sleep or when I am in meditation. Although I was not aware of it, he was with me in the early days when I was writing about the spiritual experiences and is always with me when I take his dictations while auto-writing at the computer. Sometimes he even awakens me during the night or very early in the morning. By comparison, my contact with, and communications with the other three angels, and now Jules, has been quite brief. The others seemed to have come through only after Archie had established a belief within me, over a period of several weeks and in many lengthy communications.

ML has communicated with me in several short conversations. My Relationship Angel, she primarily has told me that if I want to know about, or have a need to communicate with former friends or family members who have crossed over, I should go through her. She claims responsibility for assisting in some of my "spiritual communications and dictations" and said she would be able to arrange another communication with my late wife Claricé whenever I think I am ready. She agrees that it is too soon, because I still have the strong emotional ties and I have not yet fully accepted the reality of her loss. She said what would be considered personal communications are over, and future conversations would only be on an esoteric level. When I asked about talking with her on family matters, I was reminded that Claricé is with us always and she knows what we know and therefore, there is nothing to discuss; *if you think it, she knows it* and this applies to all and she will guide you in whatever way she can.

I was on the fifth draft and what I hoped would be the final revision of what was the *original* or first manuscript when Archie, my angel guide, stopped me and suggested I set it aside. I was in the midst of struggling with the final edit and at first I thought I just needed a breather. Perhaps I needed some time to let my thoughts simmer in my mind before completing the manuscript and attempting to market it. This was true. I was fighting it and trying to determine if I had over-written some areas of the text and felt I was rambling at times. Also as I mentioned, a couple of my readers had said there were actually three stories in one.

During the break in editing, I had lengthy communications with Archie. He suggested that it might be helpful to my overall purpose if I would write a story focusing on the angels in my life before finishing the current manuscript. He encouraged me to ask more questions of my other angels, to get a greater understanding of how they have influenced my life. He then challenged me to write about all of the communications. He reminded me that I already had much of the material written in the form of the various dictations I had been receiving.

He said if I really wanted to, *"You could probably write the story about the 'angels in my life' in two or three weeks."*

I replied to him, *"That is quite some task you're proposing."* What I said to him was quite true. Although a significant amount of this was put together in a few weeks, I actually have been working on this story for well over a year. But he reminded me of how much I already had, including the written record of the spiritual communications and the abundance of personal "angel stories" which had been discussed and dictated from both from him and my other angels.

At the time, I had a pile of "notes" on the 4" x 6" sheets at the side of my bed, quickly written down at the times they occurred during the night. Many of which I had not taken to the computer to ask the angels for further clarification, which was a process that had developed over the first few months with Archie. From August to November of 2000, this process had become very time-consuming and exhausting. I was suffering from lack of sleep and fatigue. The communications went on and on at all hours of the night. I quickly found that if I didn't make notes and go to the computer and write it out in the morning, it would soon be forgotten like a dream.

Without the notes, I would hit a blank spot in my recollections of the night. With them – often only a word or two — I could mentally ask questions of the depths of my mind. When I did this, answers and clarification immediately came through to me. It wasn't in thought or mental answers though, the answers began to flow out through my fingers and into the computer with no preconception of content. I soon realized I was auto-writing. When I reflected back on what I had previously written about the spiritual experiences, I realized then, I was also being guided. My remembrances were too detailed and beyond normal recall. Due to my exhaustion, I began to procrastinate and did not always respond. When I did this, the communications stopped. A day or two later I would take my notes, go to the computer and type in a question about one of the notes. Immediately, the information would begin to flow again. I learned I could "choose" when to be with the angels.

Archie, who you will soon be introduced to, initially had a habit of coming through to me whenever he chose to. Teasingly at times he would tell me what he thought I should do. As stated earlier, when he comes to the forefront of my mind, normally it is when I am in the twilight state just prior to sleep. If I'm not too tired when I go to bed, he will talk about whatever is troubling me. He answers whatever questions come to my mind, or chatters on and on about something he wants to bring to my attention.

I use the word "chatters" because sometimes he will go on and on until I would plead for sleep. I often have told him he sounds like the squirrels that run over the screened garden enclosure attached to the house in my back yard. They call back and forth to each other in a chattering-like noise.

In answer to my plea for sleep, he has said to me, *"It has taken me 66 years to finally break through to you. If you think I am going to stop now, you have to think again."* As you will read, sometimes the angels can be humorous, playful and a little tricky in maneuvering us, beyond our conscious awareness and yet within the parameters of the path of God's plan for our lives.

There have been many times Archie has something that he wants to direct my attention to when I have not "listened" for him, or perhaps to him. As noted above, it took a while for me to learn that I do have a "choice" whether to listen or not. On the occasions when I am not open to him before sleep, often he will wake me for an hour or two in the middle of the night after I've had a couple of hours of sleep. Other times, he will intrude when I am in a silent meditation trying to relax or rest during the day. To get my attention, he can be quite forceful.

When he has had a lot to say at night on a few occasions, he has directed me to get out of bed and go to my computer immediately to write it down. He knows I am forgetful. I often forgot the details of the twilight messages by morning. When this happens I am only left with the essence of what was communicated, and questions. It only becomes clear again after I have gone to the computer, taken the dictation and then later read through what has been brought to me. This is the reason for the notes at my bedside.

Although to the best of my knowledge this is a true story, it is only the truth of my personal experience. I cannot say for 100% certainty that it comes from spiritual sources outside of my mind. Voices I would recognize, like my wife's Brazilian accent, I initially thought I was hearing in what has been termed "clairaudience communication," with my ears as well as in my mind. Soon I came to realize that most of it — although seemingly heard — the communications were really taking place within the "higher-self" of my mind. Even though they were in the form of voices I could recognize, or someone's usage of words or style of speaking, I quickly realized they seemed to be originating through a form of telepathic communication.

Angels in My Life

Only the first few spiritual communications and the "goodbye touch" came with any form of visual imagery, called "clairvoyance." Regarding imagery, I often wonder about the "aura," that some say they can see, the energy that encompasses the physical vehicle we call the body. I have been able to "feel" the energy or aura of my own body and I have *visually* seen my own "glow" reflected in a mirror, but there was only one time that I have been able to witness the aura of any other.

Depending on what book you read or the source of information that is believable to you, it very well may be that all angelic and spiritual communications come in a telepathic format from the energy in the universe where all spiritual life resides in another dimension. Scholars on the subject write that, sometimes the capability of experiencing these forms of communications comes about following the sudden, tragic and unexpected death of a devoted loved one. This happens most often when the departure came without complete closure, or at a time unfinished business was lingering when a loved one crossed over. At these times, it will be something more than an, "I'm okay," message. Other extreme personal traumas also can spontaneously open this channel of spiritual communication, as my own came about.

In my situation I was admittedly in shock and somewhat on a suicidal path. Perhaps my researching and focusing so much attention on the medical problems related to my wife's death was the unfinished business. I don't know the *why* of it. In addition to the spontaneity of the communications that happened with me, both Claricé and Archie have clearly stated that each of God's children do have the capability of spiritual and angelic communication. "Ask and you shall receive..." listen and believe. A trauma is not always necessary.

Some who have written on the subject say they believe that for unexplained reasons, a trauma will open one's ability "hear" in an auditory manner and to "see" by making use of what has been called the third eye for visual imagery. Others report it is as being able to reach into the super-consciousness of their mind, the ability to get in contact with the "higher-self," or soul memory, where all knowledge of the universe is located.

All in all, it is not a matter of science that can be proved or disproved. Other forms of spiritual communication are "clairsentient," through feelings, sensations and emotions, and "claircognizance," which is a sense of knowingness and certainty of new thinking or information beyond the scope of conscious awareness. Perhaps this, too, is a matter of choice. In my regard, I don't believe that it matters where or how the information comes to me, or whether it is from a higher state of my own mind or elsewhere.

The only truth *I know* is that *it is not the workings* of my conscious mind or *an attempt to satisfy needs of my ego consciousness*. I also have come to realize that it is the conscious mind and ego where much of the negative "mind talk" goes on and where evil influences that permeate the energy forces of the universe can lead us astray. It is the "higher self" where the door to the soul can be opened to listen to God, to the spirit within or to communicate with the angels. What we listen to in our minds in our daily life or spiritually is a matter of "choice." Even though the ego can bring forth positive thoughts and action, any thought that brings negativity is certainly of the ego consciousness, also called the "lower self." That which comes from the "higher self" is always positive in nature; it is where the spirit, the soul and God resides within, and therefore can only be of truth, because it is of God.

Most of what has come through to me in spiritual contacts or through Archie and the other angels at night or in meditation is a hazy memory until I sit at the computer and begin to ask questions. I ask whatever comes to mind or use the notes written during the night. When I began the transcription phase of the communications from my late wife Claricé and others, at first I thought I was just writing what I remembered and was just putting the bits and pieces together in some form of continuity. But I knew I was not recalling everything that had been said and as the silent questions in my mind began to be answered more and more details came forth.

Once Archie broke through to me, the similarity of the earlier transcription experiences and the new ones led me to realize that without my awareness, Archie and/or the other angels had been assisting me from the time I began writing them.

One fact has become very clear to me: When I sit down at the computer to begin, I generally only have a few questions in mind that relate to the experience of the night before or notes of an earlier communication. At that time, I have absolutely no idea or thought beyond the question. I don't know how Archie or the others will answer the questions or what they will direct me to write. There are no preconceptions or outlines; once I ask a question, I write whatever comes to my mind as quickly as I can. I have come to believe that at this stage I am receiving information through claircognizance, because I am not "hearing" words, they just flow like water coming over a waterfall, and they are unstoppable until the entire session has been completed.

Although I am not in any kind of trancelike state, I do find I am very focused and the sessions can last anywhere from a few minutes to several hours. The longest was two sessions in one day for a total of seven hours.

Sometimes when I pick my hands up from the keyboard to pause or take a breather, my fingers are still moving. Often the words, which I will continue to call dictations, come faster than I can type and occasionally there are missing words. But the flow does not stop... even to correct obvious typographical errors. There are other times when my fingers will stop in the middle of a phrase or statement as if the *source* is in thought. When this happens, and the final few words seem obvious to my conscious mind, I sometimes instinctively write out what is left. When I do, my fingers will then invariably be directed to hit the backspace to delete my words and different words will then be inserted and added.

It can be a very strange experience. At the end of a session when the writing is finished, I do not remember much of what I have written and could not intelligently discuss the content until after I have read it over a couple of times. It is like reading a new book or something someone else has given me to read for my comments on content. This is when the editing process begins and is both for my own understanding and for the purpose of grammar and typos. When I question the context or meaning of a phrase or segment that was added, clarification comes in the same manner as the original dictation. Because of this occasionally a phrase, or a sentence or two may sound like it is out of chronological order. Archie sometimes refers back to communications already received.

Details of most of the communications I have had with Archie and spiritually with Clarice and a couple of others, will be covered in the following pages. But, to answer a couple of obvious questions that I am sure are immediately in a reader's mind, I would like to say I am certain that *there are angels among us*. This I am as certain of as I am that the sun will rise tomorrow morning.

I also know the angels want to communicate with us and can assist us in all we do. All of human kind, every one of God's children, has angels who are assigned to him or her. Angels guide us on our daily walk on the planet Earth, which is a very small part of our universe God has created. Most of us have several angels to help us, dependent upon what we are doing and what our needs happen to be, as with those I have with me at this particular time. All you have to do is *ask... listen...believe.*

The most obvious of the questions, which came to my mind when I began reading about angels, were questions like, "Why aren't we more aware of them? If they are here to help us, why don't they make themselves obviously known and available?" And, "Why are they here? What do they do if we are not communicating with them?" Answers for myself began to come after reading more and more of the angel stories and relating them to similar experiences I have encountered recently and throughout my own life. Validation and affirmation came from reading reports of many other people's experiences that were similar enough to my own to overcome any lingering doubt.

With the assistance of my angels, once I began to look back throughout my own life, I was able to see the many times angels had intervened in my life without my knowingly asking them. With this, I really began to believe, *believing it is possible, accepting it is possible, and learning to trust the inner knowledge as it comes forth.*

In a simple example I have suggested to others, I ask the curious to look back through their own lives to the many times they have encountered one problem or another. If you will do this, you will find times when, and after many frustrating attempts at solving a problem, you have thrown up your hands in frustration and/or disgust and *uttered* the words, or mentally asked, *"How am I supposed to figure this out?"* or *"God help me!"*

You will recall occasions when the answer had come immediately after the words were uttered or the silent request was made and had seemingly come from out of nowhere. In your conscious awareness you didn't even realize you had asked for the angels' or God's help and that because of it, the request was answered. There are times when it was a very difficult problem. Dilemmas like this have happened to all of us. When the answer spontaneously appeared in our minds, we considered it a stroke of genius and sometimes thought, *"Am I great or what?"* Well, you are great, all of God's children are great, but the truth of the matter is that you were *provided* the solution to your problem. It was God given and/or sent by one of his angel messengers.

As long as a request is within God's plan for your individual life, angels will always, unknowingly come to your aid as a result of your silent requests and thoughts, such as, *"How do I do this?"* Or, even

Angels in My Life

when you're driving to *great aunt Martha's,* when you weren't quite sure of the way and you may have thought, "Is this the right street to take?" Suddenly, you get a *sense of awareness, get a feeling, or think,* "Yes, this is right!" At that precise moment however, when you were still trying to tap into your memory bank, *you suddenly knew it was right.* These are mental requests that angels can respond to; they are times when God or His angels are assisting us beyond our conscious level of awareness and in response to silent or vocalized prayers or questions.

Angels are messengers of God and He created them to assist Him with all of His creations in the universe. It doesn't matter if you pray to God, Christ, intermediaries such as saints and archangels, or any other power, which may be within your personal theological belief system; the angels are there. And if your request is within the plan God has for your life on the planet called Earth, God and His angels are there for you. This is a universal truth for those who believe in the supreme source, one God, the creator of all things, known or unknown.

Each of us has a lifetime of examples to draw upon for confirmation: those in which the angels have unknowingly helped us make it through the day. Archie and my other angels have recently reminded me of several such experiences I have had. All you have to do is think about it for a few moments. Think back and you will find many cases of angelic intervention throughout your own life. You may even discover why you are who you are.

Much of the internal mental dialogue is with and between the ego of your conscious mind — also referred to as the lower self — and your higher self. Times that we continually experience, when we think we are talking to ourselves, very often are the angels trying to contact us, or to assist us in our daily living. They can fulfill our needs when we ask questions through vocalized utterances and/or the silent mental requests.

As mentioned above, angels are always there and thankfully so, especially at the times when your life may have been in imminent danger. When — through no fault of your own — your life was or is threatened *before it is your time* to leave your life experience on Earth, angels can and do intercede. To understand this, I would like to draw upon one of the most acceptable beliefs of mankind and our belief in God: draw upon your belief in His creation of the species known as human beings. In the Bible, Christ teaches, "Ask and you shall receive." It is readily accepted that we are different from all others in what is acknowledged to be within the animal kingdom, because when God created mankind, He gave human beings the "freedom of choice." Therefore, within reasonable parameters, God will not consciously interfere in your life unless you ask for His help.

From a theological perspective I would like to point out that God *consciously* comes to your assistance or to your awareness only when you pray, when you ask for him or ask for his help, and more importantly *believe* that it can be so. You may not always get the answer you want, but you get the truth and the answer that fits God's plan for your life. It is often asked, "Why didn't God answer my prayers?" or *"Why doesn't God answer all prayers?"* Certainly an omnipotent God could do that. I know. I did that myself and hated God when my wife's life was suddenly taken. The truth I have since discovered is that prayers are answered according to His plan for your life and whatever lesson in life is yours to learn. Two beings going through the same negative experience can be prayed for, yet one will be healed and the other will pass on to the spiritual realm that mankind calls Heaven. Why? It happens exactly the way it should, because that was God's plan for each of their lives. Acceptance of this concept didn't come easy for me. Many, many communications took place before I fully accepted that Claricé's death was according to God's plan for both of our lives.

Life on Earth is a learning experience and we may not always understand the adversities in our lives, but we must trust in God that His will, will be done. Only evil acts and influences that sometimes permeate our lower selves and the susceptible ego consciousness of our minds, is beyond the realm of God; and these acts, which go beyond the parameters of our lives set by God are our *freedom of choice;* we can avoid sin and evil if we listen to the spirit within and voice of our higher selves where the soul energy and our oneness with God resides.

The "ask and you shall receive" principle applies to the angelic realm of the universe, as well as to God. Angels are God's messengers, and it has been clearly demonstrated to me that the angels will not consciously come to your assistance until you ask for them and acknowledge their awareness. They are always there, and they are quietly assisting you, but your conscious awareness will not recognize or accept what they can and will do, *until you ask for and believe in them.*

Chapter Two
More About My Angels

As mentioned in the opening chapter, it was on the night of August 24th/25th 2000 when the angels finally came through to me. After four almost sleepless nights of listening to the myriad voices traipsing through my mind and crying out for the angels, they finally made contact with me. They came to assist me with my grief.

Archie, my dominant angel guide was the first to come through to me, and during my first experience with him, he told me he had been with me all of my life. I have read that some believe that the angel that is always with you is your "guardian angel," but in my understanding, Archie almost always uses the terminology of angel guide. He says that angel guides, angels who are assigned to earthbound souls are with you for life and have never incarnated on the planet Earth. He seemed to suggest to me that guardian angels are our loved ones who have crossed over and have chosen to take on multiple functions in the spiritual realm. One of their chosen functions is to watch over those they have left behind. In most cases, during their earthly existence, guardian angels were what has come to be called, or were recognized as, soul mates. If you imagined yourself as a leaf on a branch on the tree of life, your soul mates would be those closest to you. More specifically, they would be those with whom you have an eternal spiritual relationship over and over and those farthest from you are with you less frequently, as each of you choose the paths of learning for the eternal life God has granted your soul. Archie has said that your loved ones, however, also watch over you and influence your life once they have crossed over into the spiritual realm.

This is not totally consistent with other reading in my research, but at the same time I do not believe it is very significant. Jules, my other life-long angel, who came to me later, put it to me differently. At first, I understood him to say that he was a "guardian" angel. When I asked him about the difference, his reply was, "guiding or guardian" they both can sound the same to you. Then he went on to explain that guardian angels also "guide" you, and assist you. Angel guides do the same thing, and I shouldn't concern myself or waste my time thinking about semantic differences in what I hear, perceive or read from others. As you will read later, Archie talks about how the many differences throughout the world are based on problems in communications, and come about through different semantic understanding of the various meanings of words and the many applied interpretations. Because there are continual changes in the precise meaning of words within any one language and between languages, semantics is the root source of strength as well as strife in communications among all mankind since time began.

As an example, he points out that all of the information that comes through to those who listen and are able to receive on a spiritual level, is consistent with God's intent. However, you are asked to realize that those who do receive, accept and believe in what comes to them, are first taking the information in through their own intellect and personal frame of reference based upon their own life experiences. The same is true in the manner and form of how they express what they have received. Therefore, it is understandable that when the information is received and is then passed along, it has been "filtered" to some degree by the recipient. Each receiver may put a slightly different interpretation upon the outpouring of the words and information received as he or she defines them.

How this relates to guardian angels or angel guides is found in how each of God's children who accept, hear or receive the messages, interprets them and passes them along. They can be visual, auditory, energy vibrations, by sense, by feel or telepathic and knowingness. Because Archie sometimes refers to "guiding angels" and other times "angel guides" in the same context, my understanding is that he is speaking about one and the same. However, in listening in an auditory or telepathic manner, as I believe I have received the communications, the similarity in "guiding" and "guardian" as Jules said are "sound-a-likes." This could account for some of the differences, which are reported by others and yet are really quite insignificant.

The fact that we do have angels who are with us, be it guiding or guardian, is really all that is important to believe. Archie said there are a million times a million times a million, and more angels in the spiritual realm, and that defining who or what they are with a "name" is meaningless. Knowing who they are for you and what they do and have done is what is important, not what they are named or called by others.

He said I have had many other angels assisting me throughout my life's endeavors, but at the present time there are five. Others he said are available as needed and that God has messenger angels for any specific purpose or need I may have.

Archie has been my primary contact since he came to me at the end of August 2000, and the communications I have had with him and dictations from him will be the basis for much of the text in this, the *"Angels In My Life"* story. ML, began her communications with me a couple months after Archie first came through, and Ali and Miriam, each a month or so following and as I mentioned, Jules did not add his voice until about six months after the communications began.

Angels, in the spiritual realm and their communications are of vibrational energy, much like the souls of earthlings without their bodies, or physical vehicles. Using terminology and language from the human form of semantics, verbal and written communications, our soul energy has been termed the "aura," for this writing. Since Archie has become such a dominant presence in my conscious awareness, it is sometimes difficult to determine where he leaves off and my own mental, spiritual self, conscious intellect or higher self come about in my thinking or thought processes.

I myself am not always certain, because as my awareness of their presence grows, I "sense" them almost continually in my mental processing, writing and verbal communications. Very often, I know they are with me as I listen to the internal dialogue and evaluate the source to determine if the thought pattern is from the spirit and higher self, or the ego and lower self. Many readers may also have heard of the "inner self," which in my understanding of in the use of the words, relates to a portion of the higher self that deals with emotions, feelings, instincts and intuition. It is called a "clairsentient" experience when the inner self comes into play; and this too is a truth because it is of the higher self. *A word of caution* should be injected here, however, because the "I want" nature of the ego can be quite deceptive and create false feelings and emotions. Sometimes the difference is a hard line to define and therefore should be looked at carefully. When we let ourselves be *run by feelings and emotions* it is more likely to be of ego rather than of the higher self.

The reader should assume we... one of my angels and/or myself, are both writing the words unless indicated and written in a conversational question and answer format. When this takes place, questions will be obvious and in the same style of typography as is now being used in the text, and I will make use of an *italic* type style in the *answers to the questions.*

When I use the words "I" or "we," I will often be speaking from my own spiritual self or making reference to that which comes from Archie and his friendly angelic brothers and sisters. As well, when I use the words "you" or "we," I am then making reference to all of God's children on the planet Earth. Since we are all "one" in terms of the universal energy, the specific context I am coming from, hopefully will be obvious within the framework of the message itself. My references to hearing can be either hearing, or the knowingness of my higher self, especially in references to dictations. And references to God with the word He, the commonly accepted usage, will be consistent to avoid the confusion of He, She, Father, or Mother, God as it applies to some theological, spiritual and metaphysical beliefs.

As you read, you will see a little repetition that is redundant. I have come to notice that Archie does this quite frequently, as I sometimes do myself for emphasis, but I will make an effort to keep it to a bare minimum. However, Archie has clearly pointed out that we are all in *a learning process* as we take our walk through life on God's planet Earth. Therefore, much like going to school and studying for an exam, in order to really "get it," often times we have to read it, read it and read it again to learn the lesson. The basis of his communication to me is to bring awareness and understanding that angels are God's messengers and they are here and available to help us in our life and to learn and fulfill our purpose in the current incarnation. All we have to do is ask, listen, believe, accept, and trust their words in whatever way you receive them.

Much of the internal conversations and mind-talk we have, when we think we are talking to ourselves, are the angels *trying to get through to us and to keep us on track and on God's plan for our life purpose.* Much of it goes on between the "I want" of the lower self, ego/personality and the communications of the higher self and spirit within. It is the questioning of our next step and/or to block the influence of evil intentions or negativity of the ego. The existence of angels on the spiritual plane has been mentioned in writings of the Masters since the beginning of time and is consistent with almost every religious and theological persuasion known to humankind.

Getting back to *my* angels, Archie will have a lot to say and a lot of information to pass along in the following pages. Going by the name of the initials ML is my Relationship Angel who has explained that her purpose is to assist me with my current relationships in life, family, friends, romance. If other angels are needed to assist her in these functions, if I ask, she will call out to them to take care of whatever comes about.

She is also here, as I previously stated to assist me in communicating with or getting information about loved ones, soul

Angels in My Life

mates and friends who have crossed over before me. She clearly said that if and when I am emotionally able to handle further communications with and about my late wife Claricé, she is there for me. But she has cautioned me to "give it time" before asking to speak about her or to her again. The personal issues are over but when I'm ready, I can ask for her guidance as well.

ML said that at Archie's direction she and Miriam, my angel of miracles, played an active role in assisting Claricé to come through to me in January 2000, as well as the different spiritual communications I have had with the others that will be in following chapters. Her early primary role, before I was aware of her presence was in the transcription of the communications I had prior to the arrival of Archie, when he answered my plea. I was unaware of the earlier help and, at the time I began transcribing the words that came through to me, I believed each time they were from fragments of my memory. Instead, I later found that she and Archie were the "conduit" for the words that came through and that in each of the writings only the words that were meaningful to my ongoing life experience and purpose were given to me for my transcriptions. They intentionally omitted all of the emotional and personal dialogue between Claricé and myself during the five communications that took place as well as, that which would be meaningless to others.

Omitted, was much of the communications I had with my late wife of a personal and somewhat sad, nature relative to her sudden death and leaving. In their entirety the communications were approximately seven or eight hours in total length during the five visits with her. ML said she transcribed only that which was important and that which would give me a belief in the reality of the experience. This was also true in transcribing the subsequent spiritual communications I received from the other spiritual entities.

An interesting side note about this is when I spoke of my newfound experience with one of my daughters. She replied, *"Dad, if I could do that, I would want to talk to both of my grandmas, grandpas, my friend Stephanie from school who died of cancer and a bunch of others."*

Since Claricé had mentioned in her communication that my mother, stepfather, father and others were present with her in the spiritual realm, I asked ML about it. I even wondered why I didn't have any deep-seated desire to communicate with them, I was also curious why they had not come through to me, now that I was open to making spiritual contact.

This was an easy answer for ML. She said that the reason for this is because they are at peace with themselves and their departure from their earthly existence, and that I too have been at peace with their leaving and had accepted that it was their time to go.

ML then went on to explain that communications between those who have crossed over and those who remain on the earthly plane only take place when there are troubled feelings about the departure on one side or the other. When a spiritualist, an intuitive or a psychic assists an earthbound soul with a reading or contact with a departed loved one, the message is almost always little more than, "I'm okay or I am at peace." Sometimes there are brief messages about the beauty of the Heavenly environment or references to other friends and family members who are with them, but generally it is just that they, too, are okay in the spiritual realm.

She went on to tell me that it is only in situations like my own, in which severe trauma surfaces and prevents acceptance, that lengthier communications can and will come through to those who ask, listen and believe. At these times there is a very strong purpose or a severe need to help heal the grief. In my case, she said it was both to heal my grief and to give me a purpose in life. My purpose, she reinforced, was to write and focus attention and awareness on the prevalence of breast cancer, the problematic medical community, and to communicate to my fellow beings the message that angels are a reality and they are waiting for us to ask for their assistance in our daily activities.

My contact with Ali and Miriam has been very brief. Ali, however, must be working well, because physically I am in the healthiest I have been for almost 20 years. Miriam, as you will read, reinforced my belief in angels by telling me stories of how she has been active in my life, by describing and reminding me of life threatening situations where she prevented my leaving the earthly plane before it was my time.

All three of my angel ladies are what we might call multi-faceted in earthly terminology. They are omni-present. They assist me, and others as well, at all times in their specific mode of being. The essence of angelic energy is sexless as it is with our own soul energy. Before our soul incarnates, it chooses the sex it wants to live out on the earthly plane. The same is true of all the angels. They choose their sex-identity to fit the purpose and need of the soul they are assisting and serving.

Angels in My Life

Ali, my Angel of Good Health, was responsible for bringing about my awareness of my cardiac problems in the 1980's and influencing the maintenance of my physical body throughout the years. She influences those who will make sure I have a proper diet and make sure that I seek out the medical attention required to keep my physical "vehicle" purring until I complete God's plan for my life.

Sometimes angels can be humorous. The first time she came through to me, I thought I heard the name "Alecia" and referred back to her as such. Quite indignantly she replied, "Not Alecia! It's Ali... and then slowly spelled it out for me, "A... L... I..." Archie then injected, "Also Victor, please don't call me 'Arch'... the name is Archie."

Miriam is my Angel of Miracles and has recently reminded me of times in my life when she has prevented my premature departure. In some of these cases, where I only had a brief recollection, or perhaps a distant memory of what may have been told to me, she has recalled to me detail by detail of her life saving interventions. Brief accounts for this purpose would be when I was four years old and was "bumped" off a pier by a teenager running and diving. In her story about the incident, an aunt, discovered I was missing and ran to the water to look for me. Upon finding me in the dark water, she pulled me to shore by the hair of my head. I had heard that I had almost drowned as a child, but was never aware of the details.

Another incident long forgotten that she detailed was an accident I "almost" had as a teenage driver when I lost control of the automobile, went off the road and by pure chance came to a stop with the bumper of the car just inches from crashing into the cement block wall of a small office building.

More poignant was when I was married to my second wife Heather in the mid 1970's and we had a break-in at our apartment. This story I remember very clearly and, even at the time it happened, I considered that for some reason God didn't want me to die on that day. It was in 1974, when, an intruder awakened my wife Heather and myself, in the middle of the night. It was shortly after 2 a.m. and a man was standing next to her side of the bed with a gun pointed directly at her head. He touched her shoulder and "shush-ed" with a finger at his lips. Startled, she reached for my hand under the covers and squeezed it. When I awoke and saw him standing there, I quickly sat up in the bed. As I did, he fired the gun. With angelic assistance, the bullet missed her head, went by her ear through the mattress and into the floor.

Then he ordered her to tie me up with shirts from my closet. When she did this, I held my hands and feet in such a way that she could not tie them tightly, yet when he checked them, it seemed tight to him. He then ordered my wife to go downstairs with him and when I lifted my head in protest he pistol-whipped me behind the right ear.

Unknown to both of us at that moment, Miriam caused the cylinder of the revolver to open and the remaining bullets silently fell into the thick shag carpeting. As soon as he left my line of sight, I undid my knotted shirt and went to the drawer where I kept a 22 cal target pistol and loaded it.

While I was doing this, I heard a door slam downstairs and I thought he had taken her somewhere outside. Immediately I went after them, but once outside I couldn't see them. At almost the same time, I heard a scream from inside the apartment. I ran back inside and my pistol ready, I kicked in the door of the downstairs den where he had begun to rape my wife. I hesitated firing my pistol for fear of hitting my wife. As I hesitated, he jumped up with his gun in hand and came at me. Immediately, we were face-to-face, inches apart. I pulled the trigger of my gun first, but it misfired. The bullets I had put in my gun were old, corroded and the gun hadn't been cleaned or fired in several years.

The intruder's gun, pointed at my chest and stomach area went "click, click, click". *His ammunition was upstairs lying on the bedroom carpet.* As I repeatedly pulled the trigger, my gun misfired, but then, I did get off a few shots and hit him. I can still clearly hear the, "Click, click, bang, click, click, bang, click, bang". We confronted each and began to struggle in the doorway, eventually hitting at each other with the misfiring weapons.

Because my gun was only a 22-caliber target pistol, it didn't have any knockdown power. Even though he was hit twice, with a bullet in his chest and another in his stomach, he was able to fight and struggle until he broke free and ran out the still-open front door. As he ran from me I was still attempting to fire my gun and was able to hit him once more in the back of the left knee.

To shorten a long story, he was in the hospital within 20 minutes of my call to the police and upon arrival, his condition was so bad from the stomach wound the doctors in the emergency room closed him up to stabilize him without removing the bullets. The one bullet, had deflected off a rib in the front and another in back and according to the emergency room doctor, it tore up his insides. Once the police got to him and his condition improved, his "fifth amendment rights" against self-incrimination, prevented them from having the bullets removed.

A year and a half later at trial, because it happened in the dark, neither my wife nor I could positively identify him, and without the bullets being matched, the intruder beat the charges. As weak as the story he gave in his defense, in a juryless trial, the judge found a "shadow of doubt." Our only satisfaction came from an obvious limp in his left leg from the damage by the bullet in the back of his knee and the belief that it looked like he would probably have the limp for life.

As for me, I would surely have been killed if the bullets from his 32-caliber pistol had not quietly fallen out on the carpet. When the police were at the apartment to write their report, they discovered the bullets from his gun lying on the shag carpet. An officer said, "Your guardian angel must have been with you tonight."

Every day of my life since that time has been a blessing. I still remember standing on the terrace when the police left our apartment at sun-up. As I held Heather in my arms trying to give her comfort, the tears streamed down my face as I thought that I well may have not seen such a beautiful sunrise again. That moment in time, the angels were surely with me and it is nice now to know who my angel was and to be able to give thanks again. Although I have lost touch with Heather, I hope her angel of miracles was the one who prevented her from being hit when the intruder fired his gun and that her angels have brought her peace over this unfortunate incident.

Miriam certainly has been my angel of Miracles.

Victor K. Hosler

Chapter Three
Spiritual Communications With Claricé
The First Three Visits

My wife Claricé died from metastasized breast cancer on August 19, 1999. I carried hurt and anger beyond that of her death itself, because her death was questionable. The cancer went undetected, and we were told all of her tests were negative or non-specific over a period of 612 days while she visited over a dozen doctors, all of whom, were wrong. It wasn't until I insisted on a CT scan that we were given an accurate diagnosis, which turned out to be terminal cancer. Her cancer had metastasized from the lumpectomy 20 months earlier. Undetected by a dozen or more doctors, it had spread throughout her body to her lungs, chest muscles, rib cage, liver, spine, and right leg. She died 40 days later. The failings of the medical establishment, was beyond comprehension and the resulting, intense grief tore at my heart and soaked my pillow with nightly tears. I was near being suicidal.

On the night of January 5, 2000, as I laid there with tears in my eyes one more time, I wasn't able to stop my thoughts about how much I missed Claricé and our life together. For a little over 9 ½ years, I had dedicated my life to helping her and encouraging her to follow her dreams. On this night I hated God for taking her from me so soon. In the quiet of the night I cried out aloud in anguish; *"Oh, how I wish I could talk to you one more time, Claricé."* To my astonishment, in her soft voice and with her Brazilian accent, I heard her voice. Claricé spoke to me.

(Following *in italics* were Claricé's words to me.)
"You can my love, just talk to me."
"My love?" The words rocked my world. They were her words; it was the endearing term she had always used when speaking to me. Although at first I thought I audibly heard her voice, I later determined it was only within my head. At the same time it was clear as the sound of a bell, as if she were in the room with me. With those words, a visual impression of her face and shoulders gradually appeared in my mind's eye and I "seemed" to see her lips moving as she began speaking to me.

I immediately thought I must be dreaming or that my mind was playing tricks on me; yet, instinctively, I answered her and said, "How?" At first, I spoke aloud again as I had in my anguished plea.

And she replied again. *"Like you are doing now."*

As I heard her voice in my head once more I thought, "I must be dreaming." But then I knew that I wasn't. I was awake. I may have been in the twilight state between being awake and asleep, but I knew that I wasn't dreaming. I forced my eyes open and looked at the digital clock on the VCR and it read 12:50 a.m. I said aloud once again, "No hon, it can't be. My mind must be playing tricks on me. I must be hallucinating."

- - - - -

At this point, a conversation with my late wife began. It came in two phases, beginning at about 12:45 a.m. and then her voice awoke me again in the morning. The first communication lasted until 3:30 a.m. and then it began again at 6:30 a.m. and continued until about 8:10 a.m.

Due to circumstances at the time and the length and personal content of the entire communication, as stated earlier by ML, my angel of relationships, everything we said to each other was not transcribed. Although the communication is accurate, when it was transcribed, I first thought I was doing it from memory and was just remembering bits and pieces.

As I now relate the experience, I know it was dictated to me with the assistance of ML and Archie, and the form of the writing will be like a conversation, as it seemed to me to take place. When initially transcribed in my computer, the first two communications were not separated and are as if there was only one. Also, the content will not necessarily be in the order that took place as it came to me, or discussed. ML eliminated much of the personal dialog that dealt with the pain and sadness of Claricé's death and the impact on our family. She also left out what would be meaningless to anyone other than me or the family and our children. My children from my first marriage never considered Claricé as their stepmother. They generally referred her to as their "other Mother."

I soon realized that the communication was going on in my head and I stopped speaking aloud.

- - - - -

Claricé then went on to say, *"No, your mind's not playing tricks. I am here, you just have to believe."*

"How can it be?" I asked her. And then, "Where are you?"

"I'm in Heaven."

"How can you be in Heaven and still be talking to me?"

"I said you just have to believe. Ask me some questions."

"All right, what is heaven like?"

"About that it is difficult to tell you in words. All I can say is, it is a very beautiful place to be."

"Can't you describe it?"

"Not in a way that you would understand. There are no earthly words that can describe it. It is almost like whatever you want it to be, it is. Whatever your sense of beauty is, it is."

"That's not very clear. Why or how are we doing this? I know I am not asleep and I'm not dreaming."

"No, you're not. You are quite conscious, my love. Why we are doing this? In part, it's because you need to develop your spiritual growth much farther. That also is how we are doing this. You are using your sixth sense. You have experienced it before and you have used it before, but you have never acknowledged or accepted the reality of your potential in doing so. Although you wanted to, you didn't believe it.

"Everybody has the capability of using their sixth sense. It is an innate ability, but most people do not accept it even when they are unknowingly using it. Most people generally think they are just talking to themselves or making things up to suit their needs when it happens, when in fact often they really are getting a communication or help from a loved one, God, an angel or someone else who is here in Heaven and assisting them with their daily decisions. What

people on Earth refer to as 'a woman's intuition' is a part of the sixth sense. It does seem that women have a partial instinct to use this capability moreso than men, even though men are also intuitive.

"When most people's minds are innately or instinctively using the power of the sixth sense, they are not aware of it and generally do not react and ask questions like you are doing with me now. They believe they created the new thought through their conscious mind and do not open up their heart for the possibility of spiritual communication, or they believe they are imagining it as you did yourself."

Every now and then, I would open my eyes to look at the clock, to be certain I was not dreaming. "Wow. This is almost too much." I said. "Why are you doing this now, after almost five months?" I asked her.

"Because I wanted to tell you that Rob and Kelly are having a baby... and for several other reasons.

"I have tried to talk to you before but you didn't respond. Remember, my love, I always said you never listened to me. Even now it has been difficult to get your attention. Often, when you were in bed and being very, very still I would try to whisper words of comfort to you, words to guide you through your sadness and words of love.

"I tried to get you to understand with Margie's brother George when he tried to come through to you. When I couldn't get through to you I got the impression that if I brought you to someone you knew of from your past that I could get your attention with an unusual thought or message that could not be of your own thinking."

Margie is a longtime friend of mine from my college days and her brother George died of cancer about 30 or more years ago.

"Unfortunately, you weren't really getting it. He got through and you picked up the word 'Mookie' and had an impression of George and Margie but you didn't stay with him long enough. When you called Margie in New York, to see if she understood what the word 'Mookie' meant, you had the impression it was

the word you thought he might have used to refer to her when they were children. It was my understanding that when they were small children he did not pronounce her name right; maybe it was like myself when we first met and you would help me to improve my English. When you called Margie and asked her about it, she didn't remember the name or sound and due to her religious beliefs, she didn't accept that it was a communication with him. You didn't let it continue long enough for him to relate something to her that she could have understood or identify with. You thought you were dreaming but you weren't."

I never thought to ask how she knew about Margie's brother George or how she got him to try and communicate with me. The reference she made to Rob and Kelly, our very close friends having a baby, I really questioned and I put it immediately out of my mind. Although I knew Rob would like to have a son, I also knew he and Kelly weren't planning on any more children. Kelly believed she was a high risk in a pregnancy due to her own bout with genetic breast cancer and I knew she didn't want to risk the possibility of having another daughter who could also be genetically at risk. Referring to the suggested pregnancy I said, "No, I don't think so with Rob and Kelly. My daughter Vicki and her husband Mike, I would believe.

I doubted this part of the communication and said so. Maybe I was imagining things or hallucinating, but still I didn't think so. I changed the subject then to try and satisfy some of my curiosity about what was happening between us. A bit facetiously, I asked her, "If everybody has this sixth sense capability, why don't more people use it to get in touch with the other side. If we are all psychic and have this ability to communicate, couldn't we all arrange to win the lotto with this sixth sense?"

She laughed as I remembered her to do. And as I remembered it, I saw her wide smile. *"I'm glad you asked that, my love."* she answered. *"First, regarding the lotto, if it was possible for everyone here to tell everyone there what the numbers were in advance, it wouldn't make for a very big prize, would it? What would be the point? As to everybody being psychic, as I already told you, it's your sixth sense and it is possible for anyone to access it. Anyone can develop his or her sixth sense. Again, as I said before, people just don't believe enough in their own instincts and capability.*

"Whenever someone has a <u>strong</u> feeling, about one of their loved ones who has died, generally that loved one is present with them in their current environment. Therefore, a person who goes to a psychic in order to communicate with a loved one who passed away, the loved one is generally <u>already with them</u>. The honest psychics who have developed this ability obviously can pick up on the departed one's vibrational energy in the room at the time of the reading. So when they are giving the person that came to them positive feedback about their departed loved one, they tend to accept that the psychic is doing wondrous things. The truth of the matter is that if the same person believed in their own innate ability to use their sixth sense, they could do the same communication without the psychic.

"The problem with psychics is that many of them are charlatans who have not developed their sixth sense, but instead have developed the ability to study and understand verbal clues, facial expressions, and physical mannerisms. These things can steer the false psychic in an understandable direction that the people they are conning will believe, and therefore lead them to where they can be taken advantage of."

- - - - -

When this experience first ended, I began to think of it as a "psychic" occurrence I was having. But, I have come to the conclusion that the word "psychic" sometimes has a negative connotation and it is only a word. As Claricé will state later in reference to "reincarnation," it is just a word that long ago, someone attached to an unknown and unexplainable phenomenon; it's a label for a concept.

In my particular experience, I believe my communication with Claricé was through an act of God's will. I'm sure many other communications are also. However, because of the negativity that has come about as a result of the "charlatans" Claricé referred to, there has been a shadow cast upon this type of experience by many religious communities. Many with fundamentalist Christian belief systems might say what was happening with me was in some way an act of the evil forces, and as noted earlier, that was suggested to me. I would strongly challenge this thinking, however, because I see it as a blessed event, a miracle and/or an experience that I have been fortunate enough to have. Once again, if God wanted to get the attention of the skeptic I was then, what better way to do it than make use of my wife who had recently crossed over?

At this point I began to question Claricé's command of the English language. When she left us here on earth, she still spoke with an accent, and in her every-day speech, she frequently used a wrong word or tense, especially if she was excited or anxious. In her written words, when she had time to think things out, her intellect was greater than in spontaneous speech. Although I was still hearing her accented voice in my head, it seemed the words and thoughts were much clearer than I remembered them to be.

I asked her then, "How come your speech now seems to be much better than when you were here?"

"Because now I can speak as well as you do, my love. Remember, you are putting out my ideas and words. I am only presenting you with thoughts that you process through your mind and intellect, but you still are hearing my voice because I am bringing it to you."

"You know, this is all very difficult to comprehend." I said and almost mockingly and tossed her a new question: "Have you met God?" I asked.

"Of course," she replied. *"God is the light of life. God is the light at the end of the tunnel that is so often described by people on earth who have had near-*

death experiences. God is the light of Christ's ascension. God is the light of the burning bush. God is the light of protection that surrounds those who are facing danger or the unknown. God is the halo of every saint in heaven. God is the aura of life for all of mankind. Many have seen the aura and it has even been photographed. She paused for that to sink in. Then mocking my attitude, she asked, *"What's your next question?"*

Staying within the same line of thinking, I asked: "Why are there so many differences of opinion as to what God and religion is? Why are there so many different religions, if God is the light of life?"

"Because there are many ways for mankind to come to God. Because when a man has truly found God and has him in his heart, each man wants to share the glory of God with his fellow man."

This statement is one reason a fundamentalist Christian may disbelieve in her communication to me. Many think man can only come to God through Christ as stated in the Book of John in the New Testament of the Bible. Archie deals with this premise later. Claricé continued.

"Because, in turn many men believe that because <u>God is now in his heart</u>, the manner in which He got there, is the only way. For all humankind, it is the way a man lives his life, in truth, harmony and asking forgiveness of his sins against God, that bring a man to God and Heaven. For me to say any more about it would only bring challenges or add to the confusion that currently exists among mankind and the various beliefs they hold.

"The word has been written for each man to accept and to live by God's word in whatever way or means he finds it. More important is accepting God as our almighty Creator and that life as known by mankind could not exist without Him."

"Now I want to ask you why there are so many different cultures, class structures and inequities in the world, but I believe most reasons are obviously covered under what is commonly referred to as the

'Ying and Yang' concept in life as we know it? Is that right"?

"That's true, but a better explanation is the negative (-) and positive (+) influences that God created in order for man to have free choice and to eliminate the sameness in all things that would make for a very uninteresting existence. It would be a very insignificant world if everyone were white, rich and beautiful.

"God wanted harmony in the world, a proper balance and opportunity. That is one of the purposes of free choice. But it is also that which caused the tyrannical societies around the world.

"Because God gave man free choice, many covet whatever his neighbor has and/or that which he wants without regard to his fellow man. This happens at every societal level, wherever mankind inhabits. It doesn't matter if it is the remnants of my native Kamaiura Indian tribe in Brazil, a European nation, or in the Democratic and Republican parties of the United States who are looking to elect a new President or to an individual man or families. Many in mankind covet what another man has and very often <u>is that which symbolizes power</u> over his neighbor or fellow man. Coveting what another man has, greed and avarice is against God's basic laws for humanity.

"It is why God's commandments and what's been called the 'golden rule' have been handed down through endless generations, in numerous religions and in many forms; it is the only way in which harmony can exist in the world.

"Those who come to know God, ask for forgiveness of their wrongs and live according to His will and keep His commandments will enter Heaven and be granted everlasting, eternal life. Those that do not and who deny God will suffer eternal regret and damnation.

"It's really very simple.

"Mankind itself is what makes life so complex. All it really takes to achieve a harmonious existence is to make the proper choices and follow the rules of life;

rules which are nothing more than common sense. These are of God's commandments.

"Among the most important choices man can make is really the very obvious. Change! Universally, in any situation, if a man does not like who, what or where he is in life, at any moment in time, he can choose to change it. There are always options available, on all levels of all societal structures; the least being a change of attitude relative to the circumstances of one's being."

- - - - -

I wish now that I had asked her about God's plan for our lives and more specifically regarding His plan for her life or my own. In reality though, if it were something she could have shared with me, I think she would have. If we could look into the future or at our predestination, we may not immediately understand or even like where and why it has been chosen. I'm sure that fully knowing our destiny is not in God's plan for anyone. Later, Archie does explain God's plan for both of our lives, and understanding that it was His plan has given me the acceptance I was lacking for many, many months regarding Claricé's loss.

- - - - -

I was overwhelmed and <u>chose</u> to change the topic. "What do you do all day?" I asked her.

"First off, there is no 'all day' here. Time as it is known on earth does not exist in Heaven. There is no morning, noon, night or today and tomorrow or yesterday. There is only NOW. It is always now. Time does not exist. Now is eternal.

"The only earthly words to describe it are that in Heaven, it is a <u>sense of being</u>. We no longer have earthly bodies, or ears, eyes and a nose. We don't eat, drink, go to the bathroom or have sex. Our vibrational energy is often called the aura in mankind's descriptive terminology. We just are as we are, enjoying eternal life in the Heavenly plane of existence. It is a sense of pleasurable 'being' or well being.

"In thinking about the Heavenly experience, mankind thinks in their own terms of existence and humanity, when in fact it is totally different. Again, earthly words are inadequate to describe it, but I want to make clear it is <u>Heavenly.</u>

"Most mortal beings think in their own terms and from their own frame of reference, which is the human experience. When they believe the spirit of a loved one is with them, they might wonder if the spiritual being can see what they are doing at a particular moment in time. Sometimes, perhaps, in his or her mind they believe it could be embarrassing or they could be in what they believe to be some form of compromising position or situation they wouldn't want their loved one or any spiritual being to witness.

"Thankfully, it is not like that at all. Remember, my love, I said we do not have eyes, ears or a nose to check things out. So, you don't have to worry whether or not I am checking on you to see if you are behaving yourself.

"Instead, it is a connection of our energy. When I am with you, or the kids or my family, Maria, Ida or anyone else, 'I am with you... or them'. When I am with you, I am a part of you and I experience your pleasure as well as your pain. That is partly why I want you to move on with your life. I want you to be happy, so that I can be happier here also. In part, we share in our loved one's or what you call our soul mate's experience. It is a part of the learning process that is ongoing and takes place in the spiritual realm.

"You have much work to do and you will live another 20 years, and I will bring you someone that you can live happily with until we are together again."

"Whoa!" I interrupted her. "Here I am ready and have been hoping to join you soon; now you tell me I have 20 more years and a lot of work to do. I'm not sure I like that idea. How do you know I've got 20 more years to live?"

"There is no earthly way to explain that to you. I just know. But I also know you will be productive and

Victor K. Hosler

happy because I will be your guide. You guided me for the past ten years, now it is my turn to guide you."

Later, in her final communication to me Claricé does explain this.

"I think this began when I bought you the book, 'Conversations With God' by Neale Donald Walsch. I had read it and found it helpful to me spiritually. Because of my own confusion about God from my Indian heritage and then being raised by nuns in a Catholic orphanage, I never really understood the 'feeling' or connection to God. I only accepted that He was.

"It wasn't until we began going to the Community Church with the kids that I came to love and know that God exists. I am thankful for the opportunity I had to ask Christ for forgiveness of my earthly sins and accept his baptism at the hands of Pastor Mark before I left.

"The book helped me to understand prayer and talking to God. I knew that you believed in God, but I didn't think your spiritual understanding was as strong as it could be. At the time, I thought your reading the book would help you find your place with God. I didn't understand the full intent of giving it to you as I do now.

"If you recall, after you read the book, you had a spiritual experience in assisting your friend's son who was in prison to understand where he was in his life. At that time, you wrote him a lengthy letter regarding the fact that it was the poor choices he had made in his life that was responsible for where he was. You prayed about it, and as a result, unknown to you at the time, you did have a conversation with God that assisted you in writing to him, helping him to understand himself and that making positive choices in the future will put him back on the plan God has for his life. Following that glorifying experience, you continued to grow in your understanding as you communicated with others about the <u>Conversations With God</u> book and how it had begun to affect your life.

"Now, I believe God was directing me to buy the book for you because I was going to be called home and it was necessary for me to establish a believable link of communication with you after I departed and left my earthly body. As I said earlier, I've tried to communicate with you before, but couldn't get you to understand I was there. I know your grief was overwhelming and that it probably obscured my attempts to reach out to you and get your attention.

"Getting back to your question about what I am now doing, the answer is that right now, I am with you. Other times I am with the kids, Jorge, Jorgete, Delma and my family, Maria, Ida and others. I know when you and my loved ones sense or feel I am with them. It is a change in my vibrational energy that comes about and I sometimes get frustrated that you don't realize it is a connection or that I am with you or them. Instead, I just try to direct your thinking in a positive manner, wherever you are at a particular moment. It is what many of you on earth believe your 'guardian angels' are doing.

"Sometimes, I am like our track lights in our house. I am with several loved ones at the same time. Other times, I am working with, teaching and sharing my talent with new souls that are about to be born.

"I am really very busy by earthly standards and very happy, because in the Heavenly state I can share in the joy of all my loved ones every day and not be limited by human capability and earthly constraints. I can be where I want to be, doing what I want to do, at any moment in time. I can't think of anything better to be throughout eternity. Time does not exist and I don't have to play by the rules of mankind or the earthly time clock."

"To quote you, it sounds like a nice way of 'being'." Then I asked Claricé, "Who have you seen in Heaven?" And then I added, "I guess 'seen' is a wrong word since you don't have your lovely eyes, ears and nose."

"Yes, you are right, it is not seeing. The best explanation I can give you is that it is a process of

experiencing. *However, the impression I get is that each of us is experiencing the other, as we were known in our human form. Those of whom were in your life that I never had the opportunity to meet I am experiencing through your knowledge or awareness of them. A good example of this is your father. You know I never met him, but I know he is here, with a woman with white hair and he wants you to know he is happy and proud of what you have done during your life and since he left you.*

"Also, your Mother and Pa are here and you know that I never met Pa. But I can tell you that Ma was happy to be back with him and with their loving energy; they are like honeymooners. I have also seen my Mother and my son Marcel, they are always together and he is a happy little boy now. I was surprised to find that his energy was the same as when he was taken from me. I 'feel' that my father is here, but I still don't know him. Although it is not the same as a thought process in the human form, the only way I can describe it is 'thinking.' Whenever I 'think' of someone, regardless of whether they are still in their human vehicle form or they have crossed over and are in the spiritual realm, I am with them. Everybody I have experienced is busy doing something."

So then I asked her about her late husband who passed away in 1986. "How about Roger? When you saw him again did you tell him that I had told you to tell him you were already taken?"

Clarice laughed again in the cute way she always did. *"Actually no, I know he is here, but I cannot communicate, or experience him. He is serving some kind of penance, I guess you would call it in earthly terms, and cannot be reached or accessed. That is something that is difficult to explain to you. We can only experience the good people of the world who are here, those who have asked for God's forgiveness of their earthly sins. The only understanding I can give you about Roger and others is that those who were aware of God and their sins but did not ask for His forgiveness, are serving a penance and do not have the ability to experience Heaven in a Heavenly way. It is those who have denied God and His existence as our creator and have spat upon his neighbor that are damned for eternity."*

At some point along the way, around 3:00 a.m., I said to Claricé, "I've got to get some sleep."

And, she replied, *"Alright, go to sleep, my love."*

But I didn't, I continued to ask her questions, and finally, at 3:30, I again said, "I've got to get some sleep."

Once again, she replied and said, *"Alright, my love, but quit asking me questions."*

I did drift off to sleep then, but was awakened by her again at 6:30 and we communicated until a little after eight in the morning when I drifted back to sleep and awoke at 11:00 a.m.

- - - - -

After I had coffee and my breakfast the next morning, I began to reflect on the night's events. I was feeling very peaceful and more right with the world than I had since Claricé passed away. But as I thought about everything, I really questioned whether or not I had been dreaming, hallucinating or had an active imagination. I often have very vivid dreams, but never so verbally detailed or in the context that had taken place during that night. Almost every other dream I have had or could remember was of a visual nature rather than the experience that had taken place, which was primarily of a conversational nature. Occasionally during my communication with Claricé, I did have vivid images, but it was of her smile or her laugh and her facial expressions. It wasn't like she was sitting across the table or room from me. I was seeing her in my mind's eye, what is often referred to as our third eye.

I ran over everything in my mind, from looking at the digital clock on the VCR several times, to knowing that I had forced my eyes open several times to make sure I was awake and not dreaming. My conclusion was that I had enjoyed a very rare and pleasant spiritual experience.

Once I reached this point of acceptance, I was anxious to share the experience with someone who might understand it better than I and tried to call my dear friend Donald in Michigan who had been in various positions in the priesthood of the Reorganized Church of Jesus Christ and Latter Day Saints, the church of my youth, and where I had been baptized. Don has been a man of God and faith throughout his entire life and someone as dear to me as any family member could be. I thought he might have had similar experiences to share with me. Unfortunately, he was not home at the time to take my telephone call. When I was able to relate my experience to him a couple of days later, he suggested I had been blessed and God had brought her to me to aid in healing my grief.

I try not to bother my friend Rob too much at work, but next, I decided to call him at his office. Rob and his wife Kelly were our good friends who, Claricé had earlier mentioned, were going to have a baby. I think I wanted immediate confirmation that I was not thinking irrationally and losing it or trying to overcome my grief with a dreamlike experience that I might have created on my own.

Like the good friend he is, Rob was interested in my story and listened attentively. However, when I said Claricé told me she was working with new souls who are about to be born, he was blown away.

He stopped me in mid sentence and said, "That's awesome, Victor." He paused, and then added, "I can't believe it. Let me tell you something, but you have to keep it a secret just between you and me. Alright?"

"Yes, of course." I replied.

Rob then told me, "The timing of what you've said could not be more perfect. We just found out on Sunday that Kelly is pregnant. And even better, when we were talking about it, Kelly said that she guessed Claricé was sending us an angel."

Now *I was awestruck* and Rob said, "That's amazing."

Angels in My Life

How much more there will be and what impact the experience will have on my life, I don't know. I do believe that Claricé wants me to get on with my life and leave the grieving behind. More importantly, I'm sure she wants me to tell her story.

- - - - -

Sunday night, the 9th of January another communication took place. I began asking her questions about world affairs: how we fit into the kingdom of God and I again made reference to what she said about my living another twenty years and the work she said I still had left to do.

I asked her, "What can you tell me about the illnesses and tragedies that affect so many people in the world? What about the cancer that took your life?" She didn't respond to my question about her experience. She only spoke in generalities about the illnesses and tragedies.

She said, *"Almost all sicknesses of the world are of mankind's own making: by the way they live, what they eat and how one culture relates to another. People are very often victims of the environment, which they have created themselves. A good example is the starvation in the world. With today's technology in the world, starvation and insufficiency is unnecessary and the poorer nations and cultures of the world could be improved. The greed and avarice of mankind in general is the cause of most of the world's problems.*

"As for the tragedies of the world, such as accidents, the death of a child or loved one or world calamities, there is a purpose for most, a lesson in life and as difficult as it may be to accept, it is part of the learning process that hopefully will lead to the harmony God wants in the world he created.

"Once again, there will never be a perfect world. There can only be a proper balance. That which may be thought of by some people as a perfect world is illogical and not possible in a world where mankind has a God given right of freedom to choose. It makes no more sense for everyone to be rich Black and beautiful as it does to be rich white and beautiful, - or oriental – or Jewish – or Irish, etc.

"You will learn more in the 20 years you still have ahead of you. This will be the most important time of your entire life."

"At my age," I said again, "I'm not sure I want to live another 20 years." Then I repeated what I told her previously, "I have been hoping and have also prayed that I would join you soon. I'm not sure about the work that you said was in store for me."

She said, *"Don't worry, my love, I will guide you, I will guide you, guide you, guide you."* She repeated it until I drifted off and began to sleep.

Chapter Four
A Spiritual Communication With Dick
My Teen Age Friend and Buddy

On Monday night, January 10th, I was quite surprised by another spiritual communication that came through to me. This time it was not my late wife, it was with a departed friend of mine. It was Dick, my teenage friend and buddy, who had joined the U.S. Marine Corps with me in 1951. He had led a difficult life and, unfortunately, committed suicide almost 40 years earlier, in 1963. My communication with him that night was a briefer experience, but just as clear as the one I had with Claricé, and I immediately believed that she was somehow responsible for his presence.

As in the previous communications, my words and questions to my friend Dick will be in the normal type style, like the current text and Dick's words and answers will be in *italics*. The communication came to me spontaneously, as did those with Claricé, and again it put me in awe of what was happening. Once more I wondered if it was a hallucination, my overactive creative imagination or if I might in fact, be dreaming. Some dreams do seem so real. To be certain I was awake however, I immediately looked at and then kept my eye on the digital clock of my VCR. I needed to assure myself that I was awake. His opening words came at 1:20 a.m. and are in *italics*.

"Hey Victor, good buddy, I think you're going to be surprised to hear from me."

It was a statement in the still of the night. A surprise was an understatement, and moreso, because it was a man's voice. For some reason, there was an eerie sense of recognition that it was a voice from the past, like on the telephone, when you immediately identify a voice you haven't heard in many years. Compounding this, in my half-awake state of mind, there was an expectation that if I heard a "voice in the night" it would again be that of my late wife Claricé, who had communicated with me for a third time the previous night.

"Who are you?" was my immediate response. "Your voice sounds familiar, but if anything, I was half-expecting my wife Claricé again. Do I know you?" I asked, as my foggy mind searched its memory banks for recognition of the familiar voice.

"Think, my friend." He responded. *"It's been many years since we last spoke to each other."*

"Dick?" I questioned, as I suddenly remembered and recalled his voice mannerisms. Then, as I asked the question, visual confirmation began to come to the forefront of my mind. I began to see his face as I remembered him. It wasn't from the last time I saw him, but more like he was in our early years together. His hair was neatly combed back into what we used to call a "D.A." (Or, duck's ass in the teenage terminology of the '50s.). As I studied the image, looking at his blue silk shirt, with the back of his collar turned up in the style of the time, I also saw the image of his father, as I remembered him, and a woman I assumed was his mother. They were standing in the background. After a long pause, as if he were waiting for my comprehension, I again asked, "Dick?"

"Yes!" He replied. *"I've been trying to reach you since the late eighties. Remember, back when you suddenly got the urge to contact my daughters?"*

"Yeah!" I said thoughtfully. And, gradually remembered how strange I considered it when I began to feel a compulsion to contact his daughters. The last time I saw Dick and his daughters was in 1961, and so it had been a long time since I had even thought about him or his family.

Dick and I had drifted apart when I was in college and had gone our separate ways. The last time I did see him or his family was when his daughters were toddlers, a year that I briefly worked in Detroit, Michigan. I expected to see him in the mid-1960s, after I had gone to work for Eastern Airlines, and my first wife, the kids and I had flown home to Detroit to visit our families.

I believe the year we flew home was 1965 or 1966. I had called Dick's stepmother Mary to look him up again, and it was from that call I learned about his death from her; he had taken his own life in 1963.

Angels in My Life

Following this disappointing news for the most part I forgot about Dick or his family.

Almost thirty years passed when, for some unknown reason in 1988 or 1989, I began to think of his daughters. I began wondering how they were and what had happened to them without their father. At first the thoughts were just a mild curiosity that would occasionally pass through my mind. But then, as time passed I thought about them more and more until I gradually seemed to become obsessed with the idea of contacting them.

After a moment or so I replied, "Yeah, uh huh, yes..." I remember stammering. The previous thoughts had run through my mind in seconds, but it seemed like a long pause. "Uh... you were on my mind quite a lot back then."

"*Yes, that was me, Vic.*" He said with emphasis.

The image in my mind smiled at me and I seemed to hear a light, short, *I gotcha* kind of laugh.

"*Yep, Richard Allen was trying to get in touch with his high-school buddy. Remember, that was back when you were into doing past-life regressions for your friends. I thought you were spiritually in touch or in tune at the time, and that I might be able to get through to you. You did get the message, but I couldn't get you to hear my words or to acknowledge me.*"

- - - - - -

When the time came that I did decide to contact his daughters, I didn't have the slightest idea of where to begin. I didn't even remember their names. However, as the thoughts about it and the "feeling" I had about them grew, in late 1989 or early 1990 I decided to see if Dick's stepmother, Mary, was still living.

For a while, I had stayed in touch with her after the call when she told me about Dick's death. Mary lived four doors down from where I visited and then later lived with my father and stepmother in the late 1940s through 1951, and I believe she married Dick's father in about 1948. Mary had a personality that made her the "neighborhood mom." We could always talk to her when we had problems. Mine was with my dad and my own stepmother, and both Dick and myself had routine teen-age difficulties. I have a vague recollection that in one of our last telephone conversations, Mary had told me that Dick's father had passed over also.

When the urge to contact his daughters lingered, and grew stronger, I finally checked with a long-distance information and found out that Mary was still living in her house a few doors down from where I had lived.

She was astonished when I called her and yet she still recognized my voice after so many years. It had probably been at least 15 or more years since we had last talked. When I told her why I was calling, she didn't seem surprised at all. It was like we had just talked the day before. She just said, "How lovely," a distinctive phrase, which was typical of her. She said, "I'm sure the girls would be glad to hear from one of their father's friends." She then began to tell me all about Dick's daughters; their names were Laura and Brenda and that they were both living in central Michigan with their own families.

She also informed me that Dick's former wife had remarried and was living in the same area, and then repeated that she thought his daughters would be glad to hear from me. In fact, she said she was certain that, "…they would probably be happy to hear anything about the father they hardly remembered or knew." She thought they were four and six years old when their father died and, because he had taken his own life, it was a subject that was never talked about in their home and his name was seldom mentioned as they grew through the years. They knew very little about their father but since I had been one of his closest friends, she gave me his oldest daughter Laura's telephone number.

- - - - -

"How are you talking to me? And, why are you here now?" I asked Dick. Then I followed with, what to me seemed to be an obvious question, since I had just been communicating with Claricé. "Have you met my wife?"

"No, I haven't been in direct contact with her, but I did get the 'sense or feeling' that she had recently died and that she may be assisting me in my coming through to you; I'm sorry, for your loss, I know how difficult it is. You may remember that all of my life's problems began with the loss of my mother shortly before you and I met.

"The reason I'm here with you now is that I got an impression, perhaps from Claricé because I know she

Angels in My Life

met the girls and Carol with you when you were in Michigan in 1992. A <u>knowing</u> seemed to come to me that you were now open to spiritual contact and that there was a purpose for my doing it now. It is how we learn and understand everything on the spiritual level. For you it is a mental process. Our energy, which is the life force of God, that you who are still in your earthly bodies call the aura, receives a sensation that comes with needed knowledge. It is not always a direct understanding, if not questioned, but it is how we learn and grow spiritually; and believe me, buddy, I have grown and learned much on this side."

"Have you been with your girls?" I asked, but then without waiting for an answer, I immediately said, "You must have been with them to know that I have met them. Were you there when my wife Claricé and I visited them in 1992 and met them, the girls, Carol and her husband, Bob?" Then again, before he could answer, I added, "You must know that Laura and I write to each other once or twice a year and that I stopped by to visit her when I was in Michigan, after Claricé crossed over."

"Oh yes, I have been with them continually. I can't really relate to time, because it is so different over here. It is hard to explain in a way you on earth could understand. Everything is NOW, as I'm sure your wife has told you. Although we can go back or forth in time and observe, we do not have the ability to influence what has been, or what is going to happen. We cannot influence anything that is beyond one's plan of life, or that which could alter God's plan for the universe. We can only try to influence the NOW by giving positive thoughts to those we left behind. Like I said, I have learned a lot, and know now what I missed by taking my own life."

"What happened? Why did you do it? And why did you want me to contact the girls? Laura was receptive to me, but Brenda who looks amazingly like you, has not been interested in staying in contact."

"Well, I don't think you need to be troubled by the details of what happened at the end. It is something I

would rather not go back through myself. But the why, I think you will understand.

"You knew how I was, when we were buddies. My problems started when my mother became sick and then died. I felt that she abandoned me and for some reason I could never accept it and I developed a love-hate relationship toward her, and the memory of her for leaving me. This grew and festered in me until it became a sickness, which carried over into my relationships with women throughout the remaining years of my life on earth. I also resented my father for getting married so soon after my mother died. Although I now know it wasn't true, you know that at the time, I suspected they were involved before my mother died. As nice a lady that Mary was, and as much as she tried to be my friend, as she was also to you and Paul, I resented her being dad's wife until the very end."

Paul was another friend of ours from Dick's old neighborhood and my father referred to us as the "trio of trouble".

Dick continued. *"Remember how I was with the girls we double-dated? You used to tell me you thought that, love 'em and leave 'em was my silent motto. To use an old saying that I can remember us also joking about back then, you said that I could charm their pants off before they realized it happened. My looks, smile and boyish charm became a curse for me. I had what you <u>now call</u> 'an ego that wouldn't quit.' I don't think we understood what <u>an ego</u> was at the time, but I sure was a narcissist and although it was never sexual, I might have had a bit of what psychologists call an 'Oedipus complex.'*

"Women were easy for me to get, but once I had them, I was afraid of losing them. I was sure they would eventually hurt me, so I made certain I hurt them first, so that they wouldn't hurt me. I was always sorry afterwards, but that didn't make it right. It still hurt me too. I just couldn't control the feelings I had. Unfortunately, it became the pattern of my life.

"Even at the end, the fear was with me. Because I was running around, had such a drinking problem, and had been so verbally abusive toward Carol, I knew that eventually my girls would grow to hate me also. In my soggy mind, I couldn't stay around to let that happen. Brenda was the youngest and I never did have a chance to develop a close relationship with her; not like that I had with Laura. Laura was 'daddy's little girl' and she used to crawl up on my lap when I was messed up and tell me, 'everything will be okay, daddy.' Because I was sick, I couldn't and most likely would never, ever have changed. As it turned out, I did watch over them spiritually, tried in whatever way I could to influence their lives in a positive way and was proud of them both as they grew, matured and as they are today. It was really better for them. As my life was, I wasn't any good for myself or anyone else.

"Vic, I hurt from the moment my mother died until I took my own life. I wanted to be with her so badly, that in my darkest hour, I did what I had to do to make that happen. And, when it did, I was at greater peace than I might have imagined at first. I can't say that it was pleasant, and in earth time I'm not even sure how long the first phase lasted. In the beginning it was a period of blackness and emptiness... yet peaceful; it was very much like, what I am sure, many on Earth think and believe that death really is. But, I did have, <u>some awareness of being</u>; it was a somber period of seeking forgiveness of God for every single thing I did wrong during my entire stay in my earthly body. It seemed like I was in, what Elaine and Pat, the two Catholic girls we dated when we were in high school, called purgatory.

"Once that period was over, I felt the bliss of peace and was then reunited with my mother. She was as beautiful as I remembered her to be before she got sick. Then sometime later, I don't know how long it was, dad came over also. That is who you see standing behind me; it's my dad and mother. I wanted you and the girls to know I am with them and we are at peace.

"That's nice, but why are you here now? And, why were you trying to get through to me ten years or so ago, when you say you created the urge in me to contact your girls?

"Both then and now, my reason is the same. Everyone on this side, who left their loved ones in some sort of tragic manner would like to say <u>I'm sorry</u> for whatever the reason was. We, too, feel incomplete because there was never any opportunity for closure. I would like the girls to know that everything that happened was a result of my sickness. I was weak and didn't have the strength to go on, and I don't believe there was any one who could have helped me. But now, I want them to know I am okay.

"Being with God in the spiritual realm was never my intention. In fact, because He took my mother, I hated Him until the end. I never denied Him, but I hated what He did to me in taking my mother from me. It was only in my time of darkness that God's light began to shine through. I still can't say that I fully understand why I had to lose my mother, or in fact why you had to lose your wife, or comprehend the tragedies of the world and in the universe God created. Why things like this have to happen and why it is all a part of His plan, I've yet to fully learn.

"Vic, the only reasoning I get is probably the same as you well may have gotten from your wife. The goal of life on Earth is a state of evolution and learning for mankind individually and collectively as it is on God's other planets in His universes. His only goal is to achieve a balance and/or harmony of being for all of his children. There can never be a perfect world, and it would be impossible to define a way for it to be so. Perfection is nebulous and if achieved in all things would leave no purpose for being. Therefore, your world is a place of learning and creating an atmosphere of love and harmony while each one of mankind achieves his or her individual purpose for being. The same is true of the spiritual realm. Even here, we are always working toward the God-like state of perfection, yet in our contentment of being, we

accept that it can never be totally achieved; only God is in a perfect state of being. Actually, I'm still trying to get an understanding of how it can be myself.

"*Although many here may choose another incarnation into your earthly world to aid in their learning experience, I have not resolved my last time on Earth to the point I would want to choose to do it again.*

"*As to trying to come through to you ten years or so ago in your earth time, it was for the same reason. At that time, I got the 'sense' you were in contact with the spiritual realm when you were doing the past-life regressions. To use one of your earthly terms, I thought I could 'channel' through to you. You got the message, but not the words. When this happened, Laura was facing similar difficulties in her marriage that I had put her mother through. In my spiritual observation of her, I could sense the negative vibrations in which she was comparing her situation to her mother's with me. She was not thinking well of me, because that was all she knew.*

"*Victor, I wanted you to reach out to her and let her know that her dad was not all bad. For whatever excuse, her husband may have presented at the time, for his behavior, the <u>reason</u> may well have been much deeper. I thought that if you could share something about me that was good, she might look for the good in him even though their marriage was failing and they were separated. There is good in all of God's children and for those who have gotten off track, as I did myself, you often have to dig a little deeper to find the good in all.*

"*After you finally did call Laura, I was with you and assisted you in remembering many of our times together when you wrote her a detailed letter and sent her pictures of me from better times, before and when we were in the Marine Corps. It was after our basic training in Parris Island when I unfortunately began drinking heavily and I tried to drown my sorrows. That was the beginning of my downhill slide, but I'm sure it would have come about with or without being in* the Corps. *Although I wished you hadn't talked me into joining, it didn't have a thing to do with my problems.*

"Even though it was Laura I was concerned about at the time, I wanted you to contact both of my girls. I really wanted both her and Brenda to know that I wasn't always as bad as I was with their mother. When you knew me I may have been a horse's ass with the girls, but on the surface you knew I was a nice guy and we did have many good times together. I just wanted them to know that, and to know that now I am all right. I wish I could have taken away their pain and I know it still may have been hard for them to understand, but they really were better off as things turned out. With that, now I'll let you go to sleep, unless there is something else you want to ask me."

"Not really. I'm still questioning whether or not I am hallucinating or just have an active imagination. Claricé comes to me, and now you? I don't know what else to say or ask."

"Just believe it, Victor. My sense of it is that she brought me through to you in order for you to accept the reality of spiritual communications. Just believe that it is so, and sleep well my friend."

With those words, the imagery dissipated and I drifted off to sleep once again.

As I hesitated and procrastinated about calling Laura and telling her about the communication with her dad, several times Dick came back with bits of information to help me understand what we call Heaven and the spiritual realm. Each time, however, he would ask me when I was going to come into full acceptance and pass his messages along to his daughter.

Chapter Five
Auto Writing Awareness

Tuesday evening, the 11th of January 2000, I decided to begin to try and put the experiences I was having with both Claricé and then Dick into the computer so that I wouldn't forget the details. Already the events, and what had been communicated to me were becoming mixed up in my mind. I knew if I didn't write them down or put them into the computer, there were some things Claricé had said and what we talked about that I would forget and leave out. As well, there some personal details of a sad nature relative to our life and her illness, I wouldn't even want to go over again. I had to sort it all out in my mind. Any guilt I might have carried as happens with most people who lose a mate, had immediately dissipated after the experiences with her, but there was much that was communicated that I knew I would want to read, and read again.

I knew I couldn't *remember everything* from her and now I had the added meeting and communication with Dick, my teenage friend.

When I first began to write, I struggled as I attempted to explain my communication with Claricé. However, once I began writing the details, trying to remember and getting into the communications I had with her, the words suddenly began to flow from my fingertips without thought or processing. Once again, it was an unusual experience and at the time, I didn't even consider that I might be getting help from other sources. I didn't even understand that I might be tapping into my higher self and subconscious mind where all memories of the present incarnation and past incarnations are stored.

I had heard about auto writing by some authors and even had attempted it in the past. There was the experience Claricé related to in her communication regarding my friend's son who had been troubled. I had prayed and asked for guidance, but never really was aware that it had come through. As well, when I first wrote to Dick's daughter. He mentioned he was assisting me when he said he "helped me remember" our good times to pass along to his daughters. All in all, I did not have much experience or faith in my ability to auto write.

As I began transcribing my thoughts and remembrances of the communications with my late wife and the memories began to flow, I began to think and feel that I may be experiencing the process of auto-writing. The memories were flowing too freely and without serious thought, as is often required to bring forth in depth memories;

especially sad memories or those that normally one might want to block out. I believed at the time that for some reason and in some way, Claricé had begun to guide me from the spiritual dimension. As this thought entered my mind, I remembered the final words she said two nights earlier on the 9th when she repeated the words, "I will guide you, guide you… guide you…" until I drifted off to sleep.

The transcription of my communication with my friend Dick took place a few days later. Much later, after I made contact with my angels and became fully aware of auto writing, I was given information to the contrary from ML, my Angel of Relationships. She informed me that she, Archie and Miriam were responsible for assisting both Claricé and Dick in coming through to me, and when the communications were dictated to me, it was Archie who was guiding my thought processes and bringing the information from the communications back to me. It was coming from them and the impression of their thoughts being placed in my mind that were coming through my fingertips. It was her however who was helping me to organize the transcription in a meaningful manner. I know now that any transcriptions regarding personal relationships are and will be brought to me with the assistance of ML.

Chapter Six
Claricé's Return

Wednesday, January 12, 2000 Claricé woke me at about 4:00 a.m. When I first woke up, I felt refreshed and in the new communication we began having she sounded concerned and it seemed to be significant. Claricé was with me for a little over an hour and a half

This time I wanted to get the thoughts down while they were fresh in my mind, so I got out of bed when it ended at about 5:35 a.m. to continue the writing that had begun the night before. I went to the computer immediately following her departure from my mind. There were two primary points she wanted to communicate during the early morning of January 12.

The first was in regard to the question of reincarnation that came up from my friend Rob, when I was discussing my communications with Claricé. The second was in regard to Dick, my teenage friend and buddy who had committed suicide.

As many readers may also be, a good part of my immediate family are what is commonly referred to as "Born Again Christians:" fundamentalists who believe quite literally that every word in the Bible as written is the "true and only word of God." Knowing this, Claricé apparently thought I might get questions regarding her reference to reincarnation and those she acknowledged who were in the heavenly environment. She also thought that my friend Dick, who had committed suicide and was now in heaven, would bring questions from them as well.

Rob had questioned how those she mentioned could still be in heaven if there really was such a thing as reincarnation. Referring to Claricé's mention of "ma and pa, and my dad and the woman with white hair," he asked me the question, "Vic, if reincarnation is possible, wouldn't they have been reincarnated already instead of still being in heaven? Wouldn't they be on earth and living another life?" His questions came from a position of disbelief.

Because this came about regarding my communications with Clarice, she must have decided to come to me again to clarify the subject matter in a way that I could explain it reasonably. Although he didn't have a clear understanding about whether or not those who commit suicide could enter heaven, my friend Rob also questioned that as well.

Victor K. Hosler

    For many Christians, reincarnation and those who commit suicide going to heaven is contrary to their beliefs and their understanding of the Biblical position and Christ's teaching. As well, Claricé may have been with me in spirit when I attempted to give Rob my understanding and a spontaneous reply to his questions on the telephone.

- - - - - -

    When I woke up at 4:30 in the morning and looked at the clock, I began thinking about the reincarnation discussion with Rob. With this thought in mind, I immediately sensed that Claricé was with me, so I asked aloud, "If you are here with me Claricé, how can I explain reincarnation in a way that Rob can understand it without compromising his beliefs or creating unnecessary controversy?"

    The tone of Claricé's voice in my head appeared concerned, but eager to discuss it and she began by saying, *"Yes, I am here. First off, my love, my discussions with you are not intended to stir up questions about God, Christ or the Bible with our kids or anyone else. It is best to understand that words, in any language, are necessary tools for mankind to have a means of communication between one to another. They are only words.*

    "Once again, God has given man free choice. Therefore, the actual words were written by man, who chose the words he believed would express the thoughts and 'word' of God as they were understood at the various times, different places and languages they were written in. The Word of God as it was written, and other documents claimed to be the word of God, will continue to create controversy for eons to come, and it would be pointless, for me, or you, to continue discussing it. I really cannot address the issue beyond what I have said.

    "It is the same thing in my communicating with you at this moment; they are my thoughts and ideas of understanding expressed to you in thought and put forth in your own words, even though in your mind you are hearing them in my voice. By the way when I refer to or say something is of my thoughts, it is for your

understanding only. We don't have 'thoughts' as it is expressed in your earthly language or terminology. When something is asked of us or we want to pass some information along, we just do it from a position of knowing.

"A further discussion of what is called reincarnation can be explained in terms of cellular biology and how one cell in a living organism splits and begins to multiply. Rob implied that life begins in the womb. It does; the sperm joins and fertilizes the egg to become a seed for a physical vehicle in which the soul will reside.

"There is no question among believers that we are all God's children; therefore our 'soul' comes from — and at the direction or discretion — of our Heavenly Father. In mankind's understanding, why is it so hard to believe that a soul could give off a small part of itself and then multiply to become another... and another, when that is exactly what happens to the first cell in the womb?

"Whether or not there is such a thing as reincarnation, it is nothing more than a matter of semantics and the word itself. You must remember that God began with Adam and Eve. They are two people, two souls who throughout all of the time on earth and through God's will have 'split' and multiplied to become billions of souls and billions of people. If you also consider all who have died since the world began, the billions grow to trillions or zillions and more."

I said, "Rob mentioned his believing as 'faith.' My belief in what I am 'hearing' or writing is also due to faith — my faith that there is purpose to the communication that I am having and that it is actually coming from or being guided by you."

"Yes, you have to have faith to believe in the unknown and that is what this experience is for you. There is much that mankind does not know or understand about life. Mankind must accept much of <u>what is</u>, on the basis of his or her own individual belief through their faith, study and understanding.

"This is why I had to convince you of the truth or reality in what we are and have been doing. By having you communicate with your friend Dick and then later having you call his daughter, Laura, in Michigan to confirm the many details of his life and Laura's life, I could convince you to believe in the reality of my communication with you. Some of the facts or events Dick related to you were previously unknown to you. I knew that Laura's confirmation would assist you in your belief. It was necessary for you to believe and to have faith that the new experiences you were having are in truth, a reality.

"Remember what I said before? All of the believers in God, <u>the good people</u>, are in heaven. When Rob recalled that I said your Mother and Pa were here, Rob questioned that if they were in fact there, how could there be such a thing as reincarnation? Wouldn't they have been reincarnated, he asked? Once again you have to have faith in the unknown.

"But, once more, doesn't it make some sense that if God wants harmony in the world, that he would continually bring forth more of the good souls? One small part of a good soul is taken and put in the womb by the hand of God prior to birth. All souls come from and are a part of God. Therefore, is it not reasonable to assume that because God wants harmony in the world he would fill the world with good souls? As well, sometimes a soul will choose to continue the learning process in the spiritual realm and have a new incarnation on Earth as well. When this happens, a soul splits and one part remains and the other takes on a new life. Sometimes, the two souls will rejoin to become one again and other times each stay separate. When they stay apart, each soul will then have all past memory of previous incarnations. This accounts for the increases in number of souls on Earth as well as soul groups incarnating together over a period of several lifetimes.

"As a cell with its soul multiplies to become a human being, every cell in the body is a part of the original cell (good soul) and has the experience of all

Angels in My Life

earlier life. If a single cell with a soul created by God can split to become two, four, eight, sixteen and so on until it becomes a new human being, is it unreasonable to accept the possibility that part of a good soul in heaven could be chosen by God to create a new soul or being, as he created Adam and Eve and then the rest of mankind as you know it? If you take this logic all the way back in the family tree of life you would get back to Adam and Eve.

"It has reasonably been proved that a man's talent and perhaps intellect is not always a learned experience. Talent is generally accepted to be a God given gift. It is a part of the soul. However, how this talent is used and developed in the physical vehicle/body is by mankind's God given choice.

"In the growth of the human race and experience over thousands of years, the world has evolved into what you know it to be today. It is far from a perfect world, but I believe there is universal acceptance that it came about through the talent and creativity of those who have chosen to use their God given gifts in a positive manner.

"The ongoing improvements in the world and with mankind strongly suggest the talents and intellect of the good souls are passed down by God. Little else can account for the child prodigies of the world. For most of them, it is not a genetic gift or a learned experience. It is an innate ability they were given at God's direction and passed on when their soul was created and joined the fetus in the womb. But it does originate from the learned experience of the souls who have walked the Earth before them.

"Perhaps taking a little from this one and a little from that one, based on their life's experiences is God's way of creating the harmonious world he wants.

"Getting back to the positive (+) and negative (-) attributes of the world, or what is often referred to in earthly terms as 'Ying – Yang', God could create all to be one or the other. However, once more it would be a pretty boring existence if everything and everybody were to be the same. Instead, it is an on-going

experience of growth and development in the world as He determines what is needed to achieve the level of perfection and harmony He wants and not necessarily the perfect world.

"Reincarnation is only a word, created in the past by a man in an attempt to explain an unknown but experienced phenomenon and has created controversy for years and years. I have not tried to define reincarnation, my love, because to do so would just add to the controversy, confusion and debate. I have only attempted to give you some thoughts on why the idea or word itself may have come about. Belief, disbelief, faith or lack thereof is every man's choice alone, and a judgment of right or wrong belongs only to God.

"With that last statement, I will get into your communication the other night with your friend Dick. As I said earlier, I created that experience for you with him in order for you to believe in the reality of the communication I was having with you and to show you the ability you have to use your sixth sense in this manner.

"I sensed that you communicating with Dick, almost 40 years after his departure from his earthly difficulties, would assure you the truth of our experience as well as that with him. Further, as mentioned above, when you were able to confirm the details of his life and Laura's, there were details that you were unaware of until your communication with him, and then later, with his daughter Laura; I knew then that you could accept my coming to you in this way.

"Before you get into a debate with the family over your seeing or experiencing Dick in Heaven with his mother and father after he killed himself, I'll try to give you my sense of how that can be.

"It is accepted among many believers in God, our creator in Heaven, that suicide is what has been called a mortal sin. Since it is not known specifically the circumstances in Dick's mind at his moment of death, it is not the responsibility of mankind to place *judgment on what might or might not have been. Judgment of mankind's endeavors while in his earthly body belongs to God alone. We do know that Dick led a very troubled life, both as you knew him over a ten-year period and as he related his sorrow to you during your brief visit and communication with him.*

"We know Dick was a man who was never able to come to terms with or overcome the death of his mother when he was in his early teens. It was something that tormented him throughout the balance of his life on earth.

"Assume for a moment that at the moment of his death he may have said, or thought, 'Forgive me Father, I just cannot take it any longer. I know I am living a terrible life and I don't know how to change it.' That is hypothetical of course, but it does border on a confession of his sin of suicide and we do know God offers redemption for all sinners.

"As it is with those who are here that we cannot experience or communicate with, because they are serving what I'm calling a penance, perhaps it was so with your friend Dick. In your communication with him he fully expressed sorrow and his apology to those he left behind. He spoke of being in darkness before finding the light of God.

"Later, when you spoke with his daughter Laura she said she was grateful for your call and accepted this acknowledgement and said it brought her a sense of peace over his death that she had never had before. Perhaps Dick did not come to know God in time for his immediate salvation, but because you experienced him to be happy and in Heaven with both his mother and father, his redemption from God must have been received.

"No man should judge, but have faith in his experience of God and of what is, for himself. My love, I hope this keeps you out of trouble and a religious debate with the kids."

When she left me that morning, I hesitated and my mind was clear once again and back on the moment of the day.

Claricé had departed once more and I was left with a thought that came immediately to mind of a phrase I heard many years ago. "Whatever is, is... and no man can change it. You can only change that which is to come by the choices you make as you face each new day."

- - - - -

The final communication with Claricé was on the night of January 16/17, 2000, and was relatively brief. I had been upset that day because I had just learned that our good friend Kelly had experienced a miscarriage in her pregnancy. This caused me some doubt about my communications with Claricé. There wasn't going to be a baby now. Our friends, Rob and Kelly, and I wondered why she mentioned the pregnancy to me when it seems she could also have known about the miscarriage. I had thought it was some sort of prediction by her.

- - - - -

When she came through to me, Claricé said, *"I'm sorry about Kelly losing the baby. I know everyone is disappointed.*

"There is something you must understand, my love. When I told you I was working with new souls who were about to be born and that Kelly and Rob were going to have a baby, Rob and you assumed I was talking about them. It was just a coincidence in timing. I wasn't predicting, or forecasting the future, no more than I would, if I could give you the Lotto numbers or anything else. It just so happened that I was spiritually with Rob and Kelly when she took the pregnancy test, when they found out she was pregnant.

"When I came to you and told you about it a couple of nights later, I was only sharing news that I knew you would want to hear and would normally have heard about quite soon anyway. You know Rob and Kelly, or your family, are not particularly good about keeping secrets from one another. Furthermore, if I could have looked ahead and found out there was a problem with the joining of the seeds, I would not have told you about it, because it would be inappropriate under the circumstances that I exist in the spiritual world.

"It is not possible to communicate anything to those we have left behind that if known could, or would, affect the course of history and God's plan for humanity. I also know from being with them since that time, that their happiness over the pregnancy has caused them to discuss the possibility of trying again when the time is right.

"For Kelly, there never will be a satisfactory answer for the loss she encountered over the pregnancy, miscarriage and the pain that was caused. She is in the same position as you, my love. Her pain is no less than is yours. As you may never find satisfaction in the reason for God calling me home, there is no reason that would give Kelly an understanding of her loss either. She can only accept that for reasons unknown, it was the will of God.

"In regard to the communication about the pregnancy, it was exactly as you were told. I was only trying to cheer you up in your grief with some joyous news. Could I have known that Kelly would miscarry, the answer is obviously yes if I had considered looking ahead. However, even though all information is available, we are not omniscient at all times. As you do on earth, if we need or want information, in a sense we have to look for it also. Because of the pain that was added to her burden, it was unfortunate that I did not look ahead. If I had, I certainly would have looked for something else to cheer you up. As you are trying so hard to do, you both have to accept that for whatever the reason, both losses were God's will.

"Regarding the future and everything being <u>now</u> on this side is true, but it's a difficult concept to follow from your point of view. Information about everything, past, present and future is available to us here, but there is little point in looking ahead at it, because it is something we cannot communicate to our loved ones and others we left behind. The only information we can convey regarding the future is that which cannot change the outcome of what is to be in God's plan for your lives and the universe.

"When I said that you have twenty more years to live, I was not predicting the future then either. God's plan for your life is in what has been called in human terminology, the 'book of life' in 'the hall of records' and this was one of the first things I went to check out when I settled on this side. I wanted to know when you would be with me again. You still have your God given freedom of choice; therefore in the coming years, something you do could create a cause of an earlier demise than God's plan for you. In all lives, God's plan is not always followed perfectly; there are many things that could still affect the outcome of your life by the choices you will make. I'm going to leave you now my love."

With that, the image of Claricé faded from my mind's eye. Although she had said, "I'm going to leave you now, my love." little did I know that would be the last communication I would have from her.

I lay there quite some time, thinking about the communications I'd been having. As I did, a suggestion came to mind that my communicating with Claricé was a matter of belief. You have to listen and believe that you are not imagining it. In the quiet of the night there are voices to be heard, or a knowingness that seems to come about. If you ask questions and listen, they will be answered, but you have to listen and believe.

Like a prayer, when you ask God for guidance and He gives you a solution or answer, the words come into your mind, without identifiable sound or voice because God has no voice, <u>God IS</u>. I have come to believe that words from loved ones in the spiritual realm can come to your mind with recognition of voice and speech mannerisms or pure knowing, when you are open to believing. When for no reason or pre-thought you have a sense or feeling of a loved one's presence, I now believe they generally are with you, watching over you and giving you guidance from within the higher recesses of your mind where, what is called the spirit, super consciousness or higher self resides. Believe and you will receive!

Chapter Seven
A Spiritual Communication With Sally

The following communication, as did the ones from Claricé and Dick, spontaneously began in the quiet of the night and with no preconceived thought or intention on my part on the night of May 16, 2000. Although I occasionally think of her I had no specific recollection of the last time she had been in my thoughts.

Sally was the mother of my first wife Jean and my children's grandmother. She said that she had come to me because she had *an experience* of Claricé after she crossed over, and was given a sensation or awareness that my mind was suddenly open to spiritual contact. Her reason for coming through to me was because she had concerns about the state of her daughter's health and also because she wanted to clear up some misconceptions or issues of doubt regarding her death in 1967.

Her daughter Jean and I have remained close friends throughout the 30 years since our divorce, and Sally knew that Jean was still carrying negative feelings and thoughts relative to her questionable, but accidental drug overdose. She knew I would be able to share this message with Jean. The communication was so unexpected, that when it began, I was once more uncertain of its reality. Through my doubt however, she came back again and again, with her communications taking place over several nights.

What Sally had to say was both surprising to me — and yet, revealing — in regard to her experience in and of the spiritual realm. In addition to giving me the information regarding her sickness and death, she told me a story about a subsequent life and a second accidental death. She told me about her own reincarnation and of being born again into another family and the lessons she was to learn during that particular lifetime.

Once more, I found the entire experience somewhat unbelievable, yet what else could it be, and why was it happening? As the number of my spiritual contacts began to grow, so did my belief in their reality. For me they brought an affirmation of my late wife's communications with me and that my new purpose in life was spiritual growth and that I was to put my skepticism behind me.

There is much more to the universe that God, our Supreme Being, created which is truly beyond the scope of understanding in the conscious mind of our earthly bodies. More and more I have come to believe that each of us must get in touch with our higher consciousness, the higher self, the soul, *God's Light* and the Christ within.

During the period of time following my first spiritual communication with Claricé and this one with Sally, my personal research led me to the Bible as well many books on spirituality, angels and the paranormal. Sharing some of my experiences has been met with doubt by some, but in my research and reading, much of what has been communicated to me, through both my spiritual and the later angelic visits, has reinforced the reality of their content.

When Claricé, my late wife first communicated with me and I was in doubt and denial, I facetiously asked her if she had met God. Claricé then replied, *"Of course. God is the light of life. God is the light at the end of the tunnel that is so often described by people on earth who have had near death experiences. God is the light of Christ's ascension. God is the light of the burning bush. God is the light of protection that surrounds those who are facing danger or the unknown. God is the halo of every saint in heaven. God is the aura of life for all of mankind. God is the Light."*

When she was with me in her earthly body or vehicle, those <u>specific words</u> were never previously spoken or discussed between us, nor did I ever previously have any personal thoughts along this line. My intention is not to preach, recommend or quote chapter and verse from the Bible, but here are a few quotations anyone could readily find: Jesus said, "I am *the light of the world.*" and "Ye are *the light of the world.*" He also said, "In Him was life and the life *was the light* of humanity." One specific quotation I would like to offer is from the New American Bible, which also supports Claricé's communication. The quote is from John 1:1-5 which states: "In the beginning was the Word, and the Word was with God... All things came to be through Him, and without Him nothing came to be. Through Him was life, and this life *was the light of the human race*; the *light shines* in the darkness, and the darkness has not over come it." This was an affirmation that was beyond any doubt remaining in my mind.

Sally's communications took place between the nights of May 16 and May 31, 2000. There were two spiritual contacts that were rather lengthy and a few others, which were fragmentary and broken, as I fought my early doubts and attempted to push them aside to get some much needed sleep and rest. The experience of hearing voices in the night had been upsetting and deprived me of restful sleep as much as it was awe-inspiring.

Angels in My Life

I was still not certain if what was happening with me was a series of hallucinations or the result of an overactive creative imagination. However, it then made sense to me that by Claricé bringing me other spiritual communications, she was finding a way for me to truly believe in the reality of her contact with me at a time when I was doubtful. Her communications, I believe now, were intended to bring me comfort and assurance that she was okay and that we would one day meet again in the spiritual, heavenly plane of eternal existence. She clearly told me that my years ahead were to discover and share my spirituality.

In each of the five different spiritual communications that have come to me, the entities coming through were concerned about the mental and/or physical health or the well being of loved ones left behind.

- - - - -

Sally's first words came to me in the still of the night.

"Hi Vic." she said, *"Would you like to have a cup of coffee and a pep pill..."* (There was a pause and sense of a smile in her words) *...then help me rid up the house?"*

I didn't have a visual recognition as I had with Claricé and Dick and I was somewhat startled, at the unexpected visit; but this was the third spiritual entity to come through to me and I immediately recognized the unusual phrase she had often used in the past. It was one the family would tease her about many years ago.

"Sally?" I asked.

"Yes!" She replied, and then asked, *"Surprised?"*

"Yes, and no!" I responded. "Nothing really seems to surprise me these days."

When her daughter Jean and I were first married, the words in her question, "then help me rid up the house?" was common western Pennsylvania slang terminology that she used for cleaning up the house. It gave me instant recognition.

Sally had a distinctive Pennsylvania accent as well as word usage. To this day, I don't know what the little "pep pills" were, but at the time, she had an endless supply of them. Whenever she wanted some work done around the house, whether it was to paint a wall, fix something in the house or to scrub and wax the floors, she would pop tiny yellow pills into her husband's or my morning coffee. Shortly afterward, she would ask for help doing something. Because the pills energized us, we would readily fulfill her request without question. It was quite some time before her little "trick" was discovered; and when it was, it became a family joke.

"What are you doing here?" I asked her.

"I'm really worried about Jean Hope."

She almost always referred to her daughter by her full name.

"She has become so concerned over her recent health problems, I am afraid she may worry herself into leaving her physical body before it is really necessary. Her concern over her health, dying and leaving everybody and not being able be around to see all of her grandchildren grow up and get married, might make her condition worse than it really is.

"I know that in recent months you have gained a clearer understanding of the spiritual planes in the communications you have had with your late wife Claricé. By the way," she injected, *"she is a lovely spirit and I am sorry for your loss. I know how good you were for each other, but be assured, you will be together again."*

"Is she with you?" I asked.

"No, I experienced her and she showed me the way to you, but I believe she is a much older soul. She is already on a higher spiritual plane with the teachers."

"What can I do about Jean's problems?" I asked.

"Before I get into that, I want to make sure you understand something. You may already know this, but I want to clarify it for you. In all, I have been here quite a long time in your Earth years and I have been able to learn a great deal. Everything I've learned here about the earthly and spiritual planes and understanding of them is not quite the way we learned from the religious teachings many of us experienced while in our physical bodies and living in the earthly

world God created. Many interpretations we were given are questionable, but it is best that I do not get into a lot of what I have learned during my time here. Without authority or proof, and there is no way to give you that, much more disbelief would come about regarding your experiences. Any explanation I could offer is nothing more than mere words, which would be met with more doubt. Everyone, each of God's children will learn the truth when the time is right for them, or when they cross over.

"What is important now, regarding Jean Hope, is her health and well being. I think you have come to understand that God does have a divine plan for the universe. This includes a plan of learning during each individual's life on earth as a human being, as well as learning in the spiritual planes of eternity. Life on Earth and in the spiritual universe is a continual process of learning and moving toward a God-like perfection of our energy.

"When one learns what they can, or are supposed to, during a particular incarnation on the earthly plane, the soul of mankind leaves their physical bodies and returns to the spiritual plane. That however, does not mean your life on the earthly plane is totally predestined.

"Remember our Heavenly Father, God, our Creator gave each of His children 'free choice.' This means that even though there is a plan, each child of God can change the plan and will not always get back on course. Two good examples I can give you of this are: My own life as Sally in the physical plane of Earth during the lifetime in which I gave birth to Jean Hope and her brother Jack. The same is true for your friend Dick, whose energy I was able to experience through Claricé. Both of us made some very wrong decisions that led us to prematurely leave our physical bodies before our planned time on Earth was to come about.

"Regarding Jean Hope's health, it is not my place to say how much time she may or may not have in the plan for her life, but I can tell you that she must stop worrying about herself and develop a frame of mind in

which she will live out God's planned time for her. However, the stress carried by her worry may hasten the death of her physical body if she does not begin to believe that she is a perfect child of God. Perfect, just the way she is, in spite of the health problems she has recently experienced. She is in charge, but she must take charge. She just has to listen to the God within her heart, soul and spirit and do what is right for her to live and improve her own healing. It is a decision she can make. Much healing of the physical being can be done within her self-energy. Like every one of His children, her energy, her everlasting spirit was given free choice.

I interrupted her. "Wow, that's quite an observation. If you don't mind, let me ask you this, as I also asked Claricé. When we were together, you never spoke as clearly and distinctly as you are doing now. I recognize and remember your voice, your Pennsylvania accent and the expression 'rid up the house.' I also remember the 'pep pills' and the way you almost always referred to Jean as 'Jean Hope', but there seems to be much more clarity of thought in your words and what you are saying now. How did this come about?"

"Well, I will give you a couple of reasons. First off, as Claricé has probably told you, I am only planting the information within your mind. You are processing the information and then formulating the meaning into words; yet, you are hearing them in a way that you will recognize them as my voice, in order to accept the reality that the communication is coming from me.

"Secondly, as you well know, while on the earthly plane, my mind had not really been clear for many years. This is the next subject I want to bring to your attention so you can find a way to share with Jean Hope my regrets and apology for the manner of my physical existence during my life on Earth and how it ended.

"In one simple word, it was the drugs!

"Before I get into discussing my problems, I do want to say that I loved Jean Hope and Jack with all of my heart. When each of them arrived their father and I could not have been happier. Unfortunately, as problems began in our marriage, the drinking, the fighting and everything else, I was not as good of a mother as I could have been and wanted to be. I did not express the love that Jean Hope needed and wanted. It was the same with Jack also, but he was Glen's little man and he did seem to get more attention, even though I didn't realize it at the time.

"When my head was clear, I always promised myself I would make it up to Jean and tell her how much I loved her, but it was always forgotten in the fog that followed the drugs. It was a regret I always carried. As Jean Hope grew up and then married you, I could never find a way to express it or explain my real problems to her.

"Whether the problems I had were lessons I had to learn in that particular life on Earth or a continual string of bad choices I made, I haven't yet been able to fully determine, but I'm sure I will learn soon. I'll get into my pain and addiction later. For now, I just wanted to point out that most of that life was not a very happy time for me and I know that it affected those around me. Unfortunately this created havoc and pain in our family life more than I want to recall even now.

"As I believe Jean Hope will remember, her father Glen always had a severe drinking problem. He was an alcoholic and during our last few years together, when I was drinking with him before we divorced, I became like him and developed my own dependency. I now believe that was what led to my sickness and later addiction to the drugs as well. I wasn't a very nice person during those times.

"Later, after I married her step-father Ron, I almost stopped drinking. Ron enjoyed his beer, and I often shared one with him, but we didn't drink heavily; he wasn't a drunk and was a good provider, whereas her father only worked when he was sober. Ron really was a wonderful man who deserved more than he got living with me.

"I'm not certain whether it was the withdrawal from drinking so much after Glen and I split up, our stressful life, or the problems we had; but this was about the same time the severe migraines began with their blinding headaches and the vomiting.

"Soon thereafter, doctor 'C' came into my life and for about the next 15 or so years I became addicted to Demerol and other narcotics he would prescribe to control the pain and effects of the migraine headaches. When I was down and out of it, he also prescribed 'uppers' of different sorts, including the little yellow 'pep pills' I would take in order for me to wake up enough to be able to function.

"This is why I mentioned the pep pills for your coffee when I first called out to you; it was just to remind you. I knew you would remember them, and that it would get your attention. Fortunately, I didn't give them to you too often; but whenever I wanted Ron to wash the floor, paint the walls or to do anything else around the house I would drop one or two in his coffee. They never failed to get results. He immediately became energized and would do almost anything I asked of him. But he also liked his television. I had to use the pills to get things done around the house, because I was always too sick. I think Ron was the original 'couch potato.' I don't remember how long it was, but eventually he learned not to take coffee from me unless he saw me pour it in a fresh cup with his own eyes.

"Vic, I can't tell you how hard I tried to get off the pills, but I just didn't have the strength. Later, even here in the spiritual realm, it was satisfying for my soul when I learned doctor 'C' had been arrested, convicted and sent to prison for all the damage he had done to me and to so many other lives. He died in prison, as he should have. He had an evil streak of greed and only prescribed drugs, which would control his patient's symptoms and make them believe they felt better.

Angels in My Life

"Once his patients were hooked on his drugs, we would have to continually go back to him for more. To use your common druggie terminology of today, his office visits provided our 'fix' and he got rich. He even instructed each of his patients to go to several different drug stores so that the number of prescriptions he wrote would not be noticeable. The times when Ron would not let me go to him, I was able to secretly go to other doctors or sources I learned about in talking with other patients. Although I knew it was wrong and others who were hooked knew it was wrong, we were all <u>in need</u>, and convinced ourselves we were doing it for our pain and didn't consider ourselves addicts or addicted. We convinced ourselves it wasn't like a heavy addiction to hard drugs and the problems prevalent in your world today. We were fooled... and we were fools.

"Whenever I was not on the drugs, I was really very sorry for what I couldn't control. In the final months of my physical existence, Ron knew I was getting pills somewhere and he would often find them and flush them down the toilet. But, I always had more hidden or knew where to get them and would get more when he was at work and hide them.

"As my condition worsened, Ron and I began to constantly fight over the pills and he wouldn't let me go to doctor 'C' any longer. The night I overdosed and crossed over to the spiritual plane, he struggled with me to get a bottle of pills out of my hands. That is when I fell against and between the tub and toilet and got the bruises and the blood got on my pajama top. He didn't intentionally hurt me or cause the death of my physical body. He was angry and did get the pills, but as soon as he left the bathroom, there were more. I locked the bathroom door and got the pills I had hidden inside of an empty cold cream skin cleanser jar under the bathroom sink.

"But I want Jean Hope to know, even though suicide was considered to be a possibility in my death, it was not true. I did not intentionally end my physical life; the overdose was an accident. I admit I knew an *accidental overdose was possible, because I was out of it and had lost control; but I didn't knowingly take too much.*

"Because of the pain and grief I caused everyone and the way my life had been, I was surprised when I crossed over and I became aware of being in the heavenly plane. Even more, I was thankful for the presence of God during my earthly life. The Lord knew I had prayed and begged for strength and forgiveness over and over; but I didn't or couldn't find the strength or means within myself to overcome my addiction.

"Here it is beautiful, peaceful and timeless. It is a far better time than my life on earth had been because of the choices I made and the direction my life had taken. Regarding Jean's concern over her leaving your kids and grandchildren, and perhaps not being around when the grandchildren get married or the great-grandchildren are born, it is really nothing to worry about. Every one of God's children will face the same concern to one degree or another before their time on Earth is over.

"In my own situation, because of my addiction and the condition of my life while on the earthly plane, I was not really able to enjoy my kids, let alone my grandchildren. Since I have been in the spiritual plane, I have been able to share in my kid's lives, my grandchildren's lives and all of my great-grandchildren more than I ever could have imagined. Over here, we do not have the awareness of physical touch as you know it and the overt love being given and returned as it is experienced in your earthly physical bodies. I do, however, miss the back and forth communication and the 'touch' of a loved one. You are the only one of the humankind that I have been able to communicate with. The many times I have been with Jean or Jack or tried to communicate with others, they don't listen... and don't believe it when they have heard me. For me, though, it has been far better since I have been gone than it was, or ever could have been, with the problems I had. This though cannot be said

for all mortals, because life on the earthly plane of existence can be beautiful for most if they make the right choices during their physical lives on Earth. Even with those who feel or who have lack and insufficiency can choose to make more of their lives than they know and enhance their earthly learning, if they would have faith and listen to God and the spirit within.

"I know Jean has enjoyed her kids and grandchildren and will continue to do so. That is what I want her to be able to do for as long as God has planned for her. She must take better care of herself so that this can be.

"As I am sure Claricé has probably told you, here we can choose to be with whomever we want and whenever we want to; with one or all, it is our choosing. I know that for most humans, this is a hard concept to understand in earthly terms and based upon current and past religious teachings. With the exception of being able to talk back and forth and the physical act of touching and being with each other, our experience with our loved ones that we leave behind does become a satisfying state of being. I have been with and will continue to be with all of you more than you will ever know or understand.

"That is of course, until all of you eventually join us over here. But each of you should know that myself, Claricé and all of your loved ones will be here to welcome you with open arms when you cross over and learn the joy, love and peace in the eternal life of the heavenly plane that God has planned for your soul.

"Vic, because I know you have studied and gained a broader understanding of the spiritual world, I want to share something else with you. You are now in a different state of mind than are many of your kind on the earthly plane. I know that you have come to understand and are growing in your awareness of the spiritual life and the many planes of learning that is and will be available to you. I also know you understand that there are no physical 'bodies' to identify with on this side and that recognition and

realization of your loved ones on this side will be through your sense of and awareness of them, based on your experience of being together when they were in their earthly bodies.

"In a sense, you 'see' them as you knew them. Another difficult concept for earthlings to grasp is that in addition to being with your loved ones and friends on a spiritual level, you will also be able to experience other relatives, and friends of relatives whom you've never met on the earthly plane. You will be able to do this through your loved one's or a friend's experience of them when they were in their earthly bodies. This was how I was able to experience your wife Claricé, whom I never met and your friend Dick; as well, this was how Claricé was able to experience myself, your father, and others whom she had never met while in her earthly body.

"Life on Earth or in the spiritual world is a continuous journey from one plane to another in which we continue to learn and move closer and closer to God-like perfection. It is an eternal journey of joy. The perfection we seek is a day in eternity when all of us will recognize that we truly are spiritually joined and then realize <u>we are one with God,</u> the Father and Creator of all that is.

"The creation of man in God's image has often been misunderstood. God is life, that which flows through all of his creations, not only mankind. The words in the Scripture that state 'Man was made in God's image' have often been accepted to mean that Man's physical presence and form in the earthly plane was created to look like God in shape and his physical being.

"Conceptually, this came about because when God did come into the world he chose the physical form of a human for His presence, as His Son Jesus Christ, and as time passed and Christ's teaching continued to grow, this form was then understood to be in the 'likeness of,' or image of God' by many of mankind. Later the early master artists who portrayed God in the human form perpetuated this concept.

"Although it is an acceptable image for a belief in God, it does not mean that the physical being or presence of mankind looks like God Himself. Instead, it is more like that of an artist like your wife, who created pictures from the images in her mind. The images, which were in her mind, are those that she put into her paintings. It does not mean she was creating images of herself or her physical being in her paintings. It is the same manner in which God 'created' mankind, all physical forms on Earth, the universe, heavens and all that is. He created all that is in whatever image He determined the likeness of all should be.

"This is where you get back into semantics and theological debate. Likeness is a derivative of the word like and has many, many meanings. God created everything in a manner and form that would be pleasing to Him and in a form that would be consistent with that which He wanted to create. Without going further, once again semantics and the meanings of the words and translations in numerous languages throughout history is what has given birth to your multi-dimensional religious societies and differences in belief systems.

"God is light. God is life. God is love. God is the energy that created all things known, both living and that without life as known to man and throughout the universe. Much of what He created is thought of as inanimate, but in the broadest understanding of life, all creations of God have a degree of life, down to the smallest of atoms and atomic sub-particles with their neutrons and protons revolving around the nucleus and will continue to grow in God's universe and in His world, which is ever changing.

"Much of the controversy in your multi-dimensional religious philosophies is a result of semantics as has been mentioned; words made up from alphabetical letters or symbols in many languages used for communication among and between all of mankind. The word reincarnation, which has brought about so much theological debate, is a perfect example

of semantic confusion. It, too, is only a word that many really do not understand. The scriptures of the Old Testament and New Testament clearly state that God, our Creator, gave mankind 'free choice.' But, 'free choice' was not given to the 'vehicle' that is called your body, or whatever name your physical presence responds to. The body, or vehicle with your name of Victor, in which your divine energy resides will and can only live once as it is Biblically stated. Your freedom of choice was given to your eternal energy, which is genderless. Your spirit within and soul choose to live as sons or daughters of God the Almighty, prior to conception, within the heart and mind of your physical body/vehicle.

"After death of the physical vehicle, that mankind has labeled the 'body' and your parents gave the name of Victor, it will return to the earth from which it was created. It is the 'circle of life' for all things in the world created by God. Your soul and life energy of God can choose to be incarnated again to continue your journey of learning. Your soul can do this throughout the eternal life God has granted our 'being' which is the energy of God. In some cases it is because the lessons you still have to learn may be more practical to learn in an earthly body. Other souls may 'choose' to learn their needed lessons only in the spiritual environment or realm of one of the seven planes of eternal life. Still other souls may want both, and the soul can split into two, or more, to more quickly achieve their goal of learning and then, if they choose, come back together to rejoin at a later time! Remember, some of God's creatures, called lower life forms, such as earthworms and others in the language of mankind, can be split in two, three or more with all parts becoming a new life. It is the same with the eternal soul.

"God our Father, the light of life may also determine that a particular soul in making his earthly choices and learning experience has developed special qualities, talents and skills which <u>He</u> may want to perpetuate. God can take a part of a soul to create an

entirely new being for the purpose of creating preferred characteristics and/or talents which will aid in developing the earthly planet He created and add beauty, joy and harmony in your world.

"Many cannot understand this concept, but I believe you do. I am aware of your experiences of performing past life regressions through the art of hypnotism. As souls in the heavenly spirit world, you can choose what you need to learn and do to continue what is required of you throughout your eternal life. Some souls choose their time to incarnate again based upon what they need to learn; perhaps over and over again; other souls will even choose the parents they want and the lifestyle they want if it is consistent with what they have to learn, while others choose to stay in the spiritual world to learn. It is a matter of your eternal soul's freedom of choice. A broader acceptance among mankind of the concept of reincarnation would give a clearer understanding and explanation of your world's maladies.

"The spirit world is filled with a million times a million times a million and more souls consisting of students, teachers and master teachers, greeters, guides, angels and what is known on earth as guardian angels, saints of God and others too numerous to itemize or mention.

"The importance of going into reincarnation as I have just outlined it for you, is to explain what happened to me shortly after leaving my former physical presence on Earth during the life I was your mother-in-law, Sally. When I crossed over, my greeter led me to my spiritual indoctrination in which I was immediately directed to meet with the master teachers. At that time I was instructed that I should return to Earth to gain understanding of the pain and misery of my illness, what it did to others and the effects of the chemical addiction that ended that life experience in the earthly world. Time as it is known on earth doesn't exist over here. What was a little over three years in Earth time was practically immediate for me once I crossed over.

"The group of master teachers instructed my spirit to incarnate right away. They also instructed my soul energy to select a lifestyle which would aid in understanding what had happened in my previous incarnation and how I had gotten so far off course and made so many wrong decisions during that lifetime. My soul was then divided and a part of it became a new incarnation while the remainder went on to study in the spiritual realm. This was a choice my soul energy made to maximize my learning experience based upon the difficulties of my previous incarnation.

"In 1971 a part of my spirit self re-entered your world and the earthly plane again. As stated above, believers of this experience have labeled the process 'reincarnation' in your earthly terminology. My father's name was Frank and he was a lawyer; my mother was a homemaker named Susan and when I was born they gave me the name of Beverly. With them, we lived in Philadelphia, and I had a more upscale life style than that of my preceding incarnation as Sally. Both parents had also come from what you know as an upscale life style. As Beverly, I was a good student during my formative years and I finished high school by the time I was sixteen and entered college when I was only seventeen years of age. I studied pre-med in college and went on to become a doctor. I completed my internship and was in my second year of residency to become a Doctor of Internal Medicine when I was involved in an automobile accident with a drunk driver and was killed.

"As it was with your Claricé, my purpose of learning in that life was complete. For the person who was intoxicated and responsible for causing the accident that took my life as Beverly, the experience was a part of their learning process also; one which their physical being had to move through, as well as accommodating the plan of both our lives. Vic, there are no accidents in life and it continues according to God's divine plan.

"I ended that particular incarnation in March of 1998 and returned to the spiritual plane. When the *soul named Beverly re-entered the spiritual realm, the two souls of energy were fused into one again. When it happened Vic, it was like there were two small colorful tornados, or auras in your earthly terminology, of different hues; at first they were twisting alone, then slowly they moved closer and closer toward one another to meet, blending their colors, twirling to become one again.*

"As a student and physician during that brief existence on the earthly plane, I was able to learn and gain understanding of most of the problems I encountered and the wrong turns I made during the life in the physical plane as Sally. I learned many of the lessons in life that I was required to go through.

"I'm going to leave you now, but want to thank you for being who you are and opening your spirituality so that I could have this communication with you. I know Jean does not believe as you do, and understanding may be difficult for her. But I am concerned and worried that if she doesn't take care of herself and quit worrying so much about her problems, and everyone else's problems, the stress of it all may not let her live out the life God has planned for her to its fullest potential. "God bless you Vic, I've always loved you and know that you loved me in spite of my failing and frailties."

- - - - -

Throughout the communications with Sally, I hardly spoke or asked questions. She just wanted me to listen and didn't even wait for me to say goodbye at any time. She would just leave my mind. A few times, when there were fragmentary communications, I recognized her voice but didn't reply. Instead I would try to push the words out of my mind, because I was fighting my doubt and trying to get needed sleep.

The full communication with her over several nights was the third that I had with spiritual beings from the other side. The conversations have been lengthy and also in bits and pieces. When I initially transcribed the communication from Sally, it was several weeks after it had occurred. Once more when I began, I assumed it was being written from memory and to the best of my recollection, but again the words flowed into and through my mind quickly and without time for preconception or conscious thought and into the computer through my fingertips. I have since been told that this transcription also was being guided by M.L., my angel of relationships.

Will I have additional spiritual communications or hear from any of them again? I couldn't say and actually, I don't try. Those I've had were spontaneous and each came with a message for a loved one.

Chapter Eight
Spiritual Communications With Barry and John
Barry Continues His Practical Jokes

Barry, with the nickname of "Bear" or "The Bear" was a close friend and client of Claricé prior to our marriage. Afterward, he and his wife Patricia became our very good friends. Because of his outgoing, friendly personality and knowledge about Claricé's background, it was he whom I called upon and asked to give the eulogy at her memorial service. As well, it was he whom I went to for his emotional support later in the day, as we celebrated her life with family and friends in our home and then afterward, I spoke with him several times during my early stages of grief in the weeks that followed.

To my great shock, I got a telephone call from his wife Patricia the following April in which she told me that Barry had suffered a sudden and massive coronary which took his life. He, too, was only 53 years old — the same age as my wife was when she crossed over.

About three months later, a period during which I was not having any spiritual communications but was still troubled by a continual stream of unidentifiable voices in my head, a clear voice came out of the mix of broken words and phrases. It was like standing alone among many voices at a party, and then someone steps up to you and speaks.

- - - - - -

This time, I heard:

"Hey Victor; Barry here, how you doing?"

My immediate reaction and thought was "<u>not again</u>." But once more, like the ones earlier, it was a very identifiable voice. Bear was a salesman's salesman and sometimes had a strong, forthright voice. It had been such a short time since he passed over that hearing his voice, even in view of what I had been experiencing, was the farthest thing from my mind. "Bear?" I asked, in a puzzled, quizzical tone. (I want to point out that even in mental communication the same voice inflections and mannerisms take place as if you were speaking aloud.)

His presence did not come with clear visual imagery, but the inner eye at the front of my mind still brought forth a sense of his smiling face with the slight overlap at the inner corners of his upper front teeth. This was more like a memory; it wasn't the clear image of his being, like I had of Claricé and Dick, and was more similar to my "sense" of a visual, memory recognition of Sally, based upon her voice mannerisms. I've found that my conscious memories of people, and/or events are not well defined unless there is something specifically referenced that brings about a clear focus.

"Yes, it's the Bear." He responded. And then said, "I want you to do me a favor."

"Yes, gladly." I said to him. "But what happened to you?" I questioned. "I had no idea you had a problem."

"First things first," he replied. "I want you to call Dutch and give her a message for me."

"Dutch" was his nickname for his wife Patricia, who is from Holland. Several years earlier, after he and his wife were first married, Claricé had designed their personal "Dutch and the Bear" stationery.

"Of course..." I said, with hesitation and some reluctance. I wasn't sure what he wanted to say, and at the same time I also wasn't sure if I wanted to act as a "go-between." I was very resistant to acting in the manner of what is commonly called a "medium" in regard to spiritual communications. I believed that function or role would bring heavy responsibility with it and it was something I didn't believe I wanted to do or was the purpose of what was happening with me. Passing the messages to my first wife and Dick's daughters both had troubled me somewhat. As I did when I did Past Life Regressions in the earlier years, I wanted to be cautious and not mess with other people's minds. At the same time, I knew I couldn't refuse "*The Bear*." As it turned out, the message was brief and the strange, but the simple request stimulated my interest. Barry's entire communication was quite short when compared to the others. He said:

"What I want you to do is to call Dutch and tell her to look under the drawer."

"<u>What?</u>" I asked with emphasis and curiosity.

"I want you to call her and tell her to look under the drawer," he repeated the request.

"What else?" I added.

"Nothing,.." he replied, and then he said, *"She'll understand the message."*

"You're sure?"

"Yes Victor, my man, that's all."

"All right, but tell me what happened? I never knew you had any heart problems."

"Well, I really didn't <u>know</u> about it either. For quite awhile, I thought I was only having indigestion. It was only a few months before my fatal heart attack that I began to suspect I had heart trouble. It was probably brought to my attention because I often thought about <u>our</u> Claricé and how quickly her passing had come about.

I liked his personal reference to my wife. I knew he loved her as a very close friend. I let him continue.

"At first I was a little afraid of what I might find out, because I began to notice that something about the indigestion was different from the earlier bouts I'd had; but still, I kept putting off making an appointment for a physical and kept telling Pat not to worry. I finally made an appointment with a cardiologist, but it was too late. The appointment was for a week after I felt the massive pain and blacked out. I was wrong. That's really all I have to say now; I'm still adjusting to my new environment."

"Have you run into Claricé?" I asked him, but there was silence in my mind. I quickly realized he was already gone. He didn't answer me.

- - - - - -

Because it was a short and strange message, I wasn't sure whether to pass it along to Dutch or not. It really didn't make any sense to me, and when I had talked to her shortly after his death, she also told me that she knew he had been having problems with indigestion and had found out after the autopsy that he had made a doctor's appointment for the week following his heart attack.

So this information I got from him wasn't really new for me, or her. I couldn't understand the importance of the message and waited a few days before deciding to give it to her. I didn't want to cause her any unnecessary grief; I was very familiar with the pain and I knew what she would be going through.

Finally after almost a week, I began to consider that there might be something valuable hidden "under the drawer." His wife Pat had also told me that she was considering selling the house. While most of the time I felt comfortable living in my home with the memories of Claricé all around me, Pat felt differently. She also had told me she was not able to maintain the house and yard without Barry. I finally decided to give her a call, just in case the message was important.

She knew about my communications with Claricé from an earlier conversation in which I had shared my experience with her. So, when she answered the telephone I stammered awkwardly... uhh... ahh... and then told her I had something strange to tell her. She wasn't surprised at all. I quickly passed along Bear's message that she was to "look under the drawer."

"You too?" She said. Then she told me, "Victor, I swear Barry has been here also." She said, "I keep finding the kitchen cupboard doors open, when I know that I closed them. And in the bedroom, twice a bottom dresser drawer has been open when I didn't open it." She continued, telling me, "These were a couple of the things I used to nag Barry over. He was always leaving drawers and cupboard doors open." She paused a moment as if in thought, then said, "I don't know which drawer to look under, and I'm on my way out to an appointment, so I'll look tomorrow and give you a call back."

Two days later, Patricia returned my call. I could immediately hear a sense of humor in her voice. She said, "Victor, that son-of-a-gun is still doing it to me. Do you know what I found under a drawer? I pulled open his desk drawer and one of those big, black, soft-plastic Halloween spiders fell out and scared the life out of me. It was another one of his practical jokes. That is all that was there... and I checked under all of the dresser drawers in the house. I think that was his way of telling me he's okay, that he's still the same old Bear." We laughed about it together and Pat joked that she was, "disappointed not to have found a valuable document or envelope of money."

- - - - -

John's Coming Through ML Was A Surprise

The communication from John was equally questionable and didn't come through until the end of the third week of September, almost a month following my introduction to Archie, my life-long dominant angel guide. It is included here because at the time it came through it was more like the spiritual communications I had been receiving. His message however was brought to me from ML whom I had learned from Archie was my angel of relationships. Although John's wife Michele has been a very dear friend, like a big sister to me, for almost forty years, I had only been in John's presence very briefly and only a couple of times. During the years of his marriage to Michele, we were geographically apart; they live in New York and I lived in South Florida. My ongoing friendship with my "big sister" was almost always by telephone. At first I questioned his message because I really didn't know him and again, was somewhat reluctant to pass it along. After reading over the transcription several times in as many days, I saw no harm in the content and decided it might bring Michele an amount of comfort and continued reassurance of his love awaiting her in the spiritual plane. My good friend is Jewish and believes in angels and when I called her said she would be happy to receive the message ML brought to me from John.

"ML," I began, "Archie said you have a message for me to give to my friend Michele from her husband John."

"Yes, like the communication you got from your mother-in-law Sally for Jean, he is also concerned about Michele's health. It is the same problem Jean is facing, due to both their ages and recent health problems. Michele, like Jean, worries too much about others, all of her family, but more about her son-in-law's difficult situation; as well, she worries about everyone beside her family and so many other of her friends that it is putting a severe strain on her. She still has much time left in God's plan for her life, but if she doesn't settle down and quit worrying about things that are out of her control, she will cause herself more difficulty than is necessary. Again, like Jean, she has to quit worrying about things that are beyond her control and take care of her self.

"There is much John wants to tell her, but let's continue with her health first. This may sound ridiculous, but she could ease the pain in her walking if she would try to send it away. This isn't a simple procedure, but it can work. In many ways, you on Earth can help to heal yourselves. God gave each of you this ability but you have to believe you can do it.

"First she has to believe that she can order the pain to leave her and let her physical self begin to heal. This is a process that has to be done on a daily basis for several weeks; mentally she must focus her energy and awareness on the areas of pain until she begins to feel and recognize a noticeable relief. This can happen and the recognition will provide her with the incentive to continue. Michele must begin with a prayer, asking our God to assist her and to strengthen her back and legs.

"This should be done each morning. When she finishes the prayer, then ask God to help her focus directly on the source of the pain. Imagine what it looks like and when she has this in focus, hold the picture of the pain source in her mind and begin six to twelve breathing exercises where she will breath deeply in through the nose and exhale in a loud whoosh through her mouth. This action discharges negative energy that accumulates in weak areas and dispels it with the outpouring of the breath.

"As she does this, she must visualize the cause of her pain leaving her lower torso and legs as she thinks the words, "_leave me alone pain. I am healthy._" Most of the pain originates in her back, but there is a weakness of her knees also. Gradually she will begin to notice the pain lessening. Like everything else, it takes time and practice in order to get results.

"Michele like you, Victor, experienced the loss of her most precious love after only a relatively short period of time. Why? You both have asked over and over.

"What you both must understand is that life is a lesson and Michele, like you, was scheduled to be with your loved one for a determined length of time in

God's plan for each of your lives. As you know, <u>one of your lessons</u> was to learn to give up control. You had to always be in control. Archie tried to get through to you for sixty-six years, but it wasn't until after Clarice's crossing over and finally communicating with you, that you gave up control and turned your life over to the God Force, the Holy Spirit within you. Then it was several more months before you would acknowledge Archie your Angel Guide, and finally began talking to him, writing for him and letting him assist you in your daily walk.

"*One of the things Michele had to learn in this life is self-reliance. In her earlier years and prior to her marriage to John and his crossing over, and for a little while afterwards she felt she had to have someone take care of her. She didn't think she could really take care of herself.*

"*This attitude came from a previous incarnation when she was bed-ridden due to partial paralysis, when her back was hurt from being thrown from a horse and buggy as a child in that lifetime on the earthly plane. She was totally dependent on others for everything. When she planned this life with the masters before her birth, she chose a life plan where she would learn independence and self-sufficiency. She has struggled and continues to struggle with learning this. For the most part she has done well physically, but financial and emotional dependence has been a struggle. The injury in the previous lifetime was also a partial source of the pain in her back and legs throughout her present life in her earthly body.*

"*John's problems stemmed from being too concerned about the welfare of his fellow associates, family members and almost all other people around him until he reached a point where it affected his health and he wore himself down and became vulnerable to his disease. Often, like attracts like; John was concerned of those around him as Michele is concerned... worried about those around her.*

"*Victor, does this not sound like the communications relative to your own health problems?*

It should, because it is. Your earlier problems resulted from your business worries and those who depended on you for their livelihood and were a great part of your early health difficulties. Claricé taught you to be concerned about your health and to listen to your body. When you gave her control, you learned to listen...and now, you do quite well because of her. This too, was a reason for your coming together during this particular lifetime.

"To Michele, John would say he was sorry he could not have been there for you during your long and troubled times and those of the family. But, lessons were learned according to those, which were planned for each of your lives before you were born. God did give man free choice, however, and undisciplined concern and worry, can also do things that could hasten a demise earlier than God's plan.

"And, of course, we are always faced with the devilish angels. I call them devilish angels, because sometimes their purpose in the universe is to tempt us and get us off track a little so that we must make the right choices and return to the right path God wants for us. Remember Adam, Eve and the forbidden fruit? Many theologies will dispute this and will lay it on what they call "the devil, evil serpent or fallen angel" but that is really a misnomer. As God set the stage for tempting Adam and Eve, so he did with human kind when he gave the soul free choice. Devilish little angels try to tempt you by seeding the 'I want' of the ego self of your being and to get you to do bad things as good things. It is part of the universal law God has created for an understanding of all things. You earthlings call it Einstein's theory of relativity, but it's really God's theory of how your world works.

"You cannot know one thing without the other... good/bad... hot/cold... happy/sad...something, without being able to experience nothing, etc. It's all part of the learning process of making the right choices.

"Michele, John wants to assure you of his continued love for you and to know that he will be waiting to be with you again. You are soul mates who

have been together in past lives and will be again. He says he has been very busy working on policy matters for the learning council for souls for many of your earthly years. Here, he said it has not seemed to be such a very long time, because on the spiritual plane we don't know time as you relate to it there on your Earth. Everything here is really NOW! It's a difficult concept for earthlings to understand.

"Michele, John wants you to make more time for Michele and less time for worry over everybody else. You have much abundance in your life. Try to focus on that which will give you pleasure and quit worrying about things that are beyond your control. Spend your time bringing love, joy and harmony to your family, friends and the world. That is what God wants for all mankind. A harmonious world filled with love is the balance He is looking for... Perfection of life on Earth is virtually impossible. Only God is perfection.

"Michele, you like Victor, and every other soul in the universe have angel guides, often called guardian angels, with you at all times. There are literally millions of angels serving God's every purpose. You have several available to assist you in whatever way you have a need. God assigns each angel specific tasks and all you have to do is call upon them to assist you and they will be there for you. You just have to believe and listen; they will guide you.

"Thank you Victor for letting me bring John's message to Michele... and thanks to Archie also. Fondly, ML your relationship guide."

Victor K. Hosler

Epilogue Part One
Questioning Myself and My Motives

When this new spirituality phase in my life began, I was excited, saddened and very much confused. Excited of course because at first I was certain I "heard" my wife Claricé's voice once again. The emotional rush of the first two communications with her on January 5th 2000 was beyond any words I could use to describe it. I was so thrilled to hear her voice again I wanted it to go on and on… and on. My grief, which had been so intense, was momentarily released. She was back! That is all I cared about and the world could have happily ended for me at that moment.

I was in so much awe of the experience sadness did not come about until I realized I could not continue the communications with her after they ended on the 17th. Logical reasoning that it could not go on was difficult to accept… especially in view of the other communications that had begun to come through from my teenage friend, Sally, my former mother-in-law and the others. Until my rational mind returned, I wondered why, "If it happened once, actually 5 times with her and then the others, why it couldn't continue? Why are we not more aware of their spiritual presence if they are so close to us, as Claricé said they were, and that we could make contact by using what is called our sixth sense?"

The confusion began to come with the other spiritual contacts that were made with me. All in all none of it fit my convenient Christian belief system or my skeptical nature regarding spirits, psychics and other paranormal happenings. Most I had read about or saw demonstrations of on stage or television, I thought were some kind of gimmick or trickery. Now that it was happening to me, I couldn't really explain it. I was of a doubtful mind and reluctant to pass on the communications from my friend Dick, Sally, Barry and John to those the messages were intended for.

I really didn't want people to think I had "lost it" in my grief and at the same time, didn't want the messages rejected by them. Although I sensed some skepticism when I did decide to pass them along, for the most part I was pleasantly surprised when those they were meant for did warmly receive them. I believe this was because each of the communications contained some information I was most likely not to have known. I was apprehensive before each phone call, I felt somewhat responsible if there had been a negative reaction. It made me uncomfortable and I quickly decided that I did not want to become a medium for this sort of thing. Perhaps this is why the spiritual communications soon ended.

I did however meet much doubt from others. The Pastor of the fundamentalist church my wife and I had been attending said it couldn't be true. Because a part of Claricé's communication did not agree with his understanding of the Bible, He said, "It had to be evil spirits masquerading as Claricé." Others, both family and some friends who were "Born Again Christians" began to think I had truly lost it in my grief. When I continued to meet resistance, I soon learned to be selective in who I would talk about my experiences and began to seek out new, like-minded friends.

One new friend, Kim, who I met in a Hospice Grief Support Group, introduced me to the First Unity Church of St. Petersburg. Unity's Mission Statement is, "To encourage awareness of Spirit within and inspire a way of life that brings love, freedom, peace and joy." As well, Unity churches embrace diversity of all faiths, and belief systems. I found that this church was more open to acceptance of my newly developed belief system as well as my experiences. The first service I attended, the message echoed part of my wife's first communication and I knew I had found my spiritual home.

During the early experiences, I needed some confirmation, so I became a reader of all things spiritual and found much support in my reading. The books in the Bibliography have all been read in the past 2½ years. Fortunately, in my retirement, I had more time for reading than most. In my reading, I discovered that many, many others have had, similar experiences and have reported on, or have written books about them. There are far too many that have been experienced for they're not to be some truth in all of the unexplainable phenomenon, spiritual and paranormal happenings and miracles. Even in the Christian Bible, it clearly states, *"If you believe, all things are possible."* With this in mind, there is no living being that can disprove my experiences no more than I myself can actually prove that they have happened.

Belief is the key factor and, believing is the biggest change that has come over me. This onetime convenient Christian who believed in only as much as I felt was necessary… just in case it was all true, has made a 180 degree change in mind and spirit. My doubtful mind has been replaced with an inner knowing-ness that has come about me in regards to believing in what has happened and having a daily relationship with God. The Bible says, "Judge not that you be judged." Because of this, no one is entitled to discount your experience just because they have not experienced the same thing themselves. Any time you verbally express disagreement in another's experience you are making a judgment, which then is against God's word. In reference to His works, in the Book of John, Christ clearly states, "I tell you the truth, *anyone* who has faith in me will do what I have been doing. He will do even greater things than these, because I am going to the Father."

Victor K. Hosler

PART TWO

The Angels Begin To Speak

Victor K. Hosler

Chapter Nine
Archie Arrives
To Take My Pain Away

One year following the death of my beloved wife, I was still experiencing the extreme pain and grief that was brought upon me by her passing. When the first spiritual communication from Claricé came through to me, I was on a "high;" and, unfortunately when they stopped after the fifth visit from her, I realized it was something I could not continue, and quickly slipped back into depression and grief. I found the spiritual interventions with the others to be interesting and surprising, but they did not bring me comfort in the healing of my grief.

For many months I had tried to deal with my anguish by reading almost any new thought book I could find to help me understand. I read books on Death and Dying, Communicating with Lost Loved Ones, Searching for Souls, Hello From Heaven, Seat of the Soul, We Don't Die and anything else I thought might aid in my understanding, including most of the latest writings covering spiritual subjects by people who were guests on the many daytime talk shows and late night television cable channels. Although I received a slight degree of comfort and understanding of my experiences, nothing was making the "pain" go away.

Nights were sleepless and my physician had prescribed medication that I had begun taking for the sleep deprivation. I had never felt any loss so greatly! The nights were long and I really thought I might be "losing it," because I continually heard a cacophony of mixed voices running through my head for hours upon hours as I tossed and turned in my bed.

I had heard about and joined a Tampa, Florida discussion group about the "Conversations With God" series of books by Neale Donald Walsch. It was the first book in the series, that I mentioned earlier that my wife had bought for me shortly before her death. She mentioned the book in the first communication I had with her. It was also one of the books I had read in my quest for spiritual knowledge. After my second or third meeting with the group, there was some discussion about books on communicating with your Angels called "Angelspeake."

This was a direction I had not considered. For some unknown reason in my prowling through the shelves of spiritual material in the local bookstores, I had passed over books about angels as I searched for something that would give me some comfort and relief. I have always been aware of Angels as they have been depicted and are related to in the Bible, religious teachings, theologies, painting of the Masters and even in one of my late wife's paintings, the one I used for the cover of this story. Immediately following her death and prior to any spiritual contact, I had spoken to family and friends pointing to what she had called "the Angel of the Night" in the painting and said that perhaps Clarice was now "my guardian angel" and she would be watching over me.

I don't believe I understood then how true that statement might have been. This work of art by her was painted a few years before we met and like most of Claricé's work, she had an interesting story about the Brazilian culture and why it was painted. Certainly unknown to her at the time, today it appears to me to have been an early premonition of what was to be. I see the lonely figure under the "tree of life" as myself, looking out over the land, searching for my purpose in life without her. The Angel of the Night is floating in a nighttime sky, just as Claricé came to me in the night aiding my quest for understanding. In the painting, the Angel of the Night is bringing the heavens with her, a new moon and a cluster of new stars. Perhaps the moon and stars are symbolic of a new beginning and my newfound purpose in life. Perhaps the cherub angels sliding down into the painting are representative of Archie and Jules, my life-long angels, whom I have now acknowledged and are at my service.

I never previously thought too much about angels, but did mention the books to Shirley, a good friend of mine in Miami. She said she was unaware of the "Angelspeake" series, but she did say she had a couple of books about angels. One was "Ask Your Angels" and the second was "The Angels Within Us." She loaned them to me to read.

After completing the first book, "Ask Your Angels," I began to get a glimmer of understanding. Clarity was coming through to me. After reading the second book, I wanted to learn more about angels. I went out then to purchase the "Angelspeake" series that was mentioned in my discussion group. There were three books in the series (listed in the bibliography), which were written by two sisters with the purpose of sharing their individual experience of learning about and communicating with the Angels. More and more clarity began to come through as I read them and I became increasingly eager to understand more. I wondered and thought, "Can we really communicate with angels?" I had believed that something like this had only happened in the Biblical times of Christ, that God only sent His Angels to assist in the teachings of Jesus Christ and His disciples.

Finally, during the nights immediately following August 19, the date of my wife's death a year earlier, I was lying in my bed experiencing the extreme pain of grief, time and time again. With tears running down my face, I could hear the myriad of voices that were about to drive me over the edge. In my agony, I suddenly remembered the words, which were in each of the books on angels. All of them said you have to ask for your angels when you want help or are in need. With this thought in mind and with a tinge of desperation coursing through my brain and body, I spoke aloud several times and asked, "If all of you talking up there are the angels, who are you? Talk to me, and tell me who are you?" And, then in my agony, I asked, *"When is this pain going to end?"*

I asked the questions nightly, on the 20th, the 21st, the 22nd, and the 23rd. I didn't get any response. I felt I was near the breaking point, from the voices, tossing and turning and lack of sound sleep. I was pleading for relief.

All the sudden, during the night of August 24th and morning of the 25th 2000, a male voice came into my mind in response to my questions and said:

"Hello Victor, I'm Archie. I'm glad you finally have asked for me. I think that now you are ready to listen."

"Archie?" I thought and questioned what I was hearing in my head and mind. There was no identifiable voice of recognition as I had with the spiritual contacts.

"Yes, Archie, I am your Angel Guide. I've been with you throughout your life. And, Victor, your pain will soon be gone."

The name caught me by surprise. Any preconceived notion I had of angels was that of guardian angels who were relatives who had lived on earth and at one time or another had died and gone to heaven. The mental exchange I had that first night with Archie, went back and forth and continued for quite some time. I was certain I wouldn't be able to recall everything he told me the first night we connected, but it was such a revelation I wanted to remember every word. Just before I finally drifted off to sleep, I thought about the words in the "Angelspeake" books that said, "You must write it down". Then, in my half-asleep mind, I vaguely remembered that Archie had told me to go to the computer the next day and ask my questions again.

By the time I fell asleep, it must have been around six o'clock in the morning; light was already beginning to come through the window. I slept peacefully and restfully for the first time in many months and didn't waken until just before noon.

While I had my late-morning coffee and some breakfast, I began to think about what I had at first thought was a vivid dream of an angel contacting me. But then just as quickly, I realized and knew I had been awake. Just as the spiritual communications that had come to me previously, the angel communication was taking place within my mind, in what I later determined to be that of my higher self. I knew I had not been dreaming and I accepted for the first time that I had communicated with an Angel.

There are times in our lives when we imagine things and have dreams, but there are also times when you have a clear knowingness about an experienced truth. This I know had been my truth.

I immediately left my breakfast and went to the computer to turn it on. I went to my Word program and typed in my first greeting to "Archie", my Angel Guide and my new friend as he had suggested. I was very curious as to what would happen. The following is a transcription of the first message I received. Archie's responses to my words, and questions are *in the italic typography*. To my surprise, I was auto-writing once again.

- - - - -

Archie Speaks... Through My Fingers!

"Good afternoon Archie."

"Good afternoon Victor. I'm glad you acknowledged me and accepted my presence. And, finally, now that you have sat down to write and ask me the questions that are on your mind, how are you today?"

"I'm fine. I hardly know where to begin my questions. So I will start with this." I repeated my first questions of the communication during the night. "Who are you really? Have I known of you before or have I been in contact with you?"

"Yes, you have been with me...or I should say I have always been with you. I have guided some of

your past writings. I am your daily guide... I have also guided you through past difficulties when you were unaware of my presence. I think you will find it interesting to ask me questions about your past. Most recently, since your awakening, I assisted Claricé in coming through to you. You were difficult to communicate with in the beginning and for some reason it was my energy that was able to break through to you. There are many angels here to assist you but I will talk about them later and then introduce you to them and their purpose in your life. I'm afraid your preconceived and structured ideas and lifestyle have been blocking my earlier attempts and others who have attempted to communicate with you. Later, ask me more about your friend Dick, Sally and others who have impacted your life and have come into your mind where situations at the time may have seemed strange in the way and how they occurred. Also ask me about walk-in angels and the many guardian angels who have also been there for you and have guided much of your life's activities and growth. Ask about Claricé also.

"A couple of nights ago when you finally decided to ask my name, you had questions about when the pain would go away? I'm sorry I waited a few nights to come through to you, but this time I wanted to be sure you were ready to listen and understand there are many souls and angels in the spiritual realm who are always here to guide you.

"It is important to understand that the pain you are feeling is Claricé's love for you and your love for her which is everlasting and eternal. Her spirit is with you when you feel what you call 'the pain.' Remember back to your experiences of your feeling love for her when she was with you, and the love you knew she had for you. It was really the same, identical feelings you are now experiencing as pain. The difference is in your perception and attachment to the accompanying emotions. Because you still miss her greatly, a state of sorrow comes upon you when you think of her, talk about her and have the feelings you describe as *painful, and that which brings your tears. The fact is what you are experiencing is Claricé's and your love for one another. This will never leave you. When you change your attitude and let the sorrow go, when you think of her, the same feelings will bring you pleasure, and the tears you may still shed will be of joy and not pain.*

"Remember the past for a moment. Remember when the two of you held each other in a loving embrace. Remember how pleasurable the feeling of the energy of love was. Remember how it flowed through and between you... and how it kept expanding until it seemed like it would burst from your body. You wanted to shout out and tell the world of your intense love. In those times, it was an exquisite feeling of pleasure that was so strong, it was <u>almost painful</u>, yet you recognized it as a loving, blissful feeling in which you wanted to squeeze each other so tightly your energy could almost have become one. It is an example of the fine line that so often exists between pain and pleasure.

"The same thing continues to be true today. The difference is that her physical presence in her human form is absent from the picture you had of your life and this is a missing element, the loss you accept as creating the pain. What you must realize is that when you feel what you call the 'pain' because of her absence, it is really the ongoing love you share that you are experiencing. At those times, know that Claricé is with you... embracing you and letting you know she is with you at that moment, and she is there for you, to guide you and is still very much in love with you, and in her present form experiences your ongoing love for her.

"Claricé wants you to let your sorrow go! Instead, relish the love that you shared in the past and that which is shared between you in your two worlds today. You can still miss her and at the same time enjoy the love she brought and still brings into your life. She has much to do where she is today. The transition was difficult for her, but she knew it was her time to leave

Angels in My Life

because it was of God's plan for her being, and this awareness is what brought her peace in her final hours. It was difficult for you also, but now, with your acceptance, you know of your purpose and that you have much to do throughout the balance of your life on Earth.

"As you will recall, when the two of you met, you were both at a crossroads in your lives. When she made the transition, once again you were both at a crossroads in your lives. She was looking for new directions, but the work she was doing was out of your mutual need and necessity, and not in keeping with God's plan for her life in her earthly plane of existence.

Claricé is a very highly developed soul and had reached her spiritual growth and learning on the planet Earth and it was time for her to come home. This then, created a necessity for you, too. Although she was unaware of it at the time, she did have an inner awareness that you would have to find a new direction or purpose in your life to fill the emptiness that was to come. Claricé pointed you in that direction before she left you. When she bought you Conversations With God – Book One five months before her passing, she stated in her inscription that it was to "...help you heal your spirit." The period of time you were together on the earthly plane was only a small part of God's plan for both of your lives. It was a ten-year segment in which you were learning together. Now you have both turned the corner to begin new chapters in your eternal lives in the universe God created.

"As you begin to accept the reality of the work you both have to do, your sorrow will lessen to the point where you will find pure joy when you experience her love and 'feel' when she is with you. Because of your work schedules in your different planes of existence, it will become less and less than you have been experiencing since she left you. At the same time, I want to assure you that when you are ready, she will speak to you again. I want to say though, in future

communications you may have with Clarice, discussions of or the emotion of your romantic love during your earthly time together would not serve your purpose. As previously mentioned, future spiritual communications with her will be of guidance to you on an esoteric level relating to how each of your lives fit in the universe God created. New, romantic love is at your doorstep; let it come to you. In the meantime, when you are ready, you can ask of her through me, or through one of the angels that are always with you.

"In your nightly quest for information and relief of the pain, you have also been asking about your angels and who they were over the past few nights. Victor, you have several around you most of the time, but many others are available as you need them. As you will soon discover, in addition to myself, MIRIAM is one of your angels, and ALI is another one. Another angel that is with you is called ML. ML is your angel of relationships and will be the one you are to communicate with if you want information from or about Claricé or any other friend or relative who has made the transition.

If you ask it of me, I will bring ML or any other angel to you. Questions you have for the angels you will have to ask them directly. I do not speak for them, but I can pass along information to them or from them. The other angels around you have specific tasks and when something in your life develops where information is needed from God, or from an angel serving a particular purpose, the proper one will make itself available to you. Angels are the messengers of God.

"Not mentioned to you earlier, but who has been brought through to you since you began this manuscript is "Jules." Sometimes, during initial contacts with earthlings such as yourself, we don't want to burden you with too much information at one time. The 'voices' you were hearing when you had difficulty adjusting to your life without Claricé and when you were having trouble sleeping, were many of your angels, guardian angels and angel guides alike.

All of them were trying to come through to you at the same time and wanted to help you. Because you were reaching out in desperation, the vibrations of my energy field finally tuned into your own. I was the dominant force in your presence and took on the responsibility to bring you to understanding.

"Although both Jules and myself have been with you your entire life, my activities were always more prevalent during your formative years and to help you in your daily activities along the way. Jules became more active later in your life. Although always with you, we both have a planned purpose and, as Jules told you, he has been more involved in the mentoring processes of your life. His specialty is teaching and he passes this along to you and through you. As you proceed on your spiritual journey, you may well hear more from Jules than you will from me. My role has always been more directed to your day to day existence and bringing supporting angels to you for the specific needs which were required along the journey of your life.

In the beginning, when you first acknowledged my presence, it was more important for me to establish your belief in our work than to have you asking questions of both of us at the same time. Prior to your acceptance of your angels, look how confused you became when, spiritually, both your mother-in-law Sally and your friend Dick appeared to you one night at the same time. From my observation when that happened, it was like you were a 'rag doll' being pulled back and forth between them. I really thought it was rather humorous.

Victor K. Hosler

Chapter Ten
Archie Defines The Truth

I was in awe following the first communications with Archie, my dominant angel guide. I went through a period of disbelief as I did with the earlier spiritual communications with my late wife Claricé. Once again I wondered if I was hallucinating or listening to my active, creative imagination to assuage my grief. After the first night, for several weeks Archie was with me almost every night in communications and daily in the auto writing.

Quickly I began to become *concerned about the truth* in the words I was putting on paper. I recalled that he had answered the question about truth in one of our sessions so I said to him:

"Archie, I am concerned about what I am writing. I'm not a trained psychologist or authority with a string of the alphabet after my name. Where do I get the right to put forth these thoughts on paper with the intention that others will one day read them?" Archie answered:

"Well, my first reaction is to tell you that in the country where you reside, you have the guarantee of Freedom of Speech. That alone gives you the right, and God gave you the freedom of choice as your birthright, which becomes your authority. So, don't worry about it. You have the choice to write it and your fellow man has the choice to read it, not read it, believe it or disbelieve it. Do not be concerned. This is your purpose today, just listen to what we say and put the words out for those who choose to read or hear them."

Archie continued. *"During our first night, you asked about truth and I gave you a quick answer. Ask it again."*

"My question about truth was how do I know that the answers I get to my questions are the truth and that I am not just making up the answers I want to hear with my conscious mind to satisfy my ego?"

"First, now that you have accessed your 'higher self,' the answers to all of the questions you directly

ask are coming from God. And God doesn't lie! You must remember that angels are messengers from God.

"Although I am your guide, I also am an angel. Angels can and do appear in many forms. They choose to come to you and others in whatever way that is acceptable to you, so you will believe in their presence. Many of the books you have read spell out for you the many ways an angel guide or a lost loved one can come through to you. Simply put, it is in any way you will believe in them. They come to you for a specific need or to answer a special question you may have. They also fulfill your silent and uttered requests whenever they can and as long as it is within God's plan for your individual life experience.

"Some angels have precise assignments, as in my being assigned to you. In earthly terms, in the work place you might call our assignments 'job descriptions.' When there is a perceived and urgent need for it to be, as it was in your situation, angels also assist in bringing a departed loved one through to those they have left behind. Departed loved ones also can become angels. To use an earthly term, they are your guardian angels and for the balance of your period of time on the earthly plane they are with you as needed or until you are at peace with their departure."

"When you first opened the door to the pathway and allowed me to come through to you, it was crucial for you to become aware of and discover your higher self. You were once again at the depths of your despair and from your reading, you realized you had to <u>ask</u>; you did, and it was given. You saw the truth in asking. You had earlier asked to speak to Claricé 'just one more time' and she came through and answered you. The doorway to your higher self opened just a little. As your communications continued, it opened more and more until you finally asked for your angels; then I came to you.

"The truth you are seeking is in and from the spirit and your higher self. Only in silence will you hear the divine guidance of God, the angels or loved ones who have crossed over. As long as you keep the door open

and listen, you will have peace, love, joy and bliss in your life."

"The spirit or angels cannot and do not lie. Only God's truth can come from the spiritual planes of heaven. And yes, I did intentionally use the plural term 'planes.' Although some earthlings who are connected spiritually interpret it differently, the consensus is that there are seven planes of learning, in the totality of the spiritual realm of what mankind refers to as heaven. The number really doesn't matter. Acceptance of the reality that there is more to eternal life than that which you know of in your earthly bodies, and that life itself is a learning process is what counts. Eternal life means that the essence of your soul will never die. Death, as it is called on Earth is only a transition from one place of learning to another; it's much like graduating from your earthly high schools and going on to college.

"Another answer to the truth of what you hear or write is that within the soul energy of every being of God's creation is the full knowledge of God, the oneness of the universe and of life itself. You, Victor, are guided to write the truth. You must remember that the souls of mankind emanate directly from God and there is a continuum of connected energy that radiates out from God, to every humankind, being or creation of God. God is...all that is!

"In earthly terms relating to the spiritual world, this energy of life or the soul has been called the 'aura'. Because the energy of all mankind is brought forth to all of the children and creations of God, this is a direct link and connection to everything that is and all knowledge that has ever existed throughout the intellectual growth and development of mankind and all of the universes of God. All things in the universe, broken down to the smallest of microscopic particles are made up of intelligence. This is clearly shown in the makeup of an atom and its subatomic particles, which are always in motion. This energy of the life force comes with intelligence, the intelligence of God your creator. Does it not take some form of

intelligence for a seedpod to open, begin to grow and a flower to spring forth and bloom? Does it not take some form of intelligence for the procreation of all in the animal kingdom? Humankind has been led to believe they are the only intelligent species on your planet Earth or beyond in the universe they are a part of, when in reality as stated, every creation of God has some degree of intelligence."

"Therefore, when you are communicating with your guides, angels or departed loved ones only the truth can prevail, because they are drawing out of the untapped recesses of your mind-energy the knowledge that has been there from the beginning of time. This is the total knowledge of God, the all knowing. The worldly tree of life began with God and the spark of life identified itself in human terms as the soul or spirit and, therefore, we are all connected and striving to become one with God as it was in the beginning. This is where true perfection can be found, only with God. God is all."

"All humankind was given the freedom of choice. Unfortunately, there are many, many easier paths for one to follow than getting in touch with the truth of their individual spirituality. To follow the will of God is a daily experience of having a relationship with God. You must speak to God or one of His messengers as you are faced with life's day to day dilemmas. 'Ask and you shall receive,' Christ tells you in the Bible. But you must ask! God's answers may not always be what you expect, but they are God's will. And in times of adversity, you may not always understand it, as it was with your loss of Claricé."

"Many, many nights, days, weeks and months passed before you received clarity and began to understand that God had other plans for the two of you. You two are soul mates and have been together for eons and will be together eternally. Your present separation is but a brief interruption in your time together. But there are other soul mates as well. Look to the branch of a tree and how a larger branch gives off two, each of which then give off three, each then

which then give off four or more. The leaves closest to you on your branch of the tree are what mankind has labeled your 'soul mates.' Those near to you will be with you several lifetimes. You will meet and meet again. Like begets like, growing and learning together. In your earthly incarnations you seek each other out and often feel a sense of recognition, and randomly identify with one another when you meet without forethought or reason.

"One of the bigger problems, which fit the mold of 'truths' most earthlings have been given, was in their early youth. It is during this period that they are forming their fundamental and basic personal ideas and belief systems about life as they are learning it. And, too, this is not isolated to your modern industrial world's religious philosophies. There are those on your earthly plane who have not had the opportunity to understand or use their God given innate abilities due to the circumstances of their origin of birth in cultures with lack.

"Without getting into words that stimulate debate, the simple truth of the matter is that God is a LOVING God. God is a forgiving God. Many due to early theological teachings, have been brought up with a belief in a 'fear of God.' They've been led to believe that God will punish them and they will burn in hell for eternity for minor indiscretions and come to God, out of 'fear' rather than LOVE.

"Fear, dread, negativity, helplessness, gluttony, avarice, greed, lust and evil intentions are earthborn creations of mankind, the ego and conscious awareness. All negative thoughts or considerations are evil influences, which come through the susceptibility of the lower mind-self and ego. There were times in the early life and the learning of humankind when it was necessary for God to instill fear of retribution. Early mankind, as you, were given free choice, but the intellect of early man lacked an awareness of the potential of their being.

"Jesus and the Master Teachers, before and after His birth, brought forth and taught the meaning of life

and love of your fellow man. Although there is still much to do in your world, the negative attributes of the conscious mind, man's ego and greed have begun to be replaced by love and giving, of and for one another. God has no religion. God is all. The freedom to choose belief systems, which fit each man's individuality, is what gave birth to religious differences, yet you are all on a path to the Supreme power.

"Mankind only has to look at the progress of your world as it is known today to understand the magnificence and power of God's love since the time of the Master Teachers and birth of Christ. One only has to look at the technological advances of the past century or throughout the millennia. Man himself did not 'invent' the marvels and creations of the past. They were born of a perceived necessity, of course. But the <u>ideas,</u> the thinking process, the thoughts and knowledge originated with the magnificence of the God force within the minds of mankind since time began.

"Without God there is nothing. Before God, there was nothing. At the same time it would be impossible to be aware of 'nothing' without having an awareness of 'something'. In man's understanding of universal law, you cannot know one without the experience of the other; you would not know pleasure if you didn't know pain, or happiness without sadness, good without knowing bad, etc."

"In earlier days, life was different. By today's standards, all earlier life was much more difficult than you know of it now. Through 'choice' you made the world what it is today. Mankind chose to make things different or better. In every step along the way, the positive results were from positive choices created from positive thoughts brought to you through the messengers of God who showed you the way to access the potential of God within your own minds where the knowledge of all resides.

"Victor, it is like the truth in and belief of the existence of God. Would you believe that the understanding of and the image of God, in whatever *form is acceptable to a man's belief, since time began was one of God's earliest miracles? This came with the freedom of choice given to the humankind of God's creations. In order for any belief in God to exist, every man must have an image that fits a belief that is acceptable to his own thinking. Any other answer would only confuse the unexplainable. God is the light...for without light, there would be darkness...or nothing at all!"*

"I understand what you have said, but as I took a break and read back over the communication I have transcribed, it doesn't clarify the source of the truth you are bringing to me. Some of what I have written sounds rather obvious while other bits and pieces sound like it may be something I have read or heard before. I've read so many books over the past months, and throughout the years I'm beginning to question the source. Let me ask you about the "truth" once again in this particular circumstance." Archie replied as follows:

"That too is an easy question to deal with Victor. You well may have heard it all before. It could have been in the exact words or words that explain something in a similar manner. It is very likely, but not in the sense of plagiarizing or that you are making up the answers yourself. Metaphors, which you, or I may use to give an example, are obvious choices and certainly have been stated over and over again. The family tree or tree of life is an example that is commonly used to show how families, groups and societal cultures grow and evolve.

"Let me speak only of recent times for the moment. The 'spiritual revolution' if I may use one of your earthly terminologies, and call it that, has been in a rapidly progressive movement in your part of the world, as well as elsewhere, for over fifty years; really since shortly following the end of your Second World War.

"People have been looking for 'something,' more than their day-to-day routines, existence and theological teachings. They believe there has to be

more than they have been receiving through their religions and traditional means. They want joy and satisfaction to grow along with the growth in the quality of life that has taken place since the technological revolution that followed the Second World War on your planet Earth.

"During the difficult early years of the twentieth century, and throughout what was called your worldwide 'depression years' the various religious teachings and theological beliefs were growing and generally satisfying for many earthlings. However the industrial revolution and worldly transition, which took place as a result of and following the Second World War years, brought prosperity to many around your globe. With this and the peace that had come, much of humanity thought happiness and joy would follow. It didn't. Missing still was an overall inner satisfaction with life. In spite of their different religious beliefs and an improved economy, there was an awareness of emptiness that persisted and brought about a spiritual shift that began to grow. Many of your world actively began searching for that elusive 'something' which would give them the fulfillment which they believed was lacking.

"Consider for a moment the dozens and dozens of authors who have written thousands of what you call new thought or self help books to fulfill the quest for the answers mankind has been searching for. Much of what has been written is of divine guidance being given to you and others who listen through the author's angels, guides, the spirit within and knowingness of the higher self. Your question about truth is most appropriate. The truth and/or acceptance of what has been written in the past and what will be written in the future is a matter of an individuals need and belief. This refers to both the writers and the readers. Once again, this is where freedom of choice comes into the picture and each of mankind must accept only that which is within their individual belief system and/or capability of belief and understanding.

"As the shift in spirituality has moved forward, much of mankind began to question, and did not understand, the reasoning behind a fear of God that was instilled in them during their youth and early theology. Mankind's intellect over the past thirty to forty of your earth years has been changing, growing and choosing to accept a God that wants only love, joy, peace and harmony in the world He created. Today, mankind wants what God wants for the world you live in.

"More and more of God's children are coming to him in search of the loving God, the Holy Spirit that lives within their heart and soul, and is now being shown to them though their religious, theological and spiritual leaders, guides and angels. What has been and will be told to you in future communications, the identical words will be, and are being, repeated over and over again to all who are willing to listen.

"You are a writer and a good communicator. You, and many others who are ready to listen, have been chosen to pass along the understanding that love, joy and harmony can finally bring true peace to the world you live in. Your purpose is to pass along the messages you get through your angels and guides in whatever means become appropriate to you. Because the messages are being told and retold, your writing is not necessarily unique and the messages you receive have been told to many others who well may have already written about the same subject matter in words identical to those you are now putting together at my direction or words of their own interpretation based upon their personal intellect and understanding.

"The information being given to you are energy vibrations translated into verbal impressions, which stop and start periodically. They are formulated by you into your words and your particular means of expression. The pauses that come after writing a few words, or a sentence and the breaks that you take in communicating with us, is when the formulation takes place. When it comes to you in bits and pieces, your higher self takes whatever time is necessary to

assimilate and understand what is given to you so that you can write with logical continuity.

"*Although it is the <u>truth</u>, all of you still have your own intellect and frame of reference based upon your individualized personal experience for putting the thoughts together in your own words. It is also a lesson in semantics. You must remember, words are only words, and words are labels, like symbols used by mankind to communicate thoughts, ideas or concepts.*

"*When comparing words of today, with those of any language of the past, you must also realize that the intellectual growth throughout the evolution of mankind has added thousands and thousands of new words, continuously in every language, lexicon or vocabulary. Therefore when reading any translation of words written in earlier days, be it the Bible, Koran, Talmud, any other writings of the Master Teachers, theological reference books of your world's religions, or philosophy, there may be a choice, or selection from among a dozen words to use for an interpretation <u>of any one word</u> of the earliest writings and/or between languages. Accepting any writing as truth in its entirety is a matter of choice, acceptance, and faith of a man's individual belief system.*

"*In essence, don't worry about whether you are writing the truth. You will write your truth as long as you are writing from your higher self, the angels or spirit. ASK QUESTIONS...LISTEN... and just allow it to happen. Write what you receive. Realize too, your 'truth' is your truth alone and it will be disagreed with and met with negativity by many who will question your written words or the source. This has happened since the written word came into being and will continue to be throughout mankind's existence on your planet Earth.*

Early writers of 'the word' in any religious theology were continually met with doubt, as have been those, which have been called 'inspired writings' in more recent centuries, such as Joseph Smith's Book of Mormon, and your contemporary authors and writers of today. Your God given freedom of choice is your gift from God, and rightfully so.

Victor K. Hosler

Chapter Eleven
Archie's Insight on Prosperity vs. Abundance

Following Archie's arrival in my life at the end of August 2000, he was with me almost constantly. At night there were the discussions and my questions to him, and in the daytime I was at my computer, taking dictation from him and auto-writing. As previously mentioned, although I was knowingly awake, the nightly discussions still had a dreamlike quality to them and by morning when I got out of bed I was only left with the questions and "essence" of what had come about before I had gone to sleep or during the night when he would awaken me.

It wasn't until late October or early November 2000 that I learned I could "choose" when to be with him and the other angels or not. At the same time a sense of knowingness came upon me and I knew they would always be there for me whenever I would choose to be with them.

Because of redundancies caused by my going back over material for clarification, I am eliminating the chronology because it doesn't serve any further purpose. However, for continuity I will maintain the casual conversational style, with the greetings and closure as they came to me and were ended. Often, Archie and the other angels you will meet use my life experiences as a foundational basis for explaining various concepts when they respond to my questions about life, as has been done previously.

Often, too, you will find they can be repetitious and make the same point over again when it applies to a different situation; or they will return to a previously discussed concept or explanation when it is necessary and related to the context of the subject presently being communicated to me. Archie has said they will repeat something until it is learned, the same as our earthly schools.

He begins the next discussion relating to the manner in which I personally experienced "prosperity and abundance" during my life.

- - - - -

Prosperity vs. Abundance

"Good afternoon Archie. I got off to a slow start today, but last night you kept chattering away until the early morning so I guess you have a lot more to discuss with me." I was again at my computer ready to tackle the subjects of the previous night.

"Victor, that perhaps is the understatement of the new millennium for you. Prepare to work 'your fingers to the bone' to quote one of your earthly clichés. If I can use the example of how your life plan has developed, as it came about and where your life has gone throughout the years, I believe I can clarify the intent of concepts that can enhance the quality of life for you and those you will communicate with.

"When I speak of 'prosperity', as in prosperity vs. abundance, I am relating it to putting the quest for the 'almighty dollar' or monetary as a primary purpose and goal. This seems to be a quite common goal of mankind in your world today, both in your country and others throughout the world.

"Many of you want more than you need and for some, more than they could spend in their lifetime on the planet Earth. With true <u>'abundance' in your life</u>, having enough currency to supply your basic needs and reasonable pleasures in life requires a level of prosperity also, but not as a primary goal in life. You, Victor, are a good example of having experienced the extreme difference between 'prosperity and abundance' in which I speak. As I stated earlier in our discussions, most people are caught up in the idea that <u>prosperity</u>, as a goal, will bring them happiness or satisfaction into their lives.

"During what you and I have agreed to call your fifteen-year mid-life crisis, actually more like seventeen years, you were in your own 'prosperity' phase and on the treadmill to accumulate more and more worldly goods. You were relatively secure financially; you lived in a fine home as well as having other properties; you traveled extensively and you did and/or bought almost anything you wanted. This period included a couple of marriages, which came about for all the wrong reasons, as well as romantic affairs and a live-in significant other.

Angels in My Life

"*Perhaps I should give you a quick review of those years; taken alone, these years could be a story within themselves, so we will just skim the surface to show you how 'chasing the almighty dollar' contributed to the several bumps in your road of life, broken relationships, heath problems with your heart and mini-strokes. Prosperity gave you spurts of pleasure and many good times, but it didn't bring you true happiness, peace, joy or the fulfillment of real love in your life.*

"*Isn't it nice how you have improved physically and that you now enjoy the good health that came about in the ten years you experienced your life with Claricé? With her once you gave up your quest for prosperity, you had true 'abundance' in your lives as well as joy love and happiness.*

"*Victor you were falsely high on life during those years as you chased the elusive brass ring of financial success and prosperity. We know it came about due to poverty in your early life during the depression years, and you thought you had to take 'control' of your own destiny. But, think about what you went through — the several kinds of business you got into once you left the corporate world and began this quest for the almighty dollar. Let me remind you of your business ventures during this period.*

"*There were a couple early design studio adventures, before you founded the company, which grew to become a small full service advertising agency. Then, was the addition of a typography department and later a photo studio to your agency. And still later, your motion picture titling and animation studio. Then there was also the travel agency you had with your second wife Heather. There were outdoor advertising businesses in both California and Florida, and, the 'but wait there is more' pitch on late-night TV for your perfume business venture. Then you should also consider the effect of 'black Friday,' where you took a 'big hit' in the small stock market crash of 1987.*

"Along with this, take a look also at your personal life. After your second divorce, you were so afraid of commitment that you chose female relationships so far away from where you lived that you couldn't get too seriously involved. Because you could afford the long distance romances, you played it very, very safe: in Puerto Rico and Panama; in Santa Barbara *and* San Francisco; in Lansing, Michigan, and New York. Did I forget any?

"Victor, is it any wonder you were a massive coronary waiting to happen? How many highs and lows can one person take in such a short period of time? You have to thank God for 'Ali,' your angel of good health; somehow she was able to influence those around you that you were heading for trouble. It was your friend, who later became your 'significant other,' and her mother that Ali, in her role as a walk-in angel got them to get through to you. They encouraged you to have the physical exam that led to the quad bipass that saved your life.

"It wasn't until you had to close your agency and film business and almost went broke, and then met Claricé that you were able to find true 'abundance' in your life. Surprising isn't it... broke, but with abundance. You were to learn this lesson in life. Everything that led up to and during your entire time together with Claricé was all a part of God's plan for your life. Things do not happen by accident.

"Later, and shortly after you met when you had the three mini-strokes, it was Claricé who began to encourage your early retirement. She convinced you in her own way that money or 'prosperity' was not necessary for happiness between the two of you; that the love you shared was the important ingredient in your lives.

"You had been on the same path then, as your good friend Bear took. As mentioned earlier, he suffered a massive and fatal coronary at only 53 years of age. Like him, you were disregarding the warning signs. Whether or not this was a part of God's plan for his life is not for me to say to you. However, we *certainly know it became a lesson in his life just past and that will benefit the future of the spiritual journey of his soul.*

"It was in the early 1980's when we first thought we could get through to you. We could see the path you were on. When you had your heart surgery in 1983, which was a result of stress and your many over-indulgences, a heart attack to end your life was not in your life plan. Even still, this lifestyle and quest for prosperity continued for several more years. As we waited for the time that Claricé was to come into your life, we tried and tried to get your attention. Even though we were unable to get through to you, everything you experienced was a part of what you were to learn during this incarnation, and you remained within the parameters of God's plan for your life.

"When you began your serious writing, unbeknownst to you and with our intent to awaken you, all of your stories have had angelic guidance and were of a spiritual nature. Even the first manuscript you wrote, the one taken on by your agent/publisher that never quite made it to press, was guided.

A walk-in angel visited your good friend Shirley and influenced her to encourage your writing from the beginning. That story which began as a hand written sixty-five page concept for a short story, with Shirley's encouragement and editing, turned out to be a lengthy supernatural, contemporary romance. But it was also a story that had a lot of truth in it; truths that are a part of many fictional stories from a writer's mind.

"You got into hypnosis and doing past life regressions in the mid-eighties. At the time, you thought it was research for writing a fictional story on reincarnation. It wasn't. Once again, I and the other angels, who were then with you, were trying to get your attention. This story was based on reality. It was about Christel, your friend from Germany who now lives with her French husband in southern France. When you met, she was a foreign exchange student, who had just completed her studies at the University of

Miami. It was an unusual experience for you, meeting her briefly for only a part of one day in 1960, the day before she was to return to her homeland. There was an indescribable attraction between the two of you at that time.

"After being together for only a few hours in the company of 20 others on a one-day sail off the coast of Miami, you became obsessed to contact her. This obsession got you in contact with her by telephone and resulted in your becoming pen pals for several months. Eventually this brief contact drew you together as friends. Ten years later, you subsequently developed a relationship with her, her husband and family, that continues to this day. Your families have visited each other's homes and from that brief encounter, you have now been friends for over forty years. You did not meet by chance and have significantly influenced each other's lives. Christel has inspired much of your early writing, and you have inspired her artistry throughout the years.

"Christel is one of your eternal soul mates. You have been together before; as brother and sister siblings in one life, the basis of the story you later began writing, and as lovers in another incarnation. This was the reason for your immediate attraction and identity of each other and the strong bond that has developed over forty years in which you have strongly and creatively influenced each other's lives. The entire story of Christel and you is much too long for this particular writing, but with the attraction you had for one another, it is worth pointing out that it was good that the two of you have remained on different continents divided by your Atlantic ocean.

"Victor, you always had to be in control of your life and for most of your life, you were not about to let us in. We knew that many times we were close, by the subject matter in your writing, the indications that came through during your years of doing past-life regressions and the compulsion to contact your friend Dick's daughters after he tried to get through to you; that is why we never really have given up on you.

"Claricé and you were meant to be together exactly as your lives turned out. When the time for you to meet was getting close, you were living with your significant other, in the later stage of your mid-life crisis years. We had to get a little devious and tricky, as angels can and sometimes do. We had to create your break-up and we had to do this by tempting her fate with another. We had to split the two of you apart to make room for Claricé in your life. I might add that this too, was a lesson in life your friend had to learn.

"Later, once the initial course of your life with Claricé was determined we again had to become more involved. You were still not letting us in or to be heard. Claricé strongly encouraged your early retirement because of her concerns for your health; she wanted you both to sell everything you had and leave Miami. The plan was for the two of you to simplify your lives.

"You don't think the little motor scooter 'accident' when you were on your honeymoon in Cozumel was really an <u>accident</u>, do you? No, it was something we had to do to assure your retirement. A little puff of wind into the bag you held between your knees caused you to lose control. We did have a little hand <u>in breaking your hand</u>! Pardon the 'pun' as you on earth would refer to it in my example. But we did arrange it to happen, and the reconstructive surgery required on your hand assured your retirement.

"Claricé loved your stories and wanted you to get back to your writing again. She was going to find work and you were supposed to write. Instead, once you moved to St Petersburg and you settled into your new home and marriage, you took control again; you began to guide her career instead of writing. As it happened, this did turn out all right. You encouraged her to follow her own dreams and she became and was accepted as a very fine artist. It was only in the last year or two, when the time for the two of you to part again was coming near, that unknown to you, we began to get through to you both. Due to difficulties on the art show circuit and Claricé's early stage

illness, both of you began to give up control of your lives, and started looking to God for answers.

"You will have to agree that true 'abundance' only came into your life when Claricé entered it. It was a time when you were in a state of financial recovery not prosperity. But you became abundantly happy as the beautiful relationship developed between the two of you; and then also, the good relationship which came about between both families, American and Brazilian alike. All of your activities together, including the remodeling and designing of your new home, your business in Mexico and touring the art show circuit brought you closer together and brought you joy... even though you soon discovered that term 'starving artist' was not a cliché, but is in fact, a truism. You certainly did not return to prosperity on the art show circuit.

"Once you stopped chasing prosperity Victor, you found the "abundance" that brought the two of you much happiness and peace within. Even during the troublesome period that came as a result of your touring and the onset of her illness, the abundance of your love for one another saw you through a most difficult time. In the end, she found peace with the knowledge she would soon be leaving you. You held each other in silence; nothing more needed to be said between you; you had your eternal love!

"Although Claricé's crossing over was a devastating loss and has brought you great sorrow, this too was a necessary part of the plan for both of your lives. Claricé is a wise older soul. This is not in terms longevity as you on Earth think in relation to time, but more in the sense that she has accepted and moved through much of her spiritual learning. The soul itself is ageless. The energy called the 'soul' is one with God; and God has much more work in store for her, her talent and gifts. It wasn't until she arrived on this side that we were finally able to get through to you. Her communications with you were the wake-up call that finally caught your attention.

"We know that at that moment of realization, you turned your life over to God, the Creator of all. Your reading and research over the past months have shown you that the metaphysical world is consistent with the teaching of Christ and God's word. Opening yourself to hear from and communicate with God myself and the angels who are with you has opened your mind to the opportunity Claricé wanted for you when you first met. Write. Write. Write. It is a large part of your purpose for your remaining years.

"I also know that, based upon your reading of the books on angels, communicating with me and with the other angels, you have begun to find peace over Claricé's departure. Confidence in the knowingness of your eternal life and that you will meet again can be very healing. As your sorrow begins to dissipate and is replaced with greater understanding, the painful experience of your grief will continue to diminish and you will recognize the emotion as your ongoing love for one another and proof that her spirit is with you. That feeling and emotion, within your heart, is identical to the love the two of you experienced as lovers embracing, as if to become one."

Archie, I want to thank you for assisting me through my grief and how you have made the loss of Claricé understandable. Your explanation of how we were brought together for a specific length of time as was spelled out in God's plan for both of our lives has indeed brought me peace, and the ongoing communications have given me hope for the future and my purpose in life. You have put me on an exciting journey and I look forward to continuing the ride. I offer my thanks to God for you and your work in my life.

Victor K. Hosler

Chapter Twelve
Archie Talks About God

"Hello Archie, in our nightly chats, you keep bringing up the question of believing in GOD and making reference to God in many ways. You seem to have been tossing it around in my mind, not just pertaining to a belief in God, but the belief in life itself — 'our' life as we know it, and the pure act of our existence and being. I've been avoiding this topic of belief systems due to the obvious and unnecessary controversy the subject could generate due to the many religious theological belief systems. But take me where you want to go; start wherever it makes sense or where you want to begin?" I had let a few weeks pass since last going to the computer to ask questions; Archie seemed impatient in his response."

"Well, hello, it's about time you got back to me. Victor we have been having the same discussion over several nights in the past weeks from different perspectives. Let me begin by saying what I am about to tell you is not intended to be sacrilegious or to question God in any way shape or form. There are many, many human interpretations of what God is or isn't. As well, I can only relate to God and His creations in the language of mankind. There are not words in the lexicon of any earthly language that would explain or be understanding of all that is beyond your planet earth or other life in the universes of God's creation.

As you know, I do believe in GOD, as most of humankind uses of the word. After all, I do work for Him! Pardon the insertion of a bit of humor. As well, Jesus Christ <u>was</u> the Son of God sent to earth for God's purpose of introducing salvation to mankind and spreading His word.

"*The big problem throughout time is and has always been, semantics. Language. <u>God is</u>! But, 'God' is also just an English word. There are many other words in as many other languages and religious* *theologies that also refer to the meaning of GOD as you use the word in your English language. No one, in any language can define or describe God. You cannot just say that God "is the essence of life itself" because all things do not have what mankind defines as life as a human being or a living creature or thing.*

"They just are; such things as a rock... sand... mineral elements or the moon... or a star... do not have life as defined in your human experience. However, as stated earlier, broken down to their sub-atomic particles, even what you call inanimate objects could be said to have life.

"A more accurate response might be that <u>God</u> is the essence of being. The fact that a human can ask a question <u>is proof of being</u>, but only in the mind of humankind inhabiting your planet. Therefore, in a manner of speaking, God only exists in your head. A rock doesn't know God, nor does the moon or stars know of God... yet they are of God. On distant planets, there is <u>intelligent</u> life and because that life is intelligent, because 'they are, or exist,' they too will have a belief in what you call a God... the same God because He created the universes.

"Consider this, and I believe I mentioned it before, humankind relates everything to their own experience and being. Intelligent life on other planets will have a different 'look' or 'being' than humankind because that particular intelligent life had a totally different experience of being, growth and the development of their particular species or culture due to the environment in which they happen to evolve.

"Semantics again comes into play very strongly. The intelligent beings will not be of a human kind, they will be something other than being as mankind appears as life on your planet Earth, which is known as the human experience. Therefore, they too, in whatever existence their 'being' happens to be (using your language and analogy because there is no other way to explain it for human understanding), they will also be children of God, because they too, whoever or whatever they are, were created by God, as was your

Angels in My Life

Earth or another planet, place or life form, animate or inanimate.

"*God doesn't look like anybody, human or any other imagined species. The only necessity is to know is that <u>God IS</u>! Without God, there wouldn't be an existence of anything... anywhere! God is <u>everything</u>! God is the "spark", the creation of all existence. Perhaps, as your scientists relate to the "big bang" theory for creation of the universe, this event was really the beginning of God's creation of <u>all that is</u>. Whether it took six days and six nights and a day of rest is insignificant. In the Heavenly realm of the spirit of God it is timeless, so your scientists very well may have chosen the right metaphor in describing it as a 'big bang' because creation was instantaneous in your standards of understanding time.*

"*And, do you know what Victor? It doesn't matter who believes what. God gave humankind the freedom of choice, and this includes the freedom to believe or not believe. Does it matter what, if anything, God may or may not look like or be? No it doesn't matter at all. God just is!*

"*The difference, which matters to humankind on your planet, comes from the illusions created within your own minds. If you believe in God, the soul and everlasting life, you will have a special harmony in your life that allows you to look beyond death to an eternal existence. This is a major contributor of the "abundance" that God wants for all of mankind, and has been mentioned before. Although most people still have a fear of death, because the unknown is an absolute, because of their religious and theological acceptance and understanding, they still look forward to joining departed loved ones in Heaven or in the Heavenly environment.*

"*Without a belief in God you cannot look beyond death, and therefore, you will have a totally different outlook in your daily living and experience. With a lack of belief, you will be more open to acceptance of the evil forces that prevail and, 'unknown to you' will influence the negativity in your thinking. This will* occur because you don't really have a reason to care about the outcome of your life or anything beyond emptiness of death in this perception.

"Now Victor, let's get back to the basics of semantics. <u>WORDS.</u> Every word, as you call each of them, and use them in all languages of mankind, were created by God. They were created as a means for the communication of thoughts, ideas and/or concepts. However, the confusion which has come about in understanding of God, Christianity and all other religious philosophies has come about because of semantics, which is the study of the meaning of words, especially as they develop and change.

"You have to remember that humankind's intellect had grown and evolved through the years, as has man's vocabulary. Words are created like anything else, on the basis of need. I have 'coined a new word' is a phrase that is often used when a new word is created based on need or purpose.

"An example of this might be the title of the original manuscript from which this story evolved. You have given the story the working title of 'LIFECLOUDS.' For you, this was a metaphor to convey to your readers the idea that the problems and bumps in the road of life can be compared to the weather. Sunshine in your life is indicative of 'the good times,' or that which makes you happy and adds to your abundance, while the clouds that appear in the sky tends to block sunshine from coming into your life. Therefore, life is like the weather, sunshine mixed with clouds and a little bit of rain. When dark days are upon you, sometimes you have to push the clouds aside to find the sunshine in your life.

"Words are created to serve a purpose. They have been in the process of creation and growth since time began, and the lexicon of language expands daily. The vocabulary in every language known to mankind since the first sound was uttered by a human being on your planet, has been in a continual state of evolution. Therefore, due to growth, the meaning of words becomes more and more complex and even more as *they are translated among the hundreds of languages that are in use on your planet today. At the time of the earliest writings many words now available for use to describe a person, place, action or thing were not available in the beginning. Therefore, modern day translations of early writings can be more specific and perhaps colorful and interesting due to the semantic growth of the language of mankind. At the same time interpretations based on the filtration and intellect of the many interpreters throughout the years have brought about questions as to the truth or accuracy of modern translations of early writings.*

"Let's face it by using your word 'lifeclouds' as an example. If this were to become a new 'coined word' in the English language the translation process would begin to take place. An editor, translator or someone would look at the derivation of the new word...'life' and 'clouds' based upon the specific definition of the derivation of each part of the word, as they understand the intended meaning. In other languages, the editors, translators or whoever, would arrive at some kind of consensual agreement and then create a new word in their language that they 'believe' comes as close as they can come to the intended meaning of the word lifeclouds as it was put in use by its creator. The word lifeclouds as translated into the new language <u>may or may not</u> convey the purpose or meaning the creator of the original word intended in the first place. Close maybe, but not exact, and this is where misunderstood translations develop and become debatable.

"Now, go back to the beginning of time. God, the creator is all knowing and the intellect behind all things and has given human kind the ability to create sounds that became the basis for human communication. Man, Woman, Eat, Hot, Cold, etc., on, and on. From the seed of the first utterance, words became the language of mankind and have grown to include millions of words in each of over hundreds of different languages.

"Can you begin to understand why mankind is confused over what has been called <u>God's word</u>?

Actually ALL WORDS are God's words because they could not have been created without God. And man, given free choice was provided with the intellect to put meaning to the uttered sounds. But this too has changed. Man's intellect through the years has grown like an inverted pyramid. Therefore, Biblical, theological and religious confusion over 'the word' is understandable. And that is why there are so many differences of opinions. Through the years what is known as the 'Word of God' has gone through many translations and each has required many of the past scribes to draw upon the knowledge and intellect each of them possessed at that particular point in time.

"Those who choose to say, there is only 'one meaning' to each and every 'word' of God, support their belief that the words as used, were 'inspired by God'. Of course they were, all words have been, inspired by God. How the words are used or put together, in various combinations, or assortments, gave meaning to the overall context, based on the understanding and intellect of the writer/scribe at the time the translation was made for the specific 'audience' and/or language the translation is intended to be for. What many would say in response to this, is that the way the words are selected and put together were inspired by God in order for the intended meaning to go out to all mankind in what ever the language may be.

"Once again you have to look back in time. The intellect and lexicon of words used by man in whatever language was limited by the accumulated knowledge up to the particular date in time the 'Word' was written down; and even earlier, before the written word came into being, passed down through the word of mouth. Be it the words of any theological book or text, in their earliest of forms, only the words which were available to them, in their lexicon, at that particular moment in time were used in their writings.

"Mankind, wherever they are in the world, as it is known to you, when left to their own devices, select words from their own tools and personal frame

of reference, to explain or define what for many of their kind are unexplainable or difficult concepts of understanding. In the past as well as today, the intellectual complexity of life on Earth in the universe and how it may or may not have come about is mystifying to many. Conceptually, a simple explanation is beyond any known words for use in mass communication to effectively describe or explain your earthly experience. It always comes down to 'faith' in accepting the words and teachings of whatever theological beliefs mankind chooses to accept."

"All forms of life, whether it is in the earthly plane, the spiritual realm or other worlds in God's universe, is illusionary. It is a perception of reality which is a collective experience of mankind, based upon individual experiences of the soul energy, which gives life to your physical bodies, created by God for your earthly experience. This illusionary experience is a shared reality, and more specifically, within each of the perceived environments of God's creations throughout His universe.

"In a broad sense, life as known by humankind is truly an illusion, but is not a believable concept for most because of your perceivable awareness of your five known senses. However, could an intelligent energy force not of your Earth, and beyond what is understood as being within your reality, observe differences between the perceived reality of mankind's activities on the planet Earth, from the illusions electronically created and transmitted by mankind out into the universe, or from the dreamlike images which come from another dimension of time and space to flow through the illusionary minds of man?

"Mankind relates to everything within their own illusionary experience, as they know of their existence within their own perceived reality. It is the only common point of reference within mankind's reality to draw upon as earthbound beings or souls existing within their God created physical form of being.

"The imaginative minds of mankind, in both the written word and your motion picture created illusions, have stretched the imagination of the human minds throughout your planet and given forms of probable belief to the illusion of life in the beyond.

"Anything is possible within the creations of God. If and when the time comes on your planet earth for God to bring together the meeting of, and an awareness of, another intelligent life form or energy force within His universe, it will be whatever God deems is appropriate for a common understanding between the species of the two different illusionary worlds. God tells us He created many worlds. Because you do not yet know of them, does not mean they do not exist. The simple fact that you exist, and have an understanding of your own being, is proof that there is a supreme intelligence that is beyond logical reasoning of the conscious reality of the physical self. Life, as you know it, cannot be proved beyond the 'I AM' concept, yet this too is illusionary."

"The concept of <u>God</u> is a perfect example of this. That is why I often go to and use the word 'semantics.' There are no universally acceptable understandable words in any earthly, or worldly language that can explain the God force that would be acceptable to all mankind. In earthly terms, it is truly beyond any provable, comprehensible explanation.

"Each man for himself develops a 'faith' in his own belief or non-belief in God; or a belief in whatever he or she refers to as the reality of the intelligent force that created our being or our 'I AM' awareness. The 'I AM' perception cannot truly be denied by those without faith or a non-belief in a Supreme Being because in the act of 'denial' they are acknowledging the 'I AM' consciousness which came with our incarnation into our physical being and earthly presence.

"Belief beyond the 'I AM' and life beyond death of our physical bodies or 'vehicles' is where faith is required. This is one example of where true faith and freedom of choice comes into the picture and that,

which has come to him or her from their personal frame of reference and theology within whatever culture he or she happens to reside. It is important to remember that, some cultures have never had the opportunity to develop an intellectual understanding of life, of why or how they exist, or even the basic, most common understanding of a God or Supreme power as known or understood by most of humankind. But, still these cultures have the awareness of and are mystified by the 'I AM' sense of being which has brought about an alertness, that has given rise to a belief in many God's, of many descriptions."

"So, Victor, in most ways, what I have told you is obvious, so where does all of the confusion come in? The confusion comes with mankind's interpretation and understanding of what each of them believe the words to mean, and this, brought about by every man's God given freedom of choice of belief. This gets back to where I defined your 'truth' in what I say to you and you then transcribe. Your understanding and transcription is based upon your personal intellect, frame of reference and geological or environmental influences. Therefore every person on your planet of every theological persuasion is free to interpret <u>the Word</u> as he chooses to accept and understand its meaning and those who hear the voice of God or His messenger Angels.

"Victor when a man's literal interpretation of his reading of Christ's teachings tells him that Christ walked among his people and, as stated earlier, said, 'I am the truth, the way and the life...' to God or the Kingdom of Heaven. It is the truth in every one of the many references of this nature within the various texts of the written Word. But the same is true for your personal belief of what Christ meant by those words to you. You too have the freedom to believe it, as you read it, and you understand it to mean that He was speaking to His people, and those along His journey through life. Of course he asked for the word to spread to all of mankind and the peoples of His then known world. Herod and the leaders of other societies

and cultures in the known world may have wanted their people or subjects to believe they were gods and kings to be worshiped, but they were not. At that time in the very small area of His known world, He preached that believing in Him, Jesus Christ, would allow His fellow man to come to God and the Kingdom of Heaven.

"To you, a belief in God is the primary intent of the word because you have developed a 'relationship' with God. This is your truth, as another man's beliefs and convictions belong to him in his truth in which he has developed a relationship and acceptance of Christ is the primary ingredient of belief. How can there be a right or wrong way when they are one and the same?

"This can also be said for other religious persuasions and those who have not had the opportunity to know Christ. Many, due to just the magnificence of life, believe in a Supreme Being or source. For each of them it is their truth and that is the important message. Wouldn't this also apply to those who before the time of Christ worshiped a 'sun God'? After all, Jesus Christ said 'I am the light'... and 'Ye are the light.' Is not the sun God's light that gives life to humanity?

"Belief in the power of God, behind the existence of the universe is the key to abundance in your life. Non-belief is also man's choice; but as stated above the emptiness beyond death for non-believers deprives them of living their life to its fullest in a state of peace and harmony that comes with the acceptance of an eternal life.

"At the same time, the non-believers also have their free choice and in many cases, they are indifferent to the point that they don't care. Only life here and now on your planet Earth means anything to them. You find this among many with evil intentions or those with greed or seeking power over their fellow man. This obviously is where most of the trouble on your planet Earth comes about. There is worldwide greed, corruption, criminal activity and the negative

Angels in My Life

forces of evil intent among the ego consciousness of the lower self of non-believers.

"Believers in a Supreme Being only want peace love and harmony in God's world and this is the intent of all theological persuasions.

"Where believers in God, the Supreme Being, get off course, is in questioning (judging) each other's belief or belief systems. Each of you is right because God gave you freedom of choice to believe as you wish so you should stop debating the right or wrong way to believe in God. Instead believers should join forces throughout your world to face and fight off the evil forces that try to control the destiny of your planet.

"Man must understand that achieving perfection in your world is a myth. A balance between harmony, love, joy and peace is all that God wants for his world and the universe. This can only come from mankind's awareness of, and a goal of achieving, abundance in life. <u>God alone is perfection</u>. Working toward the God-like state of mind and learning the lessons of your particular purpose in life is what your incarnation on Earth is all about.

"As it was told to you in your communications with Claricé, a <u>perfect world</u> would be a pretty boring place to be. Mankind must have goals to strive for; without them there would not be incentives 'to be or not to be.' The heavenly state of the spiritual world is about as close to perfection as one could expect to reach. Even in the spiritual environment the souls of humankind are continually in a state of growth, a time of learning and achieving higher levels of understanding in their quest for oneness with the perfection that is God."

"Perfection, as applied to one's earthly endeavors for being 'perfect' in what one accomplishes, such as the 'perfect 300 game' in bowling or a 100 percent score on a test, is only a semantic label attached to a specific result. Unfortunately, in the semantics of worldly communications in all languages, 'perfection' has been misapplied and sought after as a goal for mankind to achieve in his earthly environment. I say it is a myth, because I ask the question, what would a

> *perfect world look like to you? And, Can you define perfection, as it would relate to a perfect world?' You cannot, because everyone of every culture or persuasion would have a different answer. That is why God only wants peace, joy, love and harmony in his world. He knows it cannot be perfect."*

- - - - -

Archie's communications often flow like the wind, frequently taking different directions, and then switching back and forth, sometimes becoming repetitious or redundant. Sometimes he becomes so complex I do not understand the first reading and he has to immediately clarify the intent. When I first began compiling the communications, I tried to bring specific references, or subject matters together, but found that when I would move a segment out of its original position, the intended meaning of the overall context would change and I would have to move it back.

Chapter Thirteen
Angels, God And The Ordinary Man

"What's next Archie?" I asked. "We seem to be bouncing all around the place. I want to ask you to talk about the 'common man' of which, I consider myself to be. In last nights communication you made reference to the 'Ordinary Guy from Mo-Town,' a chapter in my original 'LIFECLOUDS' manuscript. In your talks about God, you seemed to bounce all over the place. Can we communicate in a more chronological manner?"

"Victor, throughout your professional career in advertising and marketing, in communicating your client's ideas, preparing and writing presentations for their speeches, or with marketing assignments, you always took the position that you were to be a recipient of the information. You prepared for each project as if you knew nothing about the subject matter. In doing this, no matter how complex the information may have been, your goal was to create a method of presenting the details in a simplified manner that you could readily understand, and/or would create in you the desire to react or not react to the message. By using this technique, you knew that the targeted or intended audience or recipient would be able to 'get it' also.

"You are just an ordinary guy, and if I can communicate to you in a way that you can understand God, the soul, the spirit and the creation of God's universe in simpler terms, then your transcriptions could be meaningful to the many I hope choose to read what you are writing today. You, as well as others who are listening, and have also been instructed to do, are to present the ways and intention of God in a spiritual and metaphysical manner which is beyond that of former, traditional religious and theological teachings.

"With the changes that have come upon your Earth/world society, humankind today is looking for

greater understanding than has been previously sought after by the masses upon your earth.

"All right, let's go to your angels and an ordinary man again, since that is where this chapter began. Victor, you have found that YOU, an ordinary man can talk to your angels, and because your angels are messengers of God, you are thereby communicating with God in a most direct manner; this is no different than prayers to your Heavenly Father. You will find much doubt and disbelief, from many you may communicate with this about, as you proceed along this journey. Don't let it bother you and don't try to force your belief in the experience upon others. As you have, every man has to come to terms with his own belief and in his own time. Those who have not experienced what you are now experiencing may just think you are 'losing it,' just as you did when the first communications from Claricé, Dick and Sally, your former mother-in-law came through to you.

"As you have read, and come to believe through your communications and research, everyone has angels with them; and they also have the ability to talk to or communicate with their angels. The probability of common, ordinary beings, such as yourself doing this, is incredulous and beyond the belief of most people on your planet. They think that if it is possible, it is only within reach of the clergy, students of religion, Christianity, theological masters and teachers, but not of the 'ordinary man,' or woman.

"Most people in the world who have faith or a belief in one form or another accept that they can talk to or with God in the manner of prayer. A question that came up for you when your prayers for your wife Claricé were not answered and she succumbed to breast cancer, has also been asked of you. 'Why weren't your prayers answered, when in the Bible it states that if you believe, all prayers will be answered.' Unfortunately Victor, that is a misnomer in the literal translation and has brought with it much pain and anguish throughout the years. Your daughter-in-law and your wife developed breast cancer symptoms a

month apart. You created prayer chains for both of them to be cured throughout the world; in South America through Claricé's family; Europe through your friend Crystal; Canada though Claricé's friend Michele and throughout the United States with family and friends. Your daughter-in-law's family did the same. In the early stage your lovely daughter-in-law was diagnosed with a very aggressive breast cancer, already invading her lymph system and Clarice was diagnosed as not having cancer, or at the worse, possibly a 'pre-cancerous' condition.

"In the end, your daughter-in-law, with the most frightening diagnosis survived and is now nearing the 5-year period of remission, and Claricé, with the non-cancer diagnosis died within 21 months. Why? You were devastated and did not understand why prayers were answered for one, but not the other. As happy as you were for your son and his wife, it didn't make any sense to you and you even quit going to the church your families attended. The pain was too great. When your prayers for Claricé to win her battle with breast cancer were not answered, you became angry with God; in fact by your own words, you had a hatred for God. But, God is a forgiving God and He understood the anger that came from your pain and loss.

"Why? You asked, as the hatred grew within and when your prayers to join her were not answered, again and again. The miracle of her coming through to you spiritually, on January 5th 2000, finally began to give you answers. But, it was many months of spiritual and angelic communications before you came to believe and understand that God does have a life plan for every one of His children. For Claricé who was at another crossroads in her life, God had other plans for her and He called her home; it was according to His plan for each of your lives. Fortunately for you, your son and his wife, God has much more for them to do in His plan for their lives. You have learned that there is a divine plan for His universe and your lives on the planet Earth.

"Most prayers to God or a higher power — the specific name of which, depends upon each man's theological or religious preference — are requesting something from their God; other prayers give thanks to Him for their daily bread, bounty and life. Unfortunately, 'Ask and you shall receive' in this context does not always come about. Therefore, when the specific request is not given to them, doubt arises as it did with you. When prayers for a loved one's healing do not come about, the question of whether or not a God really exists torments those left behind. You wonder, 'Is God listening? Or in fact can He/She/It, even hear your prayers?' After all, there are literally millions and millions of prayer requests being put forth at any second of every day. It would take a busy God to handle each prayer personally, wouldn't it? But then 'personally' implies a man-like God. Your more common, worldly understanding is that God is omniscient, omnipresent and omnipotent. Therefore, all prayers within reason should be answered, but often times in your understanding, they are not. The truth is that if your prayer request fits the plan for your life or that of the one being prayed for, it will be answered.

"Actually, it is the angels, which enable God to be so effective. Angels, who are messengers of God, are one with God. These are angels assigned to your soul during your earthly incarnation, and those with specific responsibilities. As stated earlier, there are a million times a million times a million and more, angels fulfilling millions and millions of God's tasks and assignments at any one moment in time. To use an earthly term again, each angel has a specific 'job description.' And as well, every man, woman and child has angels assigned to assist them in achieving their life goals according to God's plan for each of their lives. Although each child of God has two angels assigned to them for life, additional angels with specific abilities, walk-in angels, are assigned as needed or available to fulfill the many different requests. The number of your attending angels can

vary daily. These angels have never incarnated to the earthly plane of existence. They are God's messengers.

"Your loved ones who have crossed over and choose to watch over you are your guardian angels and are with you as long as they 'feel' the need. While with you, they are fulfilling a dual purpose and also learning and studying in the spiritual realm. Jules may say it differently; and those who are listening as you are on the earthly plane may also hear it differently. But once more Victor, we are getting into semantics, by which you Victor are choosing the words from your experience to communicate the intended message. For you, guardian angels, is your choice of words for loved ones, friends and others who have crossed over, based upon your understanding of what I have given you, and assigned angels and walk-in angels have never incarnated on the earthly plane.

"Where the problems arise, are in the words that are chosen to explain beliefs in a Supreme Being, or God, that mankind has then built upon. Individual beliefs and word choices can be as different as night and day, depending upon the writings of the masters and teachers of the past and that which has been given to them from their forbears. It doesn't matter what theological or religious preference it happens to be, each has 'written words' as a basis for developing of their structured beliefs. Most believe in a one-way communication within their specific belief system or tenants, based upon their understanding of the words or what has been taught to them. Be it through prayer or meditation, they pray to whomever or whatever name or names they have been taught is the Supreme Being based upon their particular religious philosophy.

"There are hundreds of different Christian denominations in just your country, without considering the many non-Christian religious persuasions. Many believe that 'their way' is the only way, but there is no 'one way' to come to God, and for me to try and clarify this further would only create

unnecessary debate and rejection of the message being given to you. You have already faced this disagreement when Claricé said to you that there are many ways to come to God.

"That every man can have two-way communication about the essence of their life experience with '_their own_' Supreme Being, God, or higher power is met with doubt by many, and talking with angels or spirits is most often met with disbelief. It is a difficult idea or concept for disbelievers, doubters and others to understand or accept.

"The reasons behind this are that communications with your God, or in fact your angels or loved ones who have crossed over, is entirely a mental process as it was when you were communicating with Claricé. Granted it began by your voice asking to be able to speak to her just 'one more time' and was followed by her answer, 'You can, my love.' Initially you _thought_ you heard her respond in kind, but then soon realized that even though it was her voice and with her Brazilian accent, it happened entirely within your own mind. Many believe in the answers to prayers that sometimes come into their minds from God, but they don't listen, hear or believe in the possibility of other communications. The other words or messages, that enter their minds they believe is a part of the mind-talk or chatter that goes on in every waking hour; they think it is a part of the thinking process or just nonsense thoughts as dreams often seem to be.

"Belief was a difficult step for you and only came about because of the other communications we brought to you. That was the primary purpose of bringing your friend Dick, Sally, your former mother-in-law, Barry and — the first one that you didn't respond to — from your friend Margie's brother George. Claricé wanted to get your attention, because of her concern over your deep grief and we knew that bringing her to you would bring you to God. Because of your anguished plea, we believed you were then ready to listen and believe. Now that we have your attention, and you have come to accept it and have developed a personal *relationship with God, what you are doing now is the work Claricé said you were meant to do in her first communication with you.*

"*Initially, you were caught up in disbelief and were certain you were imagining things, hallucinating or perhaps that it was all a part of a dreamlike experience. Although you responded, you didn't understand the reality of the conversations and you determined they were going on in your head and you thought you were making it all up with your overactive creative imagination. You considered it was wishful thinking you brought on yourself to help you overcome your grief. This is a common reaction; and probably the most difficult task we angels have to overcome in order to be able to begin a dialogue with each of you who is ready to listen.*

"*As stated above, everyone hears voices in their head. In this manner, you certainly are not unique. For the most part, most people think of it as the mind-talk that goes on, and sometimes that of their conscience. And it is! But your conscience is your angels at work, generally your guiding angels, advising you of the proper path to follow in fulfilling your life plan as well as trying to keep you out of trouble when the negative voices and evil or improper thoughts permeate your mind. Negative thoughts, envy, jealousy, evil thoughts are of the 'ego' – your lower self, which often attempt to work their way into your life and steer you off the path chosen for you by God and the masters, when your life in the physical vehicle was planned. Prisons are filled with the success of evil entities. All positive thoughts, ideas and impressions are the 'truth' of your higher self and spirit where the living God resides in your being.*

"*In Biblical terms and other references, all angels are not necessarily messengers of God. There are, what has been called 'fallen angels...' angels with evil intentions that also may enter your consciousness through your lower self and the 'I want' mode of your ego. You have to beware of them as you do in your every day actions in avoiding negativity, wrong choices, and evil in others. Instead, mankind is to follow the 'golden rule' and commandments of God. The Ten Commandments are God's law for a harmonious life among your fellow man and accepted in some form or derivation in most religious theologies. By the way, we like the joke that some tell, that 'originally there were fifteen commandments, but Moses dropped one of the tablets.'*

"*Getting back to seriousness though, everyone does hear voices in their head and they have many internal discussions. In fact in the past, many who have vocalized what you are saying and writing today have been penalized, abused and even put to death for claiming to have heard 'the voices;' they were thought to be possessed by demonic or evil spirits, even though their purpose and intentions were of God. Instead, the evil was that of the non-believers. You are fortunate that day has passed, Victor. You have even joked that you thought your children were about to have you carried away by the white coats in a 'straight jacket' when you first told them of your talking to Claricé, your angels and others.*

"*Recent written information in books on the subject of angels that you have completed suggested that you 'write it down.' The purpose of this is to focus and get a complete record of a communication.*

"*For several months during your early grieving, you were bothered about the myriad voices you were hearing and bits and pieces of conversations; but you weren't truly listening. At those times you were not focused enough to hear what was being brought to you. Because of it, you were suffering, from sleep deprivation from what you called the 'noise' that was keeping you awake all night. You must be relaxed and in the twilight state of mind before sleep, or in meditation, or really listen to your thoughts, to be able hear. If you have a specific question and you are ready to listen, the Biblical words, 'Ask and you shall receive...' become a truth. This is where you <u>must listen closely</u> and trust what you are hearing. If the words you hear are of a positive nature, it is from the* *angels who are God's messengers. If there is any sense of negativity, it is from the ego-lower self or what has been termed 'fallen angels.'*

"The reason for writing it down is that when the messages come through, they are in a form of energy vibrations which are in tune with your own vibrational energy. Until you are ready to listen and focus on them, they come through like scattered words and thoughts that seemed to ramble around in your mind. You described it as noise or a cacophony of disconnected words. When this happens, it is like fragments of a dream and they are forgotten within minutes or hours. It is when you truly begin to focus on them that they suddenly come together in an understandable form. You have found this to be so in my communications with you, and it still happens when you are not really listening for me or the others. That is why you decided to keep a note pad on your nightstand. You became aware of the need to write down the bits and pieces, until you were fully open and receptive to receive the complete messages we had to give you. This then became clarified when you began to sit at your computer and ask questions relative to the brief messages or fragments. Even today, you still keep the note pad on hand and often write down a few words to remind you what we talked about the previous night.

"This was also true in regard to your conversations with Claricé. Although there was a total six or seven hours of conversation with her in the five visits you had, after they had taken place you only recalled bits and pieces each morning. It was when ML began to assist you in the transcription at the computer that the messages became clear and not dream-like. As it turned out, the total transcription only amounted to about 30 pages; this was because she only included that which was relevant to our purpose and left out anything that was of a personal nature. Omitted was that which would be meaningless to your readers and well may have brought you painful

thoughts and questions relative to grief you were then still experiencing.

"When mind-talk goes on, and you have fragmented conversations or hear the 'noise' in your head, more often than not it is during the late night or wee small hours of the morning and as stated like dreams they are quickly forgotten. In your waking hours and daily routines these same type of conversations, are thought of as you are talking to yourself; you believe that in your mind you are just thinking things through, and often you are just rehearsing your thoughts for a later discussion where you need to be perfectly clear in what you will say.

"The only time these conversations are meaningful is when you are in deep thought, solving one problem or another after which, when you come to a successful conclusion, you then credit yourself for the brilliant solution you came up with. The fact of the matter is that your 'brilliant ideas' come directly from God, through your angels or drawing upon God's innate knowledge placed within the grasp of your mental faculties, which are endless and for the most part untapped.

"Normally, and prior to the solving of a problem, somewhere in the process you silently and without conscious awareness ask a question. 'How can I do this?' Or, a different question is asked, which is beneath your level of consciousness.

"Some of the humor in all of the 'mind-talk' is that many of you imagine you are hearing the name of the next horse that is going to win the Derby or a dog that is going to win the fifth race; or perhaps you are really 'getting' the next day's Lotto numbers. You get the idea that 'somebody up there likes you' and you throw away your money, thinking God is giving you a winner. He is not. It is wishful thinking, the 'I want' greed of the ego – lower self, and it can be addictive. When the information is wrong, you are then upset with God because the horse or dog crossed the finish line last and you didn't even have three numbers right in the Lotto. Giving you prosperity in that manner is not His

purpose. If there is no logical reason for winning in these situations...it is purely a matter of what you have labeled 'luck'.

"However Victor, when the angels see a need sometimes they do work those little miracles, like Miriam did the summer before your last year of college. At that time, you had a job with your wife's uncle selling awnings and quickly found you weren't cut out for sales. You were broke and didn't know how you would be able to afford to continue your last year of school; but Miriam did slip you a message.

"Although you had never before been to a horse race, when you passed the Detroit Race track she whispered the number 812 into your ear (mind). Although you were down to the last $5.00 in your pocket, the number and a compulsive urge took you back by the race-track; once, twice, and then the third time you passed by the race track, you gave in to the urge. After you paid the $1.50 general admission price, you had $3.50 left and went up to a ticket window and naively asked if you could play the number 812.

"The man at the window looked at you strangely, but then said he could sell you an 8-12 daily double ticket. You took it! Number 8 came in and won the first race by several lengths and later after the second race, you nervously paced back and forth during a photo finish between the number 4 and number 12 horse, while the possible pay-offs were flashing across the tote board. You won that race, but Miriam was with the jockeys riding the horses. The ticket paid $316.80, which was a good payoff in 1958. You cashed the ticket immediately, and before the third race, you left the track and went to your in-laws and began throwing $20 dollar bills at your wife. For a moment, she thought maybe you were so worried about returning to school that you had committed a crime. Then, before you could even get the idea to return to the track for "more luck", your wife wrote a check for $300 to pay the next four month's apartment rent at college and put it in the mail before the sun went

down. Sometimes angels can make your luck happen, but don't ever bet the farm on it. In that situation, your returning to college was in God's plan for your life and Miriam just kept you on purpose in whatever method was available to her.

"Generally, these prayers for things or money go unanswered. For unknown reasons, other prayers also go unanswered because it is not in God's plan and people often get angry with God for not answering them.

"I want to remind you Victor that you went through that experience yourself regarding Claricé's death from breast cancer. As I said before, you asked, 'Why didn't God answer my prayers?' And you did hate God. It has taken you quite some time to accept that her death at the time it happened was a part of God's plan for both of your lives. I believe you are only now beginning to see the purpose behind it all, and how BOTH of you are entering a new chapter in the eternal life God has granted your souls, and that your love too, is eternal. The grief of death for all of humanity is a 'tough pill to swallow', to quote an old and tired metaphor.

"Communicating with angels is available to all, once mankind accepts it is possible, believes, listens and begin to write down what comes to your mind. It begins in small fragments and sentences and then builds until you begin to see the truth and then ask follow-up questions and write down the answers you receive."

Chapter Fourteen
More About Angels
Archangels, Assigned Angels, Walk-In Angels and Guardian Angels

"Hello Archie, in our nightly chats, and in several chapters of this manuscript, you often mention *walk-in angels*. In fact, one night you spent quite a bit of time explaining how they fit into God's creation of His universe, our souls and the divine plan for all that is. Now that I have caught up on writing and have taken a break, I'd like you to explain it again for me so that I don't miss anything of significance."

"Well, hello again, it's about time you got back to me with that question. I've been waiting for you to ask me about it because it is an integral part of the story we are telling. Let me begin by reminding you that all of God's angel messengers were created prior to His creation of the human species.

"In addition to the archangels mentioned throughout the Christian Bible, as stated, there are a million times a million times a million, and more angels in God's service. Relating to the 'job descriptions' in your corporate America hierarchy, archangels are the 'chiefs' like your CEOs, 'Chief Executive Officers.' More specifically, Archangels are angels of the highest order in the celestial hierarchy created by God.

"All angels were created by God in order to assist your everlasting souls during your walks of learning throughout your world and to help with your day to day problems. The planet Earth would be a more peaceful environment if all mankind understood the significance of angels, and that you can communicate with them. They are in your lives to help you, guide you and to answer any question you may have.

"Victor, I know that you now understand this through our communications and those with the other angels currently involved in your life. Most of humankind however truly does not understand that

they too can receive angel guidance and assistance. 'How can this be?' they would ask.

"The answer to this is in understanding the power of each and every human mind that God created; to have faith and belief in your innate capability, to ask and then listen for the guidance that comes through. Most ongoing thought processes of mankind are limited to whatever is required to make it through each new day without considering the workings of the 'psyche.' But the soul is more than that. Life is more than that. The human mind is more than that. The physical being or vehicle is more than that. The psyche includes the control and breadth of human capability. This includes the soul, mind and spirit. It is the totality of a person's mental components both conscious and unconscious, instinctive and selective, physical and mental reactions, and all that is available to you to make your choices as you move through your daily routines, whatever they may be.

"To simplify this, we have to look more closely at the physical vehicle/body, the lower self and the higher self; look at the psyche of your soul energy, which has been labeled the 'aura' by mankind, and encompasses all, including your complete physical vehicle/bodies.

"Next, consider your minds, which are the most complex part of an individual's psyche. The mind is truly multi-faceted and to be understood must be looked at in terms of the higher self-lower self, duality of purpose, the soul energy and how it all relates to your God given right to choose."

"Archie, that is all well and good. I have somewhat of an understanding of what you are telling me, but what has all of this to do with 'walk-in angels,' or other angel messengers?"

"Victor, some things cannot be simplified without losing their intention or purpose. I am only trying to give you an overview so that you can see where the pieces of the puzzle fit together. I think you will see how it relates to the angels in your life, as well as give understanding to your readers. To clarify things, I will have to again be a bit repetitive.

Your Higher Self and Angels

"Let's relate to the angels currently active in your life: myself, Jules, Ali, ML and Miriam. Myself, and Jules are assigned angels and we permanently reside within the higher self of your mind. God assigned us to your soul energy prior to the soul's joining with the fetus during your mother's pregnancy... your chosen parents for your current incarnation. This joining can happen anytime during the gestation period of the fetus but prior to its birth.

"Assigned angels are with you continually, from birth until you make your transition back to the spiritual realm that mankind refers to as Heaven. Assigned angels are there to guide you and assist you in all you do. For the most part, they are very much underused. Although they constantly try to guide you in keeping you on the path of God's plan for your life, their guidance is often not heard, followed or is just ignored. It seems they are most effective in answering your silent requests or utterances. When you think: How am I supposed to do this or that? They will give you the answer...if you are listening. The same thing is true when out of frustration you may utter a request: What am I supposed to do with this or that? They will give you an answer...if you are listening. In these situations, you think you suddenly figured out the answer, when in fact, the angels have guided you to or supplied you with the solution.

"In the Christian Bible it's stated, 'Ask and you shall receive.' Because God gave you the freedom of choice, angels are not overtly active unless you ask for their assistance. In their guidance, they try to influence your thoughts to keep you on your path, but they do not force God's will upon you. The unasked for guidance, which is accepted, is often thought of as being the result of the sixth sense, or more commonly know as a women's intuition. Men most often ignore their intuition or ability to use their sixth sense. Often men get what they call their 'hunches,' which

sometimes is intuition, but generally these are more bad than good because men tend to force their 'wishful thinking,' such as picking the winner of a race or winning the lotto as mentioned in the previous chapter.

"The one situation when angels become overtly active without being asked is when your life may be jeopardy and threatened before it is your time to return to the spiritual realm in God's plan for your life. When this happens, your 'angel of miracles' will take charge and intervene to prevent your premature demise. Although angels of miracles will perform other functions in bringing miracles to your life, this is where their work is most apparent and recognized by humanity.

Walk-In Angels

"This brings me to the subject of walk-in angels. Miriam, your angel of miracles is a walk-in angel, as is Ali and ML. Although there have been situations in your life where Miriam has intervened to prevent your leaving the earthly plane prior to God's plan for your life, her current involvement has been in co-creating the belief system within you to accept the reality of your spiritual and angelic communications. For you, acceptance of your wife Claricé coming through to you spiritually, five months after her transition, was truly a miracle, assisted by Miriam. Walk-in angels function within your higher self with Jules and myself.

"Beyond Miriam, Ali, and ML who are each walk-in angels, there are an endless number of walk-in angels, each with a specific purpose. All of them are available to assist every man, woman and child on your planet Earth.

"There are far too many to list here, but a sampling of walk-in angels would be: An angel of creativity; an angel of success; an angel of courage; an angel of patience; an angel of temptation; an angel of solutions; an angel of spirituality; an angel of harmony; an angel of understanding; an angel of abundance; and many, many more. Any need you have, God has an angel available to assist you...all *you have to do is quiet your mind, ask, and listen for their guidance.*

"Although Jules and I are assigned to your soul energy and presently are assisting only you, walk-in angels with specific tasks, as those mentioned above are multi dimensional.

"In her spiritual communication to you, Claricé said, 'Sometimes, I am like the track lights in our house, I shine on many at the same time...' What she meant was that her light of God can shine on and be with you spiritually and at the same time, she can also be with your children, her brother, sisters or friends. Think of the soul energy as being like electricity...it comes from one source, but it can light up one room or every room in your house.

"The same is true of walk-in angels. As stated, they are multi-dimensional and they can be with you and others at the same time. Oftentimes when you may be facing a crisis of one kind or another they silently try to assist you and guide you to keep you on God's path, even when you have not asked for them. At times when you don't listen or act upon their silent guidance, they look for other ways to get you to do what needs to be done.

"Your health is a good example to show how walk-in angels can work in this manner. Due to your heart problems which began in the early 1980s, Ali, your angel of good health has been with you almost daily. More recently she has been there to remind you to exercise, to eat a proper diet, to take your medicines and to keep your doctor's appointments.

"However, beginning in 1980 Ali had a greater purpose in your life. Due to the stress of your business activities and that of your overactive personal life during the early stage of what I call your 15-year midlife crisis, you were a massive coronary waiting to happen. You were in a similar state as that of your friend Barry and the problem that took his life. In your case, Miriam called Ali into your life for assistance. She tried to guide you, but since you weren't asking for her help, you ignored her as well as you had ignored

the symptoms of your physical vehicle's warning of an imminent heart attack.

"Like many of your kind, you assumed the on again, off again discomfort in your lower chest was heartburn or indigestion caused by your lifestyle and erratic eating habits. You were on a sabbatical from your business, rewriting your first novel and in the early stage of your relationship with the lady who was to become your significant other.

"When you didn't react to Ali's attempts to warn you, she entered the consciousness of your lady-friend and her mother. With them, she was able to bring about the awareness of the extreme shortness of breath you had developed. You had not realized the significance of it and had brushed it off as a problem remaining from the years when you were a regular smoker.

"Both your lady-friend and her mother began to warn and nag you a little about the problem until you agreed to go to a diagnostic lab for a complete medical and physical work-up. Although the seriousness of the condition was not immediately determined, you were told to go to a cardiac specialist as soon as possible.

"Your friends received Ali's guidance, from your walk-in angel visiting them. Two weeks later your cardiologist did a catherization and detected your severely blocked arteries, which were immediately corrected with heart surgery and a quad-bi pass before there was actual damage to your heart.

"So Victor, the message here is that walk-in angels can assist you in many ways. If you do not pay attention to them when their guidance is necessary, they can walk-in and out of the consciousness of others until you do get the message.

"Archangels, assigned angels and walk-in angels with specific tasks have never incarnated in human form on your planet Earth. The only angels that have incarnated on the Earthly plane are what humankind has called 'guardian angels.' Guardian angels are your loved ones, close friends or what you have termed *soul mates who have made their transition and returned to the spiritual plane of heaven. They too are multi-dimensional and work, or function through your higher self, with the Holy Spirit, which is your individual direct connection or conduit to God through your soul energy.*

Victor K. Hosler

Chapter Fifteen
How The World Works
According To Archie

"Hello Archie. Today I have come to you looking for more direction in my life and what I am to do next. I really don't know what question to ask you. I'm looking for clearer purpose in my communications that was suggested in Claricé's first visit and that you also have mentioned, beyond the healing of my grief.

"Thanks again for the help you have brought to me. Part of my life remains empty and at times, filled with sadness because of my loss, but growth and understanding is coming as I read through the dictations. More and more I can take time to think about Claricé and joyfully remember the good times, her bright smile and remember the way she looked as she walked through a room. The tears are fewer and farther apart... and I can now begin to sense them as tears of joy for what we had, rather than those of pain."

"As I believe I recently told you, you are in a learning and acceptance phase. And you will 'get it' if you take it step by step. I'm showing you how the angels have worked in your life and at the same time trying to relate this to how the world works and to enhance your belief in the experience."

"How the world works in 'simplified' terms truly interests me. Also, I want to continue to communicate with Jules and my other angels to gain a better understanding of what their roles have been and will continue to be in my life. Now that I have become aware, I am very much interested in the world events relative to God, the universe and why the differences and the perception of mankind are so varied."

"Victor this will always bring you back to the "freedom of choice" that God granted all mankind... and for that matter, much of the animal kingdom also has a somewhat limited ability to 'choose.' Animals do not have a high degree of intellectual capacity to put conscious choice into action, because they are

driven by their instinct for survival, which for them is much greater than that of mankind. However, depending on the external stimuli they experience, they do make choices. This may bring debate by some, but there is a level of choice being made. When threatened, they choose whether to run away or attack. This is not always based on instinct, but that of a creature's past experience in which there has been a learning process. There is also communication. You only have to watch the animals of a species, or even watch the goings on within a community of ants to see this process. Ants choose to stop and communicate as they pass along side of one another.

"You must also realize that angels are not exclusive to human beings. God has angels assigned to the entire animal kingdom as well. Animals, too, are earthlings, or Earth beings. The circle of life applies to all of God's creatures.

"I'm sure an animal's pain and suffering, as well as a learned awareness of their intelligence level, is that which encourages and motivates your animal rights activists. But we don't want to get too deeply into that. It is far and away from influencing how the world works. Most animals and creature's 'choices' are determined by their need for survival, and limited learning that is needed within their own species and communal form of being when applicable.

"In other communications, regarding mankind's freedom of choice which you have had, it has been said that 'greed,' because you have freedom of choice, is responsible for many of the problems on the Earth God has created. After semantic differences, this is true. Mankind of your world has not yet learned to properly handle free choice. This then goes back to 'prosperity vs. abundance' doesn't it? Humankind seems to always want what they perceive others have, that is more or better than what they have themselves. Your earthly terminology for this is the 'grass is always greener' syndrome. However, what happens is that once your grass does become greener, you then want it greener and greener. This is an excellent example of

greed taking over, in chasing prosperity rather than abundance in your earth-world lives. Once again chasing prosperity is the time consuming, spending and acquiring in excess, and wanting more than you need. Having abundance in your lives is having enough to fulfill your needs, but includes time for love, happiness, joy and a relationship with your God.

"That cannot be said for the balance of the universes, or planes of existence of intelligent energy forms. To use an earthly term, some of God's 'societal' creations, have developed a more harmonious existence than has your Earth-world.

"The many cultures in your world...be it ethnic, geographic, spiritual, religious or other theological, God-like worshipping societies, are all led by those seeking power. It is not all bad, and democracy is a good example of that. Most leaders in a democratic society believe what they are attempting to do is 'for the good of the people' and in a large part, most of it is all with good intention. However, even considering those who seek power for greed and avarice, your world will continue to be led by those who seek power; and that is as necessary as God's Ten Commandments. What are the terms your people so often use? 'Every army needs both generals and privates.' and 'The strong will lead the weak...'

"Your world does need leaders, leaders who care and understand that a problem can have many solutions or answers. Unfortunately for many cultural leaders, it is the greed, quest for power, and achieving prosperity through material riches taken by force and at random from the needs of the people. This causes much of the starvation and strife wherever it is found on the planet. Your world's problems will only be solved when mankind listens to God in whatever way he speaks and most often it is through the voice of His angel messengers. Living by the golden rule and the Ten Commandments, God's gift to Moses and the people of your world, is the only way harmony can be achieved.

"For you, Victor, this is one of the reasons I began to remind you of the work God's angels have done and how they have participated in your life. For future consideration, I will continue to do so when it is appropriate to remind you. As an example now, let me remind you again of how Miriam, your angel of miracles has worked in your life. Sometimes they intervene directly and other times they take on the role of a <u>walk-in angel</u> and enter someone else's mind to bring attention to your particular need when your life is threatened.

"To mention just a few examples, there was the time when you were four years of age and your family was enjoying a picnic and day at the beach celebrating Memorial Day. You were sitting half way down a pier looking at the fish when a couple of teenagers accidentally bumped you. You fell into the deep water and almost drowned. Your mother's sister was the one who saved your life. Miriam entered her mind to bring your distress to her attention. When she missed you, she quickly went into the water below where you were sitting. When she found you, she grabbed you by your hair and pulled you to shore.

"Then there were a few automobile accidents when you were just a teenager when she assisted you directly. One was the time you lost control when you were 'showing off,' for a girlfriend. You and the car next to you were roaring your engines waiting for the light to change. When the light turned green you both took off, and your car wavered in the loose gravel. When you over corrected in your youthful panic, Miriam stopped the car 6 inches from the cement block wall of a building. Again later in your life there was the shoot-out in your apartment when the intruder broke into your home.

"Your angels have been very active in your life even when you weren't listening or paying attention. We really do, do what we can to keep you within God's plan for your life, whether you ask for the help or not. However, our job would be much easier if you would all listen, believe, and trust that God is with you every *day and in every way and <u>ask for our guidance</u>. It is much easier when you ask."*

"Archie, during my restless, tossing and turning before sleep a few nights ago, you began to discuss the differences in what is written about the visual experience, or perception of the 'other side' or spiritual realm. It has been described by those who have had near death experiences, visitations in a dream, or have heard it described by word or what's called clairaudience from spiritual entities, or in a vision of their clairvoyant experiences."

"Yes, you were asking me for clarification of what Claricé said to you when you asked her to describe heaven. She told you there were no earthly words that could describe it; only that it is 'heavenly'. Beyond that, she also said that whatever your concept of beauty is... is what you will find. When you are on what you call the other side, what you will find is the perfection of the illusion of your personal perception of beauty, based upon your own learned, worldly experience and whatever you believe would make you happy and joyful in your new state of being.

"All spiritual entities <u>see</u> or experience what mankind has labeled Heaven differently and in their own way or what they perceive it will be. If one believes they will be met by their lost loved ones and many friends, that is what will happen. At that time it becomes a shared reality because you meet and greet whomever was in your consciousness and belief system. Those who believe they will see God as a man with a long white beard sitting on a golden throne when they pass through the pearly gates of heaven will experience exactly what they perceived it to be. Others who do not believe in reincarnation will enter Heaven with that consciousness and remain in that state until they become aware that it was their soul that was given everlasting life and not the physical vehicle called the body. There will be a realization of choice, but because the spiritual realm is timeless it doesn't matter. They will be with loved ones, angels and God in whatever form they believe in Him. If God then

wants their soul to continue their journey of learning, it will happen in the spiritual realm or on the earthly plane.

"Eternal life is energy. You must remember that your individual perceptions, from which you will then consciously relate to, can only be based upon your earthly experience, which in truth is all illusionary. This was discussed. At the time the soul of man returns to the spiritual realm, the only point of reference then, is that of your experience on the earthly plane. When the soul renews its awareness of the spiritual realm, beliefs and attitudes derived from the earthly experience become a part of their past.

"An example of this is when Claricé explained to you in her final visit how she found out you had twenty more years to live based on God's plan for your life. I want to remind you again that this particular communication came to you before you acknowledged my presence in your life. Although it was unknown to you at the time, ML your angel of relationships, assisted in bringing that communication. In part that communication was for your friends Rob and Kelly, who had a miscarriage. You thought it was a message from Claricé speaking through you to Kelly and you presented it to her in that way, but it wasn't. You let your ego-self get in between, and you forced what you received to be what your ego wanted. This brought confusion.

"There was concern over whether or not Claricé was predicting the future in her first visit when she told you that Rob and Kelly were going to have a baby. As well in the same communication, it was stated that you had twenty more years to live in God's plan for your life. That may have created the doubt over your reception of the message. As stated earlier, she wasn't predicting the future; she had spiritually been with them when Kelly took the pregnancy test, and she found you had twenty more years to live when she checked your book of life in the hall of records.

"Getting back to what she said about 'going to the hall of records,' she said that is where God's plan for

every life form is kept and available. She said she went there shortly after she arrived to see for herself how long you had to live. The 'hall of records' was her <u>word reference</u>, based on her most recent earthly experience and selected as that which she believed you would understand. Based upon her choice of words, you would naturally think in terms of a massive library or some type of storage structure because you base your understanding on your earthly experience also. Once again we get back to illusion and semantics. There are no physical structures in the spiritual realm, only the illusions that a spirit/soul brings with them from their earthly experience."

"Sometimes I think I am repeating myself, Victor, and other times, I know I am. But in communications with the other side, be it through your angels, a spiritual guide, communicating with a loved one or another spiritual entity, you are getting a mixture of two points of view: the first being the illusionary understanding of the Earth/world perspective, and the second from that of the spiritual realm from which you have no real understanding. So it too becomes illusionary in what you believe to be your personal reality. It is from different perspectives and/or frames of reference based on geographical and cultural differences on the Earth/world plane. Add to this, the different planes of cultural existence on your Earth, the many different spiritual planes, and other dimensions of the universe and the possibilities become endless. One person's perception of Outer Mongolia might be that of beauty, where another would find it to be impoverished based upon their personal illusionary experience. The same could apply to Manhattan, Los Angeles, the beaches of Cancun or the existence of beings on other planets as yet unknown to mankind and endless forms of intelligent energy in the planes of the spiritual realm.

"Isn't it interesting to note that as you say, 'beauty is in the eye of the beholder' and that the terminology applies to the spiritual world as well as it does on Earth. 'Beauty' does not have a universal definition or

explanation. Hence, beauty too, is nothing more than illusionary as it will be different for every soul in the spiritual realm and at the same time common for those with the same or complementary belief systems.

"This confusion in the meaning of words and different languages, past and present, as well as the sense or experience of knowing or cognizant awareness is what adds to the overall confusion about life, as you know it and the meaning of life, spirituality, religion and Christ as 'the' Son of God, and not just 'a' Son of God. The function of semantics leads to the many differences and belief systems among the many cultures of your world. Interpretation and perception has led mankind in circles since the beginning of time and/or beginning of intelligent life and communication in your world. True understanding only comes in experiencing your soul energy upon your return to the spiritual realm.

"This brings me back to harmony and lack of perfection, which so many would like on Earth. Because there are so many differences in interpretation, perception and understanding of the languages, past and present, throughout time in the world in which you reside, the best you can hope for and expect is harmony in the coexistence of the species of your Earth/world with God the Supreme Being.

"Remember, I pointed out before, 'perfection' as understood and desired by mankind is a myth and downright impossible. God knows this and has created the universe to survive... not perfectly, but harmoniously. But you all have to understand this. Quit trying to get it 'right'... close is good enough for God."

"The differences the angels are putting forth in the communications we who listen and are able to receive has already been explained in your definition of truth. As has been pointed out, each of us who listen, and transcribes, or writes of the communications we receive are doing so based upon our own personal intellect, our life experience and personal frame of reference, influenced by geographic, environmental and communal differences. It definitely does account for the many different interpretations and the writing in all of the books available to humans throughout the world. I can now see why there is no <u>one truth</u> and that each of mankind must seek to find his or her own truth in whatever form it comes to them and will give them a believe in God, the Supreme Being and creator of all that is and live his or her life accordingly.

"Like I said to you a few pages ago, you are just 'An Ordinary Guy' and that is why you were chosen for this communication. That too, speaking of your being ordinary, is not to belittle you; over 99.99+ percent of the world is 'ordinary', or just 'common folk' as some of you would say. It is like trying to define perfection, beautiful, normal, or so many other words that depend upon a person's individual perception of meaning, interpretation or understanding.

"In order to be understood by the greatest number of people of your intended audience or readers, you have to get down to the basics. Repeating myself again, that is how you approached your client's problems throughout your professional experience. This is what we are now doing. We have to repeat things in order to learn them. This also relates to reincarnation and choices you make with the masters in the planning stage for a new life experience in a different physical vehicle. Often you have to repeat segments of one life in another life in order to facilitate your understanding of the learning experience.

"You have read a lot of books on spirituality and metaphysics relative to communicating with our spiritual world. Most of them spelled out various complex steps, meditations, listening to recordings and various different procedures for making contact. Reaching the point you are now at did not come easy. It wasn't until you heard about and read books about angels that you discovered how simple it was to communicate with your angels that you really came to an understanding.

"I do however want to point out how you got to that state of mind. You came to believe in the possibility only through your communication with Claricé, Dick and Sally when you accepted you were not dreaming or hallucinating. The key word is 'believe;' first a belief in the experience, then a belief in the context of the communications, which then led you to a true belief in God, which brought you to your relationship with Him and you placed yourself at His service.

"Although it is not necessary to face tragic circumstances like Claricé's untimely death in order to become a believer, this is what it took for you. Anyone can communicate with their angels if they PRAY to their God and/or the angels; BREATHE to relax their mind and body; LISTEN to their mind in quiet times; TRUST their INNER KNOWING; WRITE down their questions WAIT; and ACCEPT as truth the answers received. That's the process you learned from the Angelspeake series of books. For your purposes, you have added '<u>write</u>' as an eighth step.

"As stated previously writing it down is necessary, because as you found the information you receive in the quiet times of your mind is often fragmented and seems to bounce around from subject to subject rather than staying with one thought before moving on to another. This is again what you were experiencing when you thought you were hearing the myriad of voices and noise. Your vibrational frequency and that of the spiritual realm was not in tune until you began to focus and listen, after you asked to speak with Claricé 'just one more time.' Prior to that, all you heard were bits and pieces, that you labeled a cacophony of noise that you couldn't recognize.

"When you ask your questions, write down whatever comes to your mind. If it is a brief answer that comes to you, think about it and ask a follow-up question, then another. Myself and your other angels always come through the higher self of your mind and the information will always be of a positive nature, because we are God's angel messengers. I can *maintain more continuity and finish the thoughts if you keep following up one question with another. Eventually, the more you begin to trust your, 'higher-self,' and 'inner-knowing,' the better your communication experience will go and the more you will receive. If you get anything, which you consider to be of a negative nature (anger, greed, avarice, lust, jealousy, arrogance, disrespect, and other harmful thoughts), it will be from the 'I want' of your ego lower-self, which is attempting to interfere with the communication and you must release it. Just push it out of your mind and ask your higher self and your angels to give you positive information that will aid you. Only truth comes from the spirit within and your higher self.*

"When communications are not written down, they will generally be forgotten. Communications from angels are often like a puzzle and come together one piece at a time. There is much that I want to communicate to you, and God's angels want to communicate with all who will listen. Sometimes it all comes at one time, and that is why you thought you were just hearing jumbled words or thoughts and fragments in the beginning. You weren't able to sort the voices or words out. Once you began to focus, I was able to get through to you and later you were able to pick up the communications from your other angels also. You listened and began to focus on the quiet moments of your mind. You might compare it to the computer and 'information age' that is made up of 'bites, bits and pieces' of information, fragments of unintelligible information that can only be interpreted by a computer. The mind of human kind was really God's first creation of a computer.

"In order to communicate with the spiritual realm, some people need the 'wake-up call' that has been mentioned a couple of times now and was necessary to get through to you. The ability to connect with what is called metaphysical and supernatural occurrences often coincides with times of great personal tragedy or stress. Although not always necessary, this is what

originally opened the door for you. You found that when all of your normal resources for strength no longer handled your emotional need, help arrived from where you least expected it. From God! When you asked to speak to Claricé just 'one more time' God found the way to your heart, soul and mind. He was listening, and He brought her to you not once, but five times; and He brought you others to confirm to you the reality of spiritual communications, rather than the hallucinations you began to think you were having.

"Even still you struggled with disbelief until the communications kept coming through to you, and later, I too was able to get your attention with words and thoughts that you knew were not of your conscious mind or of your ego/self. I have now told you several times that you will meet ongoing disbelief and you will continue to be met with doubt. When you shared your beautiful experience of Claricé's communication you were surprised at the doubt and negativity that followed. You cannot let this distress you.

"Just a moment ago I referred to interpretation and perception of the words and languages of the world. You won't change the world. People will believe what they choose to believe and that is their God given gift. Do not let another person's disbelief change your perception of how God is working in your life. You have given your life to God and I will not let nonbelievers change the course you are on. Your path is defined and your full purpose will follow.

"Once again semantics, interpretation and perception is a large part of the controversy that has produced so many differences in theological and religious concepts throughout your world. Everybody wants to believe that 'their way' is the only way, and for each of them, their intention is about as honorable as one can get. This applies to you also. The manner in which you have found to communicate with God and your angels is not the only way. It works for you, but may not work for others. The books you have read speak of four primary methods: clairvoyance (seeing), clairaudience (hearing), clairsentient (feeling) and

claircognizance (knowing), as has been mentioned earlier.

"We believe these are the simplest forms and can be accessed as stated above; but many find the use of mantras, various meditations, visualizations, different prayers and many other means and techniques that are available and will make access to the spiritual realm easier for them. Whatever works to enable one's spiritual communication is perfect for them. As you will recall in your early readings, you read of several techniques that you didn't think would work for you and you didn't even try them. This was our guidance. Whenever you have doubt, it will not happen, and because of your doubt we led to you to read about angels. When you did, you found your own way, as will all who want to listen and communicate. Again the key is belief, a belief in God and belief in your self and belief in the possibility. After all, if your television pictures with sound, cell phones and radio waves of all types can be received through the space of time and air, why would one doubt spiritual or angel communications and those of God directly?

"We never intend to oppose any different religious concepts or cultures because there is no perfect solution or a perfect theological or religious philosophy. Perfection is an illusion and because God has given mankind free choice, it is every man's right to believe or not believe. There is one God. God is the light it says in the Bible. Again, could He not be a Sun God or God of the Sun?

"I know you are getting tired, so it is time to bring this to a close. As we continue our discussions, I know more simplistic explanations will continue to bring you clarity and will make your writing more easily understandable. So we will try to keep it simple and bring you more clarity when you ask for it.

Victor K. Hosler

Chapter Sixteen
Changing Your Perception Can Change Your Life

As the communications kept coming through, I was becoming mentally exhausted from both receiving them during the night and then transcribing them during the day. As Claricé pointed out in her communications, they do not have the same concept of time in the spiritual realm as we do on here on earth. It has repeatedly been said to me that it is always NOW. Time as we know it is an earthly, human creation and understanding.

After several nights and days I came to recognize that I didn't always have to listen and respond to Archie, or for that matter, any of the angels. I found I can listen by *choice* and do not always have to let them in. Gradually however, I soon I became aware that they are *always with me* and I have learned to *sense them,* and schedule my time to allow myself to be with them as I feel I want to or when it is necessary.

One night after Archie had been with me for a couple of hours, I was quite tired as I had become the night of Claricé's first spiritual communication with me. That night, when Archie didn't seem to want to stop, I asked him if he was ever going to "shut up and let me sleep." He said, *"Victor, it has taken me 66 years to get through to you, if you think I am going to stop now, you better think again."* After that night, however, I did begin to recognize I did have a choice in the matter and ever since, when I am receptive and relaxed when I go to bed, Archie or one of the others will come through to me. Other times, I just don't listen. And other times still, after I have had several hours of good sleep, Archie will occasionally wake me during the night. This is normally between 2:30 and 5:30 a.m., when he has something specific to communicate or he has been listening to my thoughts or dreams and wants to answer the questions that came into my mind.

- - - - -

"Archie, I have begun to be able to change the "perception of the emotion," that came with my grief, away from that of <u>pain</u> to that of <u>love</u> as you told me I could the night you first arrived. Even still, I find it continues to be an ongoing battle with my ego-lower self over the awareness of the reality of my life without

Claricé. It still brings bouts of sadness and depression. Since I have been fighting this battle for quite some time, let me ask you:

"What can the angels do about assisting me and others with the lingering feelings of grief, guilt, despair and depression which come about as a result of adjusting to the loss of a loved one or very close friend?" He replied:

"Victor, as I know you have learned, changing your perception of what you feel is much easier said than done; but we would encourage you to make the conscious choice to take charge of your life. This must be ongoing and continuous until <u>you know</u> that with God and his angel guides, you are in charge. Only you can do it, but you and others in similar circumstances must continue to ask for our guidance as you are doing now. As with most situations, angels will not intercede unless they are asked... other than quietly guiding you or those times when your life is threatened. So it is not what we the angels can do for you, the real question you should be asking yourself is: 'What can I do?'

"If you fight it by asking the ever-present 'Why?' of any negative emotions of the ego self, you give it more power. Therefore, when you come upon an awareness of any negativity being present, you shouldn't question the whys and wherefores or how it came about, <u>you just make a choice</u> for it to be different. You have the power. You can take control. There are times when you linger in the NOT illusion even when you know that all you have to do to change it to an I CAN state of being. This NOT illusion is the negativity of the ego – lower self, holding you back. You must shift to a positive-ness of thought and being; I CAN instead of I CAN'T and I WILL instead of I WON'T

"Only you are responsible for the choices you make. When you focus your awareness on the NOW it gives you the opportunity to evaluate it and create change based upon the divine guidance of your higher self. At the same time, this recognition provides you the opportunity for a willingness to change your

perception by choosing what is to be; and, what is to be... is fulfilling your life- long goals and plan of purpose. Although you are responsible, you must also realize that every facet of life is a learning experience of your life plan as ordained by God."

"When you accept that there are no accidents, or coincidences, in life and that everything that happens, happens for a reason, you will then realize that all people you meet and situations you encounter, both negative and positive, are a part of your life's learning experience. Therefore, when you question anything in the NOW of your life, the only question of significance is what are you suppose to do with it and what are you to learn?

"What I want to do here is remind you of what you recently read in the book titled 'AWARENESS' by Anthony de Mello. I will not quote directly from his excellent book, but I will use some of <u>his thoughts and words</u> in the overall context, as I assist you in drawing his thinking from the memory banks of your higher self. Let me remind you of some of the ideas he presented regarding changing your perception when you are lost in grief, guilt or despair.

"There are times when humans on Earth ought to accept they are 'down' as far as they want to be... and say, 'I'm sick and tired of it all. Please help me.' Ask God, the angel guides or your guardian angels for their help. For many, it's only when you acknowledge that you are sick of being sick, or whatever it is that's creating your negativity, that you decide to get out of it. As long as you are consciously fighting or accepting that which is creating the 'I am sick' attitude, you are giving power to whatever it is that's troubling you. Author Anthony de Mello suggested that, 'When you fight something and as long as you fight it, you are tied to it. You give it as much power as you are using to fight it.' You have to take charge and change your perception of your being-ness. You must take action and do something else.

"This applies to sickness and ailments of the physical body as well as the negativity of the ego-lower

self in general. Often mankind lingers in the physical sickness attitude when they could redirect their negative energy to the positive state of being, by accepting their well-ness that is, instead of dwelling on what was or might have been."

"You must <u>look inside of yourself</u> to understand your place of being. If you don't know where you are at, you are tied to whatever it is that is making your life uncomfortable. If you do not know what it is that is <u>not</u> making you happy, you will not know how to change the circumstance, or realize that you can change it to be in a state of happy. When you are in doubt about what or how to effect change, all you have to do is ask. We are here to help you. Go to the silence of your mind then ask...listen...and do!

"If you do this, you will have the power to change or remove the ego's desire to cling to whatever it is that is not making you happy. It is your ego that wants sympathy and attention; but you have the power to change the negative attitude. There is little relief in receiving sympathy. You can choose it to be different. God did not create mankind to be in misery. He created with Love. There has to be an attitude of openness, and wanting to discover something new <u>to replace the old</u> or whatever is troubling you. What you need more than anything else is the desire to learn there is something more positive you can do or be. You must develop an inner awareness that the choice of your state of mind is totally yours to make. We are here to guide you toward the proper choices.

"In most circumstances, you can choose today to be different than yesterday and face a new but unknown tomorrow with anticipation rather than fear. You cannot truly be apprehensive about something you do not know; cautious or wary perhaps, but nobody can really be afraid of what is unknown. What you really fear is the loss of that which is known or comfortable, to the uncertainty of the unknown. What is known becomes a comfort zone for most and mankind is resistant to change.

"With grief, prior to the loss of your loved one, their being-ness in your life was somewhat predictable. When their physical presence is then missing, in addition to the loss, your life without them brings forth an uncertainty of the future, which you label as fear or apprehension and magnifies your experience of grief. For some of mankind it is easier to accept negativity with known limits than to venture into the uncertainty of the unknown. This is what happens with those who stay in grief, guilt or despair for an inordinate length of time. The ego places fear and apprehension on the unknown of the future. But there is truth with understanding of what is, what was and what can be. We will guide you to the truth and this truth will give you the power to release your fears and to change your perception of what will and can be, from negativity to a state of positive-ness, thus eliminating the uncertainty or dread of the unknown.

"This then changes the state of hopeless to the state of hope. When you have hope, you are creating an awareness that something can be better than what you have right now. Hope is a positive state when it comes with reasonableness, otherwise there wouldn't any purpose in hoping for anything. Hope is a driving force of your higher self that leads you in positive directions. With God's gift of the miracle of life, you have it all... right now. You are a perfect child of God. Many are hoping for better times in the future and don't even know they can have it in the now. For each of mankind, the choice is yours.

"What mankind should concentrate on, is what <u>is</u> and <u>can be</u> positive in his NOW, and become more aware of the innate ability of man to co-create his <u>now</u> in a positive state with God, through the higher self, rather than lingering in negativity of the ego-lower self?

"To create a positive understanding of the miracles in the now, pick up any leaf, blade of grass or twig from a tree; they all are creations of God. Study the beauty in anything. Author, de Mello, suggests that,' ...mankind sleep walks through life.' Don't do it. Just

Victor K. Hosler

look around you and become aware of your earthly world. Pick up a stone, one you might have just kicked aside with your shoe. Look at it and study its smooth texture and color; think about the molecular structure; think of the energy of God within. Don't look for a crack, a flaw in its surface or the fact that it is not perfectly symmetrical. Each leaf, each stone, each flower, each body of water, each child of God, everything within the miracle of your sight and hearing was created in God's image for its own individual purpose in His universe.

"You saw an example of this the time you were sitting out by the lake in back of your house meditating and randomly picked up a leaf of 'dollar weed' as it is called in your earthly terminology. You studied it with my thoughts of the energy of God in mind, and when you held it up to the light you were truly amazed. You could see an example of the experience of God's energy displayed in the leaf. It was a true 'likeness' of the God force.

"In the center was the light, as the spark of life; it was brighter than the rest, and radiating out from the center in all directions were the veins, like rays, or beams of God's light...or energy. Then, as your eyes followed each vein or ray, every one of them began to give off smaller rays to the sides in both directions; then the farther out the beams of light went, the little rays became smaller and each then gave off even smaller rays; and then they all began to connect with each of the smaller rays on both sides until they became 'web-like' and were all fully connected around the circumference of the leaf, completing the circle of life. That dollar weed, another miracle of God is a visual example of how the energy of God works in the world. It all began with a spark of life and then went out to the far reaches of His universes in all directions and all within becomes connected and a part of the whole and oneness of God."

"Anytime you are allowing your ego-lower self to focus on a negative feeling toward anyone or any situation, you're living in a NOT illusion of negativity

and your attitude within must change. When you suggest that someone else is to blame for the misery you are claiming to be in, and that he or she has to change or this has to change or that has to change, NO! That is only your perception of what needs to be and it is a false expectation. The one who needs to change is you. You cannot change who or what someone else is or change a situation, which exists in the now. You can only change what is to be... for yourself. You are only responsible for you and only you can truly change your being-ness. And sometimes this change can only be in your acceptance of what is, so that you can focus your changing of what is to what is to be. Often this can just be a change in your attitude of being-ness, based on the circumstance of the moment.

"It is appropriate and alright to feel sadness over the loss when a loved one or friend dies. It is a part of the human experience. But one has to look at his reaction to the loss to determine the power you are giving to it relative to the actual role they played and how they were a part of your life. Are you feeling sorry for yourself because they will no longer fulfill the expectations you had for their being-ness in your life? If so, it is the ego's selfish reaction of self-pity. Your reaction is a personal loss, but the 'feeling sorry for me' grief can be an over-reaction, which is a sign that your happiness was fully dependent upon this person. This is your perception that has to change. You must learn to always live in the now. They are gone from your being-ness. You can and should be grateful for the joy your loved one or friend brought you in the past, but at the same time you must accept that it is the past and move on to the positive-ness of the present and what the future can be.

"Realize that bliss, joy and happiness are based upon abundance in your life. Realize then too that abundance is brought forth to you and in you from many different sources. True abundance cannot be taken away by the loss of just one, and you will never lose the beauty of the experience of what was. This is

in your heart and of your higher self. It will always remain. When you choose it to be so, you will change your perception to discover the beauty that remains in the now. In choosing to focus on what is positive in the now, you will push the negativity of the lost expectations aside.

"Look for the 'dollar weed' miracles in your life. You cannot experience bliss, joy, happiness and abundance in your life when you are focusing on what you don't have rather than actualizing your awareness on what remains and can be. You can only experience this positive-ness when you have everything you need to be in bliss. And you do. This will come when you change your perception of what you don't have to that which is and can be. What you are aware of, you are in control of; what you are not aware of is in control of you!

"When something controls you, it is because you are giving it power and you are giving control to your ego - lower self. When you accept that you are doing so, you become aware of it, and only then can you change your perception to be free of it. You can or will experience the negative-ness when it is there, but you do not have to be affected, controlled or enslaved by it. Your awareness empowers you. Identify and acknowledge the negative feelings within you and you will have the power to change your being-ness to positive-ness and thereby change your perception of what is to be.

"Understand that feelings and emotions are in you — not in the world — but are in you. They are NOT a part of you and they are NOT who you are. Feelings are emotions and emotions are feelings, both of which play off one another and come and go at the whim of the ego. You must understand that when you change negative feelings, when you change your perception, everything changes. Only YOU have the power to change that, which is within you.

"You must accept in your heart that you have the power to change that which you want to change. The most important thing to know and remember is YOU

ARE IN CHARGE. Only you can change things by the CHOICES you make each morning and all day through. If you focus on your pain, fear, sadness or any other negative emotion, it will stay with you because you are giving it power and control. You have to shift your mind to more positive thoughts of what is, in order to change your perception and what is to be. Whether it is for a minute, hour, a day or more, you need a distraction, something that will change your focus.

"In your world, doctors in the past would give a baby's bottom a small slap to distract their attention before giving them a shot. Likewise, in order to displace negativity whenever it appears, you have to distract your attention away from the negativity and refocus your attention elsewhere to put your thoughts on positive aspects of your being... or miracles in the now.

"The same goes for guilt, grief, depression or any of the ego's negative attributes. Again, Victor, it is easier for me to say than it is for earthlings to do. But each of you must know that in some way you are choosing to be exactly where you are in mind, body or spirit. You often are just unaware that you are choosing where and who you are at any particular moment in time. The ego does that to you. Otherwise, when you are in the negative territory of being-ness, you would choose to be somewhere else and would be looking forward to the days ahead with a positive perception of your tomorrows.

"Guilt in regards to a final communication or experience with a lost loved one or friend is totally without merit. You said or did what you thought was best at the time you did it by the choices you made. At that time for both your loved one or friend and yourself, you were changing the perception of the moment from negativity to positive-ness. It was with the same intention that your loved one or friend would have said or done for you or at your request if the roles were reversed. You were not in control of or responsible for the outcome that was to be. Therefore,

you cannot change the past, but you can change the negativity in the now which resulted from positive choices of the past. You can only change what is to be by the choices you will and can make based upon your life's experience, understanding and recognition of what is, regardless of whether <u>what is</u>, is positive or negative. You can live in the positive NOW by carrying forth the joy your loved one brought into your life and setting aside the negativity of the, 'could have, should have' doubt and needless guilt. Instead, choose to have the abundance in your life that your loved one or friend would want for themselves and that you know they would want for you.

"When you are living in negativity and the NOT illusion, in order to change it you must change your perception of how things can be. Each day you must choose to wake up with a positive attitude and become aware of those things in and about your life that will bring you abundance, joy and happiness. To move away from depression, despair, guilt or whatever is troubling you, you must face each new day with a new and positive attitude and do something you didn't think you could do the day before. Hold your head high in the awareness of the new day upon you and look to bliss in your future by making the positive choices that are always brought forth from your higher self. In doing so, you will become more and more aware of the miracles in your life and less and less aware of the negativity that comes from false perceptions of what could have been or is not, and that which is brought upon you by the lower self, ego."

"It's not easy to do. I'll say it again and again. Many have been there. Many like your self have experienced hatred toward God and everything else around them when they have lost a loved one or a very good friend. When it is a personal loss, our ego-lower self spews anger under a false and perceived impression that life has been unkind to us. This happens even though such losses are daily experiences of what will and must be in every life. It is most difficult to accept that your personal loss is God's will.

The ego-self does not readily accept that most experiences in life are a part of our plan for being. To get back on track you must focus on a conscious awareness of your being-ness. Accept that you can change your perception when you choose that you want to live and that which will make you be happy. When you choose to live in joy and bliss instead of dwelling in the negativity, anger or misery of your circumstance, things begin to change. But only YOU can do it. You must choose to be happy.

"When you are in pain of any kind, you can choose for the pain to go away. You do this by choosing to focus on your awareness of the positive nature of the miracles in and about your life and your earthly world. Excruciating pain brought about by severe physical or health considerations may be beyond your capability of 'wishing it away.' At the same time, however, even severe pain can be lessened by changing your focus on the now moment. Once again, shifting your awareness away from the pain/negativity requires a distraction, which can change your perception from what is, to what can be. For whatever period of time you are choosing to focus on the miracles, positive attributes and energies of your life, you have moved away from the pain and negativity of the perceived experience. Therefore, to some degree, you can 'wish your pain away' if only for a moment or so, and this you can build upon... bit by bit.

"The conscious thought and awareness of your 'being' and the 'I AM' concept of knowingness is one of the early miracles of God that became a reality to each and every one of mankind; and with that awareness came the ability to choose our "being-ness" and who we are. I hope this gives you some understanding that you, Victor, are in charge of who and what you perceive yourself to be. When you are not happy in the NOW, you must choose positive energies or thoughts, which will create it to be different and better. Live in the NOW of your choosing rather than the ego's negativity of the NOT illusionary experience.

"Let's begin to close this by going back to the Scripture where Christ says, 'Ask and it shall be given.' Most of mankind upon your earthly world, through their thought processes, will make many silent requests when they are troubled, in grief, depression or pain. Each of your angel guides, specifically assigned by God to serve your individual needs, continually offers you whatever guidance is requested. But you can have more... you have to ask and listen. All of mankind receives the answers they request in the quiet of their minds and through the internal dialogue with their higher-self consciousness.

"Unfortunately, as you well know yourself, you and others generally do not listen or do not follow through on the advice given. You asked about this a few months ago in reference to how to help a friend who was suffering needless guilt and again recently when you went through a brief period of depression yourself. The problem is, instead of listening and acting upon the truth of your higher self, which is coming from your angel guides, you instead listen to your 'ego' who says 'poor me,' and don't get off what you earthlings call the 'pity-pot'. Know that the ego can be very, very controlling.

"Simply put, you often ask, but you don't follow through. Re-read the words I have given you. Let me repeat it. You must accept in your heart that you have the power to change that which you want to change. The most important thing to know and remember is, YOU ARE IN CHARGE. Only you can change what is to be by the CHOICES you make each morning and all day through. If you focus on your pain, it will stay with you. If you focus on your grief, it will stay with you. If you focus on being depressed, it will stay with you. If you focus on blaming someone else for YOUR current state of mind, it will stay with you on and on and on. You have to change your perception of what is... to what it can be by focusing the awareness of your mind on the more positive directions from the higher self.

"Victor, you should keep these words near your fingertips. Anytime you let what is troubling you persist beyond the point of your awareness, you are giving it power. You must listen to the voices within your higher self, those that are giving you positive choices and then DO IT. Follow though and set aside the ego's negativity. Remember what I said earlier; pick up that leaf, blade of grass or twig from a tree. Study the beauty of God's energy in the 'dollar weed' and any creation of God. Just look around you and become aware of your earthly world. Look into your memory bank and pull out positive images of the past. Every second, moment, hour, day or longer you replace a negative thought or image with one that is positive, you are taking charge of the NOW and destroying the ego's negative intentions of living the NOT illusion.

"Once again, I know it isn't easy. You have to take it one-step or moment, at a time and then build upon it. As you do this you will then again become the master of your destiny rather than being a victim of your circumstance. Only YOU have the power to change YOU. Let it be said that God gave each of you the power to choose what will be in each of your lives according to your agreements with and of His plan. Begin right this moment or the next moment you are feeling what you earthlings call 'blue' or sad. Ask your angels for guidance. Ask them what will make me feel better right now. Ask and you shall receive; then take what is given unto you. I know it isn't easy, but you can do it. You have in the past and you can do it again in the NOW. Each of you can always take back the power."

Yes, Victor, each of you can take back THE POWER. By changing your perception of the NOW, you can change your life. Shedding the illusionary attitude of NOT in the NOW is simply a matter of changing your perception and a willingness to set aside the NOT for the positive-ness of what is to be and can be in your future NOW's.

Victor K. Hosler

Chapter Seventeen
Reincarnation vs. Only Living once

While piecing together the messages received in the chapter, "A Spiritual Communication With Sally" my mind began to focus more and more on the reincarnation aspect of what had come through during her visit. Although I have conceptually believed in reincarnation for many years, I really couldn't say why nor could I speak of it with complete understanding. More than anything, I think I just wanted to believe in it; I wanted to believe there is more to life than the existence we are knowingly aware of as we traverse the earth in our physical vehicle/bodies.

In her communication, you may recall that Sally referred to her soul "splitting," with one part remaining in the spiritual realm to continue the necessary learning and the other part reincarnated to a family in Philadelphia. One night before I drifted off to sleep I was thinking more and more about what Sally had said and the probability of an afterlife.

As I thought about it, I mentally asked Archie my dominant angel guide how reincarnation really works in the world. I asked him how it applies to those like my wife Claricé, or Sally the subject of the chapter I was working on; and... how about the little children and others who die and cross over before their time; what about the deaths that come about earlier than we believed they should have. As he often does, Archie began to answer me right away and then also he discussed world calamities, war, famine and cultures with lack.

It was very enlightening but also an exhausting night. He kept me awake until about 4:30 in the morning. Near the end of the session, Archie simplified his explanations in cliché-like metaphors we are all familiar with.

He said, *"As it relates to what is known as 'karma' in metaphysics and some theologies (the quality of a person's actions in one life determines his destiny in the next life), reincarnation can be explained as, 'the circle of life or what goes around, comes around;' then also sometimes known as 'an eye for an eye and tooth for a tooth' and, 'payback is a bitch.' These are your keys for asking me more questions when you want to write a more complete story on the understanding of reincarnation."*

It was a very interesting analogy. Whatever your thoughts and questions may be about reincarnation, if you think about the metaphors for a moment, it seems to make perfect sense... or at least it does for me. When I began to write the next day, the Biblical references about "only living once" and how that relates to reincarnation also came to mind. I asked him about this.

Regarding this Archie said, *"You have to think in terms of the soul, the energy of life and the oneness you all have in being connected; that all things in the universe and all creations of God are a part of God, your Father and Creator.*

Whenever I use the word "Father" in reference to God, it is in the most common, generically accepted manner. "Father/Mother God" could also be used, but in my personal belief system, God does not have a gender identity.

Archie went on to explain, saying, *"When God gave humans free choice, He gave it to who you actually are, to your soul... or that which is generally accepted as the energy of God. He did NOT give freedom of choice to your 'body' or 'vehicle' in which your soul/spirit resides. He gave eternal life to the soul or who you really are, that which is your essence of life or being residing within the physical body/vehicle.*

"Therefore it is true that you VICTOR, BOB, TOM, JANE, SUE or whatever the NAME is which was given to you by your Earth parents for the body/vehicle in which your soul energy resides, the WHO you are named, WILL only LIVE once as it is stated in the Christian Bible.

The Christian reference to *only living once* is one of the commonly accepted interpretations from the Bible that is often used to dispute a belief in reincarnation. Archie continued.

"It is the soul, the God's energy of your being which was given the choice to continually incarnate over and over again to learn the lessons you need to learn as you strive to reach God-like perfection and

true acceptance of oneness with God. At the same time your soul energy may choose not to incarnate again and prefer to learn the needed lessons in the seven planes of what earthlings call 'heaven' or the spiritual realm."

During my writing of the above, summarized communication I got an email from a childhood friend with a question about *the purpose* of afflicted children who are born with learning disabilities. He asked if our purpose in life on earth is to learn, how can *the purpose* of these children, be explained? With his question in my mind, the following immediately came through to me.

Archie responded, *"Regarding your friend's question about inherited disabilities and afflictions, which hamper learning of the physical body/vehicle, OR most any other health related condition humans face during a particular lifetime, there is a reason for its being. The affliction or the condition is a part of the learning process. In the example of the child referred to, it very well could be the learning of humility towards one's fellow man for transgressions in a previous incarnation in which there was mistreatment or a lack of compassion and understanding of another's affliction; it could also be preparation and acceptance for learning to cope with such occurrences in another, or oneself in a future incarnation.*

"You must realize too that these are collective learning experiences. As said before, the experiences can also be a lesson for the parents or every person the afflicted one will encounter during a particular lifetime in the handicapped physical body/vehicle. Actually, it is a lesson for all. It is a part of God's overall plan for all He created. Everything in life as you know of it is an opportunity to learn... learning from direct experience, from observation or just being a part of an experience. Life as it is known in your physical body/vehicles is not perfect. But whatever your life is, it is a learning experience for the self, and an

understanding of what is required to become one with God."

I recalled then that Archie had said to me earlier, as we understand and use the word, *perfection*, perfection can only come with things like getting a score of 300 in bowling, pitching the perfect baseball game, or a 100% score on a test of knowledge.

"In most things of any other type," he said, *"perfection is a myth. Who could describe a perfect relationship?"* he asked. And then, *"Who could describe a perfect world? In any evaluation of a situation, you could have as many opinions as you have people on your planet Earth. What is perfect for one does not meet the requirement for another. All God wants for the earthly world he created is Harmony, Love, Peace, and Abundance. Perfection can only be achieved when you become one with God... only God is perfect.*

"As is often said, you must have faith. The simple fact of humankind acknowledging the commonly understood 'I AM' principal is proof of the existence of a supreme intelligent energy force that humankind has labeled God, Father/Mother God, Allah, the Supreme Being, Creator or whatever the choice is of your religious or personal theological belief system. With this awareness comes your 'faith' that there has to be some reason for your being and that purpose, in a great part, is what you have to learn."

After this communication was received I was about to write my friend about the answer I got for his question, but I still was not quite satisfied with what Archie had said to me. Something still didn't fit. So in looking for clarification I wrote out the exact question on the computer.

"Archie, my friend had said to me: 'There are still so many questions. For instance, to what purpose is the inherited disability of a child intended? If the purpose is for them to learn, why does it seem that their affliction hampers their ability to learn.'

Archie again immediately replied and said: *"The life of the child is the learning experience for the child and for those it shares its life with during the incarnation in which the affliction is being experienced. This includes its learning disability or inability. The physical act of the intellectual learning ability or capability during the child's existence or 'being' in its physical body/vehicle during a particular lifetime DOES NOT 'hamper its soul's ability to learn,' but the inability to learn is in fact a part of the learning experience of the soul energy, which is not afflicted. The affliction is that of the physical body/vehicle for the experience of its soul energy's learning, and has nothing to do with the inability or the intellectual growth of the physical body/vehicle. With the agreements made prior to birth, with the will of God, the soul energy chose the affliction for the learning experience needed, within the living environment chosen. Upon the soul's return to the spiritual realm it will have the awareness of achievement of purpose and continue its quest towards God-like perfection and oneness with God."*

This seemed clearer and reasonable to me, but it then led me to think about the questionable tragedies of the world, which are so well documented. For me there is what I consider to be a large gray area with many questions that are still beyond my understanding as well as most others. These are past and present tragedies and atrocities that I can only accept based on my faith that God must have a reason. And, without this faith, I would question God's mercy.

Often Archie responds to my thoughts before a question is asked. He then said this to me: *"Victor, for a better understanding you sometimes have to look at the BIGGER picture. Good but brief examples are the questionable worldwide tragedies that come to mind, which as you said, you and humankind often do not understand. Most recent was your World War I, followed by the impact of the stock market crash of '29, the worldwide depression, years of strife and starvation, Hitler's rise to power in Europe, World War II, the atrocities of the Holocaust and many more troubled times during the first half of the 20th century on your planet Earth.*

"Most humans have in the past and still do question the why of it. They ask, 'What was God's reason?' And, 'Why would a merciful God let all of those people suffer and die? Why did He let those tragedies take place?' And they would ask, 'How about the present world situation with the ongoing wars and millions who still face strife and starvation?'

"I want to repeat, that for a more complete understanding, you have to look at the BIG picture. The world itself is in an ongoing learning process or phase; it is not just a learning place for each individual soul's learning experience, but also for the community of souls, the community of cultures and community of nations. Your world is continually learning and evolving.

"There is no question that the atrocities committed and the deaths of millions and millions of men, women and children during the first half of the 20th century, was one of the worst periods in the history of your world. Yet, at the same time, you must look at the results. Your world and world leaders did learn! Because of that period of your history the world is a much better place, as you know it today. Even though there were additional bumps in the road in the latter half of the 20th century, a great deal of progress did take place. You will always continue to have bumps in the road, but your world will also continue to make progress.

"God gave free choice to each soul of the human species. Some who accept reincarnation can accept that the soul when planning a new incarnation with the masters will choose to be the 'victim' as a learning experience for itself and for humanity overall; others accept that the demise of the physical body/vehicle is not always predetermined due to the parameters established for being within God's plan for one's life as well as other's. Because of this, you will continually be faced with those who choose peace and progress, as well as those who are aggressors with

greed-driven ambitions and desires for power over their fellow man. The latter is of the ego. These are evil acts and intentions, which are beyond the norm and not of God's plan for the individual souls and His plan for a peaceful world. But because of man's freedom of choice, which often is ego- driven, disharmony, and evil intentions are something that will always be faced until all of mankind learns that true peace can come about.

"*Once again though, you must look at the BIG picture. If the atrocities of that dismal period of your world had not happened, would the world ever have gotten out of the depression years? From the horrors of WW II a new industrial revolution came about, and with it came greater prosperity in the world than has ever been known by mankind. Who would want to go back to the times before the depression and world wars? Even further, who would want to go back to the days of slavery... or even to the days of Christ? All earlier periods of time in the history of the planet Earth were much more difficult for the body/vehicles of all mankind than that which you are facing today. The world is growing and learning and much of it is a result of the ongoing adversity that has been and continues to be faced and conquered. Each of you want better and more because God did give mankind the freedom of choice, and through learning, you most often are CHOOSING it to be better and better.*"

"How do you relate this to reincarnation?" I asked Archie.

"*Think about it.*" He replied. "*There were millions and millions who lost their lives in your world's tragedies during the first half of the 20th century. In whatever country they resided, the greater number of those who suffered had lived difficult lives compared to the standards you know of today. Next, you might ask about the many who suffered the atrocities and innocent ones who were slaughtered in your wars.*

"*Yes, they were tragic times and the physical body/vehicles suffered greatly, but God gave their souls everlasting life. And, if you look at what earthlings labeled the 'baby-boomer and post-baby-boomer' generations, I would suggest that the millions and millions, who suffered the anguish of their physical body/vehicles in the first half of the century, have chosen much better lives and have benefited from the past strife in the second half of the century during their next incarnation and their chosen body/vehicle and life style. Those who chose to be victims in planning one life saw their rewards in a future incarnation.*

"Those who disbelieve or dispute reincarnation, for the most part, attribute the growth of the world's population to new souls being created by God. With this in mind ask yourself, why would God give the souls of humankind everlasting life and freedom of choice if they were not meant to incarnate again and again for the needed learning experiences? Why also would He create more and more new souls when there are already billions of souls who have returned to the spiritual realm with the capability He had given them for everlasting life?

"As stated, reincarnation is the, 'circle of life' and 'what goes around comes around.' Those who were the tyrants and aggressors in a previous life, you can be sure that they now understand the meaning of the 'an eye for an eye and tooth for a tooth' (Christian Bible – Exodus 21:23), for in their new learning experience of life on your planet, they would have had to agree upon a lifestyle of suffering and reparation for their past-life ill deeds. Crude cliché or not... 'Payback is a bitch' and many will learn there is a hell on earth.

"Much of how the 'world works' is a tough mouthful for many of humankind to swallow. The loss of your wife Claricé when she was still so young and had just reached the peak of her artistic abilities and creative expression is a good example to use. For her and those who have died unexpectedly in the past or as a result of atrocities such as victims of war and cultures with lack, and those who will die in the

coming years at the hands of murderers, through mayhem or killed by a drunk driver, you want to know WHY? But, generally speaking, their time of living on your planet Earth was according to the agreed upon plan of God and the Masters prior to their birth. The allotted time on Earth in their physical body/vehicles for most souls is according to the agreements made under God.

"Although for many, life and the cause of death is a part of the predetermined plan and according to the lessons to be learned during a particular incarnation, it is not always the case. It can change. As you were previously told, Victor, your wife's time on earth and the time for the two of you to be together were according to the plans for both of your lives. However, the reason, or cause of her physical vehicle's demise changed from what had been specifically determined because there was a need of purpose for an earthly lesson.

"Her case became another example of the necessity to focus awareness on the heavy concentration of unnecessary deaths from breast cancer due to misdiagnosis, medical error and lack of follow-up and less than proper diagnostics. Medical groups, insurance companies and Health Maintenance Organizations in your society today have become a major problem. Too many of them are more interested in the bottom line profit than saving lives, especially when the odds for survival are questionable, as it was in the later stage of Claricé's illness over the last six months of her being.

"Unfortunately, for you and others who lose a loved one due to any unforeseen circumstance while young or before what is perceived to be their time, there is little comfort to be had in the realization that there is or may be a purpose. The why and the doubt give rise to anger, as it did in your own life, and hatred toward those thought to be responsible. However, with your acceptance and faith that it was God's will, you gained the strength to move on with your life. It is a difficult concept to grasp, but all things do happen for

a reason. All that happens is a part of God's plan for the universes He created.

"For you, as it is for many others, the loss was personally tragic and very much misunderstood. However, when a soul has fulfilled its agreed upon life plan on earth as your Claricé had done, the demise can be that which was agreed upon prior to birth, or it can come about in any other form or means as part of a lesson to be learned on a societal or cultural level. If the death wasn't because of a particular need earlier decided upon, it well may have been to focus awareness on another of your world's problems; problems such as becoming the victim of a drunk driver or killed in a random shooting or burglary due to the prevalence of guns in your American society, or another mankind created illness that is in need of focus and attention. There is a purpose for all that is.

"These seemingly needless deaths bring about social pressures for change and correction of your ongoing worldly problems. You only have to look at your M.A.D.D. organization and other groups that have come about as a result of questionable deaths and causes. Mother's Against Drunk Drivers in your country have changed your societies' attitudes and laws in regards to drinking and driving; and statistically speaking these movements have saved lives. This reaction and type of response applies to most seemingly needless deaths.

"Victor, again, there is a purpose for all that happens. There are times also when a need develops on a societal level, which can shift the cause of a predetermined demise to a greater need. Sometimes it is because the loved ones left behind have a need for an awareness of purpose, to give understanding, as it was with your Claricé. Her death and subsequent spiritual visits and your acceptance brought about the change in your belief system and gave your life new purpose... similar now to that of the founders of the M.A.D.D. organization...to make a difference.

"Your work and writing will bring more awareness to the problems in the dissemination of information, to

those with breast cancer and their families, so they can make informed decisions regarding treatment. What is most important for each child of God to keep in mind, and to understand is that your time to be born and your time to die was determined before your soul energy incarnated and joined your physical body/vehicle before birth.

"Another example is that most of mankind's illnesses have been created by the evolution of the species. Many of these illnesses are a result of everything from attempts to extend the life of the physical body/vehicle, to improper diet, pollutants and poisons which have changed and affected your environment, to a host of other manmade created causes and effects. Cures for diseases are often not sought after or discovered until there becomes a preponderance of deaths of your physical body/vehicles resulting in high numbers, which then creates societal pressures upon the scientific and medical communities to find cures or solutions to the problems.

"Exceptions that appear to fall outside of a predetermined demise or one which has been determined just prior to the demise of a physical body/vehicle are intentional, ego-driven suicides. Other exceptions to this would be times when due to some unforeseen circumstance, such as accidents, the sudden stopping of the heart of the physical body/vehicle during a surgical process or being in the wrong place at the wrong time, a soul may be facing a possible death before completion of its agreed upon time on earth. In these situations, angels can and do intervene, as Miriam has with you; these incidents are often reported as angelic interventions and are referred to as miracles. And, they are. Many souls who have survived this type of occurrence, or have been revived after their body/vehicle seemingly quit functioning, are said to have had an N.D.E, or near death experience or even an A.D.E., an after death experience. Many, have had a glimpse of the other side and have reported that they have seen the light or

experienced the sensation of a deceased relative waiting to greet them with open arms. The circle of life and other metaphors earlier mentioned may be clichés in the language of mankind, but even more, they relate to the eternal life of the soul. Suffering in one incarnation may lead to joy in another; all according to the lessons one needs to learn. Equally so, those who cause strife in one life will certainly suffer from it in another... 'An eye for an eye and tooth for a tooth.'"

Chapter Eighteen
Bits and Pieces
Dancing Candles or Dance of Love

After I had the "touch experience" with Claricé that I earlier described, I believed it was her final goodbye to me and that I wouldn't hear from her any more. Since then I had not tried to spiritually contact her again.

Later, after I began communicating with the angels, I was told that whenever I believe I am emotionally ready to communicate with her it can and will happen.

I do talk to her quite often as I move through my day and in the environment she created in our home. She loved our home and as we were remodeling and putting it together, she often seemed to be playing house, as little girls do. Perhaps due to the artist within, Claricé had an exceptional sense of design in all she did. She made use of all the space, turning unnecessary closets into display cases for our travel treasures, and covered the walls with our art collection, and an assortment of odd dishes and unique trinkets discovered at the Salvation Army and local thrift shops. I was frequently in awe of what she brought home and surprised over how everything was used in an interesting way and seemed to belong. I still wonder if, in playing house then, she was making up for her lost, youthful years in the orphanage in Rio de Janeiro.

Sometimes when I'm beginning a task I think about it and ask her what she thinks I should do, and mentally hear her quiet laugh. This happens most often when I am cooking in the kitchen, which was Claricé's "special place" for relaxation and unwinding at the end of her day. She loved to cook and several days a week would spend 3 to 4 hours preparing the nightly dinner for just the two of us, which generally was traditionally the Brazilian dinner hour... at 9 or 10 in the evening. Always taking care of me, she never asked, or let me cook until her busy schedule of going back to school, studying and working during the final 8 months of her life. Then, she seemed surprised at my culinary skills. Now, I mentally see her smile as I go about my simple cooking style, and trying to figure out what all the spices are to be used for as I awkwardly throw a pinch of this or a tad of that into whatever dish I happen to be preparing.

The kitchen also contains one of her "special" works of art. When we remodeled the house and had the "drop ceiling" removed, she created a U-shaped, living piece of art above the cabinets. The doorway to the kitchen is directly opposite where I sit at my computer, in what has become my dining room/office. The space above the cabinets is what she called her "living, waterless aquarium" and I enjoy it enjoy it immensely — even at this moment I can look up in admiration — it keeps her close to me. Her creation is difficult to describe, but the artwork is a collection of blue and green glassware accumulated by her visits to every thrift shop, Good Will and Salvation Army Outlet in town. There must be over a hundred pieces; bottles, vases, bowls, glasses of different sizes and of all shapes in blues and greens; and clear bottles filled with seashells and dyed blue water, all backlit with fluorescent lighting. Mixed around and within the glassware, is an assortment of larger seashells, pieces of coral and colorful fish in all sizes.

She began her "fish collection" during the year we worked in Cancun when she fell in love with the beauty of the underwater world. Many of the fish are different sized wooden carvings, colorfully hand painted for the tourist market in Mexico. There's a full variety of species, from several small pairs of fish earrings hanging on the edge of glassware, to fish mounted on pieces of coral, unique fish napkin holders and even a large Yellow Tang cookie jar. I swear I can hear he laughing with me when I have to take it down each year to wash everything and then reassemble it as close as I can to the pictures I took before dismantling it the first time. The reason she called it a "living piece of art" is that it becomes new again with every washing because it is impossible to get every piece back in its original place. It has now become _our_ work of art, like so many other pieces we collaborated on in developing products for the art show circuit.

I also mentally hear a lilt of laughter as I go about performing some of her favorite household activities or washing and rearranging some of her other creations around the house. I swear I never knew how much work she really did. This is awareness I am sure many people have... especially men, who have lost a loved one. As we first awaken to the realization of being alone, it is a time of discovery. And, as we work our way through acceptance and the steps of our own, personal grieving process we learn more than we ever knew of our lost mate. I feel her presence often and sometimes, when I ask her questions, answers immediately come into my mind. Although different than in the beginning, when this happens I think about how she told me in her first communication that she was now my guardian angel. Her closing words from the one communication continue to echo through my mind —*"I will guide you... guide you...guide you."* — and I wonder if she really is giving me guidance. I believe that she is.

Very frequently, I feel her presence when I am at Sunday morning services at the First Unity Church I now attend each Sunday in St. Petersburg. About twenty minutes into the service, a period of meditation begins and almost always I feel her with me during these times of silence and listening for the enlightenment from the Spirit within.

At a recent service, following the meditation I had a new experience of a spiritual nature with her. It was shortly after the meditation had ended and the congregation had completed singing the song, *"Surely The Presence Of The Lord Is In This Place..."* This is when I most often feel, or sense, Claricé's presence the strongest. On that particular Sunday, the feeling of her presence lingered well into our pastor Alan's message.

As I listened, my eyes began to focus on the two large candles, one on each side of a flower-laden table, against the back wall and behind our minister as he delivered his sermon of the day. Above the candles and the flowers is a large and beautiful stained glass window; a depiction of Leonardo da Vinci's "The Last Supper." Although the candle flames occasionally flicker for a second or two, at that moment the flames on the candles were tall, still, and steady.

I continued feeling Claricé's presence and my mind began to drift. I was thinking about how much she would have enjoyed the services and family of new friends I have found at this church. As my thoughts wandered, I became aware that I was staring hypnotically at the candle on the right, the shorter of the two on the table behind our pastor as he delivered his sermon. The flame was still and steady with only an occasional flicker. Suddenly, I wondered if she was really spiritually present as we are told that our loved ones and guardian angels always are? When the words passed through my mind, I began to think about it, and I questioned, "How could I know?" While I considered it, new words came into my mind and I mentally asked, "If you are with me Claricé, can you give me a sign?"

At the exact moment the thought went out of my mind, the flame of the candle on the right, where my eyes were focused, began to rapidly dance. It was a back and forth and around movement, almost as if she were standing next to the table and moving her hand in a side to side wave above the flame, fanning it to make it dance for me. During the 15 or 20 seconds that the flame danced, my eyes glanced over toward the candle on the left; its flame was steady. It stood tall and remained still with very little movement.

I know that burning candles always flicker and move a little, but where these two were positioned, one on each end of the table against a wall, I thought that with whatever movement of air there might be in that specific area would cause a flickering motion that would affect both of the flames at the same time... but only the one flame was dancing for me.

My mind had wandered and the pastor's sermon was like a voice in a distant room. I smiled then with doubt in my mind, amused at my thoughts and the unexpected response of the dancing flame. I then decided there must have been a very slight movement of air that just affected the one candle, perhaps from our Pastor's walking back and forth as he delivered his weekly message.

Smiling and still feeling her presence however, I thought, "Okay, Claricé, show me again." The flames of both candles were again tall, steady and still, unmoving with no excessive flickering.

As this thought ran through my mind, I was then focused on the taller candle on the left side of the table, which at that moment was burning very steadily. As the first one had done, as soon as the thought left my mind, the candle on the left began rapidly dancing with an identical motion and for about the same length of time... dancing alone, while the one on the right remained tall, still and steady. I smiled broadly then and thought again about the song we had earlier sung, "Surely The Presence Of The Lord Is In This Place." The Lord certainly does work in mysterious ways.

I wondered then if the dancing flames were one of the Heaven-sent signs that come from loved ones who have crossed over and made their transition? Was it like a dove, a butterfly or a feather that suddenly falls, floating out of nowhere as we are told happens to let us know our loved ones are with us at some particular moment in time? Was Claricé listening to the thoughts of my mind? Was she answering me and letting me know she was with me at that moment? Or... was she waving her angelic hand over the flames — creating them to dance just for me — to remind me of the sculpture we had purchased in Brazil, on the very first trip we had taken together? The sculpture is titled "The Dance Of Love" and within it, now contains her physical remains. Was she showing me she was all right and standing there before me sharing in the service under the beautiful stained glass depiction of the Lord's Last Supper? Was it just a coincidence... or another synchronicity of life yet to be understood?

Some things you just have to accept on your faith and your belief in the experience. And for me it was an example of the words in a Biblical quotation and one of the songs the congregation sang that Sunday, "If you believe... *all things are possible.*"

- - - - -

Communicating With The Other Side

"Hello again Archie, I want to ask a few questions that you have been bringing to my mind during my nightly struggles of deciding between sleep and talking with you. One question that you seem to want to answer and you keep bringing to my attention is in regard to the act of communicating with you and/or my other angels, as well as the other entities on your side."

"Okay, Victor, I have been wanting to talk to you about that because as you are quite aware, there is much doubt among your fellow man when it comes to communicating with the 'other side.' You certainly found this to be true when you encountered so much disbelief in your own personal experiences. Everybody wants proof and this goes back to the earliest awareness of life and development of theological beliefs on your planet.

"Many who came to believe in reincarnation and who have crossed over throughout the years believed in the possibility of spiritually communicating with earthlings after death. In more recent times prior to crossing over, some have told their loved ones or other interested participants that they would communicate a secret message or some such endeavor, which could prove that it is possible.

"Unfortunately, it isn't quite as simple as that, and also, it is not what God intended. If it were all that easy, what would be the purpose of the death of the physical body in which your soul/spirit resides? Life on your planet Earth as you know of it is only a small part of your eternal life and spiritual learning process and is not meant to continue with ongoing communications with your loved ones left behind. How could any member of humankind accept the loss of the physical presence of their loved one if they could

maintain some form of daily communication with them?

"You, Victor, are in a perfect position to understand this. You did have communications with your wife Claricé after her passing. For you the experience itself was amazing and beautiful, and at first you wanted it to continue. You even tried unsuccessfully. Claricé heard you and knew you wished to speak with her some more, but she also knew that it would not be good for you emotionally. You had to accept her death and lack of physical presence, which you would not be able to do if she had kept responding to you, as she did on that first night when you cried out to her.

"Victor, the purpose of spiritual communication is strictly for guidance through your earthly journey. These communications can come from God directly, His angel messengers, other angels with specific purposes as ordered by God, loved ones and others who can assist you through the quandary or quagmire of everyday living on your earthly plane.

"You needed the guidance when Claricé came to you. And her personal visits ended when she achieved what she was meant to do. She was to help you through your grief when you were at your most desperate of times and to show you the purpose and meaning in your life that was still to come. Although her visits brought you great joy, they still came with much pain and grief. You accepted that physically she was gone and she was happy in her 'heavenly' place but the lack of her physical presence in your life was emotionally disheartening.

"Still, you continued to search for a way to reach her in reading all of the books you could find on communicating with souls who had crossed over and others who had written about having achieved spiritual communications with lost loved ones. With all of this you began to understand that your experience was not unique; many others have also experienced communications of one kind or another. This reading and research gave you a greater understanding of the *experiences you had been going through as well as shedding light on how it all fit your future purpose in life.*

"This was when you finally reached out to me. It was not until you read the books on angels that you truly began to understand. After going through so many years of your life's experience and learning you found out who it was that had kept you on the right path. And let me tell you, Victor, from my perspective, it has not always been an easy journey. Often, to use some earthly terminology, 'I threw up my hands in despair.' Your troublesome teenage years and then later in the 1970's and 1980's were tough years for me and your other angelic assistants. What we have called your fifteen-year mid-life crisis was closer to twenty. You were having such a good time exploring the possibilities of prosperity and how you could achieve more and more. You maintained control by not letting us in. In the late seventies and early eighties, when you began doing past-life regressions for research in your writing we thought we might break through to you, but we didn't. You wouldn't listen!

"Your not listening brings me to the next point in answering the original question today. In the past, as noted above, many who have crossed over have tried to communicate with those they left behind with predetermined signals, passwords or other signs of recognition. The Great Houdini, as you may well recall, is the most widely known public personality who openly acknowledged that he would do this. The truth of the matter is that he did try... and most who have crossed over do try to communicate with their loved ones remaining on the earthly plane. If for no other reason, they all want to comfort their loved ones with the message that they are happy where they are and that there is life after death of the physical vehicle.

"The problem with earthlings is that due to their parental and theological teachings during their formative years, many have developed a negative belief system. Earthlings will not take the time to

listen; and when they do 'hear the voices' as happened with you, they throw up blocks of negativity. They believe that the voices or thoughts that come into their minds are some form of internal dialogue they are creating themselves, their conscience, wishful thinking, etc. God's angel messengers are of your higher self and often are recognized as your conscience as they are continuously trying to keep you on the path God intended for your life. We, God's messengers, are the ones who try to push aside negativity and improper thoughts, the thoughts which come to your mind that are of the 'I want' of your ego-lower self. We try to discourage any evil intention from wherever it comes. Unfortunately, some earthlings get caught up in and listen to the evil intentions of the ego and allow them to prevail...this is what leads to the destructive nature that affects humanity in a negative way and precludes the harmony God wants in the world.

"Getting back to communicating with the other side then, it is not only dependent upon those who have left your worldly plane to contact you. It is also up to each of you who remain in your earthly body/vehicles to be receptive and believe in the probability. This can be by words, thought, visual images or other types of spiritual contact. Believe me, almost all who cross over try to make some kind of contact; once again however, if for no other reason, it is to let you know they are all right.

"But you who remain must have faith, believe, listen and learn to separate the negative thoughts of the ego-lower self, from the positive messages and guidance that comes through to you from your higher self where the spirit of God and Christ lives within.

"Spiritual contact almost always is only to let you know they are okay where they are. Much of it is quite subtle and has been described as the smell of perfume or cologne, the feeling of a feather brushed against your cheek, the unseen movement and feeling of a presence in the air or room. The most common recognizable experience of a love one's presence is the emotional response you sometimes 'feel' when they are

with you. The difference can be quite subtle, but it is always there.

"When you consciously create a memory of a loved one, or are reminded of them through looking at photographs or talking about them with others, they are not always present, but sometimes will join you and become part of your awareness. This can also be true when you consciously ask for their guidance and if possible they will then assist you toward the proper path.

"However, the times you will <u>know they are present</u> are those times in which there was no preconceived thought of them, when thoughts or memories pop into your mind unexpectedly and you feel their presence. When your mind is elsewhere and suddenly your thoughts are of a loved one, they have come to be with you and share in your endeavor. This will often happen at times when you are alone and your mind is processing aimless thoughts. As in driving, when you are in a semi-hypnotic state and have a clear mind. Other times it may be when you are just totally relaxed, with no worries or troubles occupying the recesses of your mind. This is the state of mind you try to reach in a meditation.

"The responsibility of contact lies within the capability of those who remain on Earth. As you have learned from the books on angels, and I have repeatedly said, all you have to do is, <u>Pray</u>, <u>Breathe deeply</u> several times for relaxation, <u>Listen</u>, <u>Write</u> down what you hear, <u>Accept</u> what you receive as <u>Truth</u> of your <u>Inner Knowing</u> and finally <u>Trust</u> that God is your guide. This is working for you Victor, because you have learned to believe; the same process can work for all if they will only believe and do.

"To close out this question, let me go back to the Houdini example. Simply stated this situation, a theatrical approach, was not a part of God's purpose for crossover communications between your world and the spiritual plane. Guidance and assisting mankind in his daily walk is the only purpose. Anything you might call gimmicky such as Houdini's intention to prove his

ability to the world or others with some secret code to locate hidden riches or looking ahead to give you the winning Lotto numbers was not your Creator's intent. Future attempts along this line will fail, as did Houdini's attempts fail, because this type of communication does not serve God's purpose. But if you listen to and speak with your angels and God, they will guide you toward the specific purpose of your path in your present life and assist you on the earthly plane.

- - - - -

Responsibility for Grief, Loss And Evil

"Thank you Archie. Now I want to see what you have to say about the WHY? This is the question I asked immediately following Claricé's death and you did give me acceptable answers that have helped me to deal with my grief. Your suggestion that the pain I experienced as grief was really the same as the love we shared together while she was with me has helped. I have begun to recognize that it was the sorrow over her physical absence that overshadowed the love. It made me realize it was her physical body being missing from my life, which was causing the pain. Most recently I have been able to push aside the pain by thinking and/or vocalizing the words "it's our love." At those times I repeat it to remind myself of the love we experienced together while she was with me and to be thankful for being able to feel and recognize it yet today. It doesn't stop my missing her presence, but I have been able to accept that it is only an interruption in our eternal lives and that we will be together again.

"So Archie, this has been consoling and worked for me, but how can I or we bring comfort to others who face similar losses. At the time of the loss, comfort does not come from the words: 'it was God's will...' or 'they're in a better place now.' An example would be in our friend's miscarriage and more recently a grandniece who, recently had to terminate her pregnancy in the sixth month. What can be said about these situations? Why does God create new life and new souls and then let the spark of life end before fruition?"

"As you were told before, any loss of a loved one, be it a fetus, a child, adult or older person is a personal loss no different than the loss of your wife. The depth and enormity of the loss is in proportion to the attachment of those who experience it. Each person needs to find their own way of moving through the painful experience of that which they feel. Each one has a totally different experience. No two are alike. There is nothing you can say or do, except to give them the comfort of understanding their pain and being there for them, in whatever way they find to deal with it. Be there for them but do not challenge their experience as some did of your own.

"Death happens to be a result of having 'been'. Plant, animal or mankind, it is the experience of 'being' that must end. For mankind, everyone who has been, in fetal stage of your physical vehicle/body or having been born into the world, your earthly body must sometime leave what you have 'been' for your soul to be returned to God who gave you the ability 'to be'. Accepting that the being-ness of your physical vehicle/body is temporary and fleeting is beyond the conscious reasoning of most and yet is a part of your learning experience on the earthly plane.

"This knowledge does not always bring comfort. There are no satisfying answers for the individual experiencing the loss. They can only come to terms with it in their own way.

"Victor, you are asking one of the bigger questions that face humankind and your earthly/world. I mention both 'humankind and your earthly/world' purposely. As the evolution of mankind has come about, most of the earthly/world's problems are of the creation of mankind itself. This is so, even in the end result of the genetic makeup of the physical bodies of man. There are times when the seed of the male and seed of the female are not compatible and are rejected immediately or soon after their joining... and as in your niece's experience, much later. This

incompatibility is the result of genetic and environmental evolution. However, just as the soul enters the embryo or fetus sometime prior to birth, the soul leaves the physical body upon death, whenever it comes about.

The soul will also occasionally reject or leave the fetus immediately when there is an incompatibility or deformity, which prevents the fetus from coming to full-term and experiencing birth as a new being. What are called full-term, stillbirths are also rejections of the soul due to a spiritual awareness of the lack of sustainability of the physical vehicle/body in its chosen earthly environment. Exceptions to this are those born with disabilities or inabilities, which are a part of their life plan, such as the question put to you earlier from your friend about children with learning disabilities.

"These situations are difficult for humankind to understand, even though the manner of, and actions of mankind throughout the evolution of the species is fully responsible for the human condition as life continues to evolve and develop on your planet. There is not however any individual responsibility or blame to be attributed or assigned. These rejections of the embryo or fetus are the result of the growth and development of mankind in your earthly/world since time began.

"The <u>creations</u> of man is where the responsibility lies; it could be the diet that has come into being throughout the years, environmental influences and factors or physical conditions that have evolved. Therefore, you have to place the blame on humanity and the world as it exists, rather than on God, the individual, or parents together. God created the humankind, but man's evolution created the human condition that is responsible for the genetic disposition of each and every human on your planet.

"For most I know this may not be a satisfactory answer, but you have to remember when God gave mankind free choice it was this free choice that has created your world as you know it today.

"God often gets the blame, but He is <u>not directly responsible</u> for everything that goes wrong.

"It is commonly accepted in most theologies that there are 'no accidents' and that 'everything happens for a reason.' With this comes the implication that God <u>is responsible</u> for all. In the sense that God created all that is this is true. This, however, goes back to the beginning of creation when the eternal soul of mankind was given the freedom of choice and everlasting life. Mankind's God-given freedom of choice (remember the 'forbidden fruit'), gave each man as well as the evolution of the world an ability to deviate from His plan, for an individual man's life as well as the divine order of all that is in God's plan for the universes He created. Remember what has been said about perfection being a myth.

"Could God stop all the negativity and evil on your planet Earth? Of course, God is omnipotent... but it wouldn't fit His plan for a harmonious world.

"When you look at time in reverse and study your individual life or the evolution of your planet earth, you are able to see the ultimate positive nature of all things that happen. Tragedies become learning experiences for achieving the positive-ness of the divine order of all things. Unfortunately, this becomes a difficult concept for mankind to understand. This is why you have to step back, and look at the BIGGER picture as noted earlier. At the time negativity occurs, it is most difficult to see the positive value of the experience. Be it in one man's life or the evolution of all the souls in the world, each is a product of their life — or the world's — experience. You could not be the person you are today without <u>every experience</u> in your past...positive and negative.

"So, let me repeat, it is commonly accepted in most theologies that there are 'no accidents' and that 'everything happens for a reason.' With this comes the implication that God <u>is responsible</u> for all.

"Confusing? Yes! Many with devout religious belief systems have difficulty assigning blame for evil on God while at the same time accept that God is responsible for 'all that is.' As well, evil as it is understood came with God giving mankind the

freedom of choice. God does not create individual acts of evil; these are created by negative influences permeating the ego-lower self of mankind itself yet they only come about due to the 'freedom of choice' He gave mankind."

- - - - -

Writing It Down

"Archie, when I speak to friends or others who are interested in what has been happening with me who would like to experience their own communications, I explain that 'writing it down' is a key ingredient in the process of spiritual or angel communications. A few times it has been suggested to me that it is easy for me to do because of my personal writing skills or capability. People express doubt and say they can't write it down like I do and most seem to have an aversion to keeping journals.

"This I understand because it was the same for myself in the past. I didn't write things down or keep anything remotely considered to be a journal or daily planner. In that sense, I have been quite disorganized most of my life and always figured things out day by day, not worrying about tomorrow. I took care of problems when and as they appeared. I believe my writing skills are beneficial, but also, they are not the "source or creativity" of the messages I transcribe.

"Victor, the answers are in front of your eyes. It's like your earthly expression of not being able to see the forest for the trees. The answer is in the words used: <u>problem</u>, <u>can't</u>, <u>don't</u> <u>want</u> and <u>doubt</u>.

"These are negative attributes of the ego-self which truly block receiving angel communications. When your writing capability is compared to another's it is being used by their ego as an excuse. The ego is grabbing for something to justify its position to reinforce the 'I can't' of the lower self to overpower intention of the higher self, which would like them to do it.

"You must remember that in the Bible, God says he will never give mankind more than he can handle. In

its most basic form, this guidance applies here also. Step by step, you must remember that God's angels are passing His messages to all who will listen. At the same time God and his angels will answer any question that is asked of them. But you do have to listen. Once again, each of mankind who listens will receive according to their own individual capability and based upon their individual frame of reference and intellect. It doesn't matter how much one writes, but more importantly that <u>something</u> is written to record the intent of the communication for future reference.

"Of course, in your case, your writing skills may enable you to transcribe in a more detailed manner than one without your particular skill. However, it is not your creative ability that is the influence here, as it is implied by the excuses being brought forth by another's ego in blocking a communication for them. It is an excuse. 'Fear and doubt,' are both attributes of the ego. Ego looks for excuses. Perhaps it is one's fear to be judged by their words. Because of your ego, Victor, you faced this dilemma as your dictations accumulated and you wanted to begin to share your writing with others. You had already faced doubt by others when you shared your communication experiences. Humankind has difficulty accepting what they cannot readily experience themselves.

"Also those who would like to communicate in this manner may fear whether or not they will receive the truth, or the true meaning of a message. The ego creates doubt within them. As long as they allow or listen to doubt of the ego they will not get the answers they seek. They have to release these fears and doubts. Let them go and let God's angels work in their lives. As long as the messages are of a positive and loving nature, ego has been overcome and is absent.

"Victor, all people are not looking to write a manuscript or book, nor is everyone being led to write in a detailed manner for publication. Each of mankind on your planet Earth has a curiosity for understanding life, but most of them just want answers for and about themselves.

"*Therefore, because it is just for themselves it is the primary reason for writing it down so it can be looked at again. I don't believe 'journaling' is quite the right word; I prefer record keeping.*

"*You know that for yourself, and you have tried to explain to others, that it is impossible to remember every communication you receive within your mind. That is not only in the case of messages from God or his angels, but in the everyday communications in your lives on the planet Earth as well. You know how difficult it is to remember something you may have heard weeks ago or months ago. Often times it is a message that you thought at the time was quite significant and worth remembering. Suddenly for one reason or another something comes up and you want to recall that incident or message but you find that it is lost somewhere within the recesses of your mind. Why? Because you didn't write it down.*

"*Every day and almost every moment, humans are receiving guidance and positive answers from the angels to the silent requests that are continually and unconsciously being made. Unless the answers are really significant or have a memorable impact on their lives, the messages are quickly forgotten. Whether mankind is conscious of it or not, it is also important when there is an awareness of asking a question of God or the angels. It must be written down or it will be forgotten.*

"*This manuscript, for you, is a good example. Although you have learned from the communications and have come to a better understanding of how life works than most, you could only discuss it conceptually.*

"*Information and knowledge is cumulative. It is all part of the educational process. As stated, it is a certainty that you don't and cannot remember everything in the 200-plus pages that have been dictated to you over the past two years. This is your record of these thoughts, words and communications. Although you don't and cannot expect to remember every word written, <u>you do and will</u> remember the* *essence of the various topics that have been under discussion. Any time you have questions, you know you can look back and review the data received for on-going guidance; you might even say this record gives you divine guidance for your life and throughout your life.*

"Anyone who can put words together in a complete sentence can keep a record of that which they receive from the angels. More important, as I have pointed out it is a great reference tool for asking other questions and follow-up questions. Everyone does not have to write a long spelled out story or manuscript as a writer might do. Instead, it might be looked at or compared to a recipe file. A master chef often relies on recipes when he wants to be very sure of an entrée he is creating. Or an architect, who builds beautiful structures, has files and files of ideas for reference. For your governmental taxes you have to keep records so that you will remember where you spent your money and how you can claim what you call your deductions.

"Use these examples as a means reinforcing the importance of writing it down; and for getting rid of the fear, doubt and the I can't of the ego lower self mindset. You can, because God and the angels are listening and waiting to assist you.

"Getting back to the examples of a chef who wants to create a variation of a successful recipe or an architect to build a better building: both will look back at the original ingredients or plans. What do they do next? They silently ask the question or think, 'how can I make this different... or better?' The words then come to his or her mind; the angels say add a pinch of this or a smidge of that and change this or that to something else. Now the chef and the architect each have a beautiful and new masterpiece. But they would not have been able to ask the right questions if they had not kept records of their earlier words, thoughts, ideas or communications they had received. The same is true for everyone in communicating with angels. If you don't write it down, even the smallest of answers to your questions, the communication will soon be

forgotten like last night's dream. You will have no record of a communication when you face the same problem or question again... or if you need further answers to cope with living your daily life."

- - - - -

How to Communicate With Your Angels

Following is the format I modified from the Angelspeake series of books to guide myself and help with my own communications with the angels. It is now an EIGHT-step process and I believe I moved some of the steps around. Under each step, where necessary, I have given an explanation of what each step means to me, and how I use it. It is my prayer that using this format might give you guidance and help you to accept and believe in angelic communications. When you listen to the inner-voice that is of the *Holy Spirit* and higher self within where *all good is available* you can begin to distinguish between that, and the voice of the ego-lower self *which brings forth both good and bad influences* and the negativity that comes and blocks your belief in what can be.

Stop for a moment and let your mind become quiet...

What thoughts are running through your mind? Right now! Probably it's, *"I can't or don't hear anything."* That is the voice of your ego throwing up the first "I can't or don't" block. At the same time, you have just completed the first step. You have acknowledged that you CAN listen to your thoughts. Now change that negative thought to, "I believe. I can." Now you have taken another step in a *positive* direction.

Think for another moment about the times you have had to come up with an excuse for doing or not doing something that was expected of you. Remember how you rehearsed different stories or scenarios. As you did this, you were listening to your thoughts. At the same time, if you recall, you were probably silently asking a question like, *"What should I tell her (or him)?"* Well, the long sad untruthful story, looking for sympathetic acceptance, was that of you ego-lower self. The voice that suggested you tell the truth and deal with the consequences in whatever way you could, was the voice of your higher self... the Holy Spirit... or your angel guide; all recognized as your conscience for this example.

The point here is to learn to listen to your mind; know and understand that the ego brings good and bad thoughts, whereas only positive thoughts and direction comes from the higher self. If you listen you can always choose what is best for your path in life.

It works for me and I believe it can work for you. As stated above, however, nothing comes easy... it takes awareness, discipline, practice and repetition as well as the Eight-steps given. Begin with a prayer; the one below adapted from the Angelspeake books, or one of your own choosing that contains a similar request.

1. Pray

Dearest Heavenly Father, Mother God
And Your Angel Messengers,
to whom God's love now commits me.
Enter this day and be at my sides,
and fill this room, with your holy and
glorious white light of protection.

Please help me to release any doubts or fears that appear,
which may keep me from hearing the words of your divine guidance.
Help me to let go of the negativity and doubts of my ego
consciousness.
Let me release anything that blocks my ability to communicate
with You God, Your angels, guides, my higher self and the Spirit
within.
Thank you God! Amen.

2. Relax and get comfortable.
Breathe deeply. Let your mind get quiet. Experience the pleasurable solitude of a meditative state for two or three minutes.

3. Ask... and Listen

Ask questions like, *"What is my dominant angels name?"* We all have two with us at all times and other walk-in angels for any specific purpose or desire. In the beginning, keep it simple. Ask a question you may have in mind. Whatever comes through, accept it and then ask for the angel's name. It most likely will be the same as the answer to your first question, and early on it will probably be that of your dominant angel guide.

The purpose of this is that it is much easier to have a conversation with a name and someone you feel you know. It can be mentally or verbally, it doesn't matter. Don't listen specifically for voices. God and his angel messengers do not have recognizable voices. I use the word listen... because a communication can come to you in any manner in which you are ready to believe in it. Listen or <u>become "aware"</u> of words that enter your mind as if it is a telepathic communication.

Spiritual communications can sometimes <u>seem</u> to have a recognizable voice as that of a loved one would have, but generally will only come if there is unfinished business or if they believe you need to know they are all right. Otherwise they are your guardian angels and will be with you as long as needed to give you silent guidance. Communications from your angel guides are the same as the mental dialogue, (monkey chatter), which goes on constantly in our heads. Often it is the angels trying to guide you but you are not listening. What you are listening for is the differences between ego negativity of the lower self and the truth of the spirit and angels of the higher self where the communications of God are received, as noted above.

4. Have a note pad available to immediately write down <u>whatever</u> name first pops into your mind.

Then direct questions to that name and make notes of anything you think you have heard or receive. The name may be simple like Mary or John or it may be just initials or something strange like JABBA. If your communication is taking place at night, just make one or two word notes for reminding you later. Like dreams, angel and spiritual communications are quickly forgotten. I make notes even in the dark, sometimes one on top of the other. The notes are only a record of the *essence of a communication*. If you try to write long drawn out statements, you will lose the flow of it. It doesn't matter if what you get sounds like nonsense at first. As you accumulate notes it will all come together for you. Remember, anything of negativity will be that of your EGO-lower self.

5. Accept whatever you get.

At this point don't worry if it is the truth, just write it down. When there is only silence, sometimes you will have *doubt* (ego) and force the answer you want to come through. This will be the ego, but when you learn to push aside the doubt in the silence, the truth or good will prevail.

6. Have Faith and Trust in the message, even if it sounds strange.

Sometimes messages come through in fragments that do not make sense until more comes through. It can look like pieces of a puzzle that do not quite fit. When this happens, I set it aside and the next day, I will ask questions about what I don't understand and generally clarity will come through.

7. Allow your Inner-Knowing and Higher Self to receive and give you the information asked for.

This is where soul memory, spiritual contact, angelic contact and communications from God are achieved. Remember the times when you have prayed to God and thought you may have gotten an answer and you acted upon it because of your belief? It is the same thing with angels or spirit. You must have faith in what you receive and *reject* the negativity of the *ego consciousness*, which will always present you with doubt. Begin by going for simple questions and answers, like the names of your angels. Once you begin to use the names, stick with them… <u>ego will tell you no</u>, but you must believe. Eventually as you ask follow-up questions and begin to see clarity, you will develop more faith, based upon the truth and logic in what you receive. Your communications will grow and multiply with practice and repetition.

8. Afterwards or the next day read your notes written down as stated in #4 above. If it is the next day and you are trying to put confusing pieces of a puzzle together, go through the steps above that you feel will be beneficial. Your higher self will guide you. Otherwise, just Pray and meditate briefly, then go to the computer, typewriter or a legal pad of paper and begin to <u>*write out the questions*</u> relative to the notes, or what you do not understand… one at a time… listen again for the quiet of the mind and then <u>write out whatever comes through</u>.

Let it build by asking follow-up questions before moving on to the next note. Repeat the process for each note. Your communications will build and accumulate. It is not necessary to keep asking, praying or begging… Just relax and allow it to happen. Be still and know that God or the angels have received your request. Know that he, she, or they are working on it and you have not been forgotten. Let go… and leave it to God and His angels is the way to let it happen. The angels say, "If you are wondering what to do next to further your spiritual quest and to find your path and truth, we can only say this. Talk to us… Talk to us. We are waiting, we are listening and we will answer your request. Listen and believe it. Christ said, 'Ask and you shall receive'. That is the truth which prevails!"

Lastly, practice… and don't become discouraged! It may take several attempts to push the blocks aside and learn to control the ego-lower self. Remember it was not until the fifth night of pleading that Archie came through to answer me.

Epilogue Part Two
The Acceptance of Angels in My Life

In August 2000 when the angels came through to me, the subject of Part Two of this narrative, an awakening to my future purpose in life and an understanding of Claricé's death came about and gave me peace I was searching for. How God works in the minds and hearts of His children and on Earth began to change my life in ways that I would not have previously imagined. Each new communication, spiritual and angelic, has given further clarification of how God does work in the universes he created. The words, "I think, therefore I am..." took on a new meaning with *the knowing of* God in my life. The spiritual visits gave me new hope in my life and the angels have given me purpose and understanding.

The pain of the loss of my wife Claricé was replaced with an inner knowingness that the ongoing emotion I was re-experiencing as pain was instead, that of the wonderful love we shared. I learned to appreciate the time we had together rather than the "what might have been" in the future. I developed a greater understanding of the need to live in the NOW rather than dwelling on the past and wondering or worrying about the future. I found that there is a purpose for all that happens and if I leave it to God and follow His guidance, awareness of His miracles become clearer and I now look forward to the future with anticipation and joy of what lies before me.

When I questioned the "truth" of my experiences and what I was receiving spiritually, I received an understanding of my truth of the truth. God's freedom of choice, given to all of mankind, leads each man to discover the truth in their own manner of belief, which will bring them peace, joy, love and happiness in their lives. A broader awareness of my freedom of choice brought with it the realization that the I AM being-ness is the result of the choices I make in my life. Therefore, when the I AM is in negativity or the NOT illusion of my life, an awareness comes about that it was a choice of the I WANT of the ego-lower self of my mind, and it is my responsibility and choice to change the perception of my being-ness to the positive path of the higher self and Spirit within.

Margie, a very dear and loving friend from my college days and me, have had friendly, ongoing discussions over differences in religions, and theological belief systems for many, many years. As a fundamentalist Christian most of her life, she had reasonable concern

Victor K. Hosler

for the future of my soul throughout my "convenient Christian" years. And, since I have developed my relationship with God in early 2000, she is still not sure about me and I am certain she shakes her head in wonder and prays for me over some of my newfound beliefs or declarations. Hopefully, when she reads this story, she will come to peace with my manner of belief.

This however points me toward Archie's many references to "semantics," the interpretation and meaning of words, the quantitative growth in words in all languages and how it influences the differences in our belief systems. In a recent conversation with her, based upon her beliefs, she made the statement that, "Satan is the God of this world." At first, my reaction was, "Oh Margie, how can you make a statement like that?" Our conversation soon ended, but I went to bed with that thought in my mind. Shortly after, Archie came through to clarify this and he said:

"Victor this is just another example of how semantics and the understanding, meaning and interpretation of words, which are only labels for concepts and statements, is responsible for much of the theological confusion on your planet Earth.

"Your questioning response to her statement shows that you still have some confusion over the bigger picture. In reality, regarding what Margie stated, you both believe the same thing but you just say it differently, using different word labels. What I have talked about and you accept is that evil does permeate the Earth and prevents the peace, love and harmony God wants for the planet. This evil began to come through the ego - lower self of your minds when God gave mankind the freedom of choice. Remember again the Biblical story of the "forbidden fruit." We agree that most of your Earth's problems are a result of the I WANT of the ego; that of the power mongers of your world wherever they reside. In all cultures, the leaders achieve their status because of their desire for power, control, money and/or greed.

"Even in your United States where conditions, because of your democratic system of government, are better than almost everywhere else, there are still evil intentions from the I WANT of the ego-lower self in many who seek the power. Change your word 'evil' to

her word 'Satan' and you are both saying the same thing except that I do not like her use of the word God in that context. Because of their quest for power and control, much of the world is run by evil intentions. Therefore, again, you are saying the same thing but using different words. You must remember that "semantics" is the study and understanding of word meanings, especially as they have developed and changed throughout the history of your world. This is what has brought about much confusion in the world relative to religions and theologies."

With that statement from Archie, once again understanding came through to me. I believe however, that the most important result of my angel communications has been in how they explained that the length of time my wife and I had together in this lifetime was in accordance with God's plan for both of our lives. Realizing and coming to a belief and a knowing-ness brought me to peace with her death. God does have a plan for each of our lives, which is written in what is generally known as, and what Claricé called, the *"book of life in the hall of records."* There is a "time to be born and a time to die" in His plan for our lives which was agreed upon before our soul joined the chosen physical vehicle for our lives in our earthly bodies. We are souls with God given eternal lives that reside in the physical vehicle called the body, not a body that happens to have a soul.

Victor K. Hosler

PART THREE

Conversations with God, Spiritual and Angel Communications –

How They Have Enhanced My Life

Victor K. Hosler

Chapter Nineteen
"Conversations with God"
It's impact on my life.

As stated earlier, I belong to a "Conversations with God" discussion group in Tampa, Florida. The discussions are about the book series written by Neale Donald Walsch, which are noted in the bibliography. At a recent meeting the question was put out to the 15 or so attendees on how "Conversations with God" (CWG) had influenced our lives. With chairs arranged in a circle each person in turn spoke about how the messages in Neale's books had impacted their lives beyond the discussions that had taken place over the past 18 months to 2 years. When it came to my turn to speak, I gave only a brief summary of the enormous influence that CWG – Book One had made on my life. It was a brief summary because when I am with those I care about, I sometimes still get emotional, regarding the details of how my wife's death had brought it all about. I found that learning what CWG has meant to others was both interesting and thought provoking.

My story is that the overall impact of Conversations with God - Book One and the CWG discussion group has significantly changed my life. They are really responsible for who I am today and the path I am presently on.

- - - - -

Synchronicities

Before moving ahead to show you the impact of Conversations with God, I want to speak more about the synchronicities in our lives that has been mentioned. In going over this, I want to apologize to my readers for the repetition in presenting information stated previously, but I feel it is important in order to show the chronology of the synchronicities and how the pieces of the puzzle of life come together when you look at them in retrospect.

When you have a series of unexpected events, which take place over an undetermined period of time, and all lead to a specific purpose and positive outcome, they are called "synchronicities." As each event takes place, we often think of them as an accident or coincidence. The nature of one event can be a happy circumstance, a tragedy or anything in between, but when they are looked at in retrospect, they can lead you to a purpose... and sometimes that one purpose can be a part of a larger purpose. A synchronicity can be one occasion — at any particular time or place — or it can be a part of a series of synchronicities that lead to a specific outcome, or in fact, collectively for a larger purpose as it is happening now with me in discovering my life and purpose.

To clarify this, I want to describe a series of events in my life, that have led me to writing *Angels In My Life* and to my newfound purpose for being. Looking back I realize that Claricé buying me the book, *Conversations with God,* put me on my present path. In truth it led me through the healing process, the grief over losing her and the realization that the timing of her death was a part of God's plan for both of our lives.

As an example, let me outline some of the events within *this particular set of synchronicities* as they began to unfold in this circumstance, beginning with the why of her buying me the *Conversations with God* books five months before her death <u>and before</u> we even knew she was ill.

As stated earlier, we had a disagreement around the end of February1999. It was nothing more than happens with most couples in a long-term relationship. At the time, neither of us could understand how it had come about or why it had become blown out of proportion to the point that we both needed our space. As with most family disagreements, the root of this one I am certain now was in our communications with one another. If you recall, Archie has said several times that communications are one of the biggest problems mankind faces in the world God has created.

Claricé was from Brazil and because her native language was Portuguese and mine English, the few disagreements we had throughout our relationship, that grew out of proportion, were almost always language based: she or I would misunderstand the true intention of what was being said... or we heard incorrectly due to the translation process.

Regardless of the language problem, I think this is true for most disagreements, be it individual relationships or those between cultures, theologies, or countries. We don't always say *precisely* what we mean, nor do we hear or understand *exactly* what the other is saying or means.

Angels in My Life

This is also true with the written word: the creator of the text or message has a purpose in mind and the words used are based upon his or her intellect and their understanding of the meaning of the words in their individual language. As well, the reader or recipient is filtering the words through his or her personal intellect and understanding. *It is all a matter of semantics*; remember Archie spoke in depth about this problem as he related it to the differences in understanding the theologies and religions of the world as well as the problems between cultures, societies and nations.

Getting back to our problem, Claricé, in "needing her space" had spent a couple weeks staying with our children as we sorted things out. In trying to find her own peace over the disagreement, which was <u>five</u> months before she crossed over, she went to a bookstore and discovered the book *Conversations with God – Book One*. Apparently during her upset, someone directed her to seek comfort and understanding in the "Conversations with God" books. Soon after she read it, she bought a copy for me and as well as one for each of our four children.

Our communications improved after that. We put it all behind us and bliss returned to our lives. Her inscription to me, inside the cover of Book One, that I will always treasure reads: *"These two books are helping me to heal my spirit. I hope they will be helpful to you as well. I love you Victor and always will. You are and will always be the man I married, my husband and my love. Claricé C. Hosler 3-28-99"*

Unfortunately, within two months, the seriousness of her illness became apparent and three and a half months later, I found out she was terminal. In another 40 days she was gone. The devastation of my loss turned into hatred toward God and His world... as well as the many doctors involved. As stated earlier I would have thrown the book away, if not for her personal inscription to me inside of the cover.

Throughout the holidays that followed, suicidal thoughts surfaced almost daily. I could see little purpose in living. Then, <u>five</u> months after she crossed over, on <u>January 5th</u> the first of the <u>five</u> spiritual visits came from her and the others. It was then I began my research into books on spirituality and metaphysics where I discovered many others had similar experiences. Then came angel visits. Through the reading came the acceptance, healing and understanding that God does have a Divine Plan for our individual lives in the universes he created.

As I look at my life today, I still miss Claricé's physical presence and always will. But acceptance and belief in my experiences have given me a new outlook on the days ahead, and I look forward to my tomorrows. In her first communication, a little over two years ago, she said I have 20 more years to live in God's plan for my life; so I face the coming years with excitement, love of life, of God and of Claricé for showing me the way.

I know many may doubt my experiences and perhaps think I am finding the synchronicities to aid in my personal healing and acceptance. But, my truth is that I now believe there are no accidents and everything happens for a purpose in the universes that God has created.

- - - - -

Conversations with God

I would like to tell the full story here because the CWG discussion group is what brought me to my belief in and the ability to communicate with angels. As well, my wife's buying me the CWG – Book One, as a gift of her love, prior to her transition was the catalyst that was the beginning. My purpose here is that perhaps there may be some inspiration for others and help for them to achieve results in their own spiritual growth, journey and understanding of how God and His angels work in our lives.

Personally, I cannot thank Neale Donald Walsch and the CWG discussion group enough for the transition that has taken place in my life and the marvelous journey I am now on. I am anxiously awaiting the mysteries that remain, of where it is going, the intrigue of it, and the continually awe-inspiring happenings, which are taking place in my life on a daily basis.

In this chapter, the reader will notice a series of **fives** underlined for emphasis. They are parts of the synchronistic puzzle and, at the end of the chapter I will give you a brief explanation of the **five-ness** connection and meaning, shown to me by an internet friend and based upon references I have found regarding the science of *numerology*.

For me, it all began on March 28 1999 when my wife Claricé gave me CWG book one and the companion workbook. (Synchronicity #1) As stated, we had just recovered from a family disagreement over almost nothing. If you recall, as a Brazilian, her first language was Portuguese. I had not understood how and why the problem had come about and I know that she too was confused about what had happened because it was so very unlike either of us. Later I determined that in part, that it must have been a result of the seriousness of her illness, which at that time was still unknown to us.

Prior to receiving this gift of her love I had been what I call a "convenient Christian" for many years. In my youth, my religious upbringing was quite strict and very regular on both Sundays and Wednesday night for prayer services; but as I became an adult I developed personal doubts. With some underlying thoughts about the war, the doubts were somewhat troubling after I joined the Marine Corps and I returned to reading the Bible. As I recall I read both the Old and the New Testament from cover to cover while on a tour of duty in Korea in what was then called a "police action." Although I had no question regarding the purpose of the Bible and I did fully believe in the life of Christ and of His purpose in coming, my doubts in the full acceptance and application of every word in the Bible as a truth in the world I knew of in 1953, doubts still grew.

Later, I studied "The Life Of Christ" as an elective in college under the G.I. Bill. Again, the lingering doubts were not about Christ, but more about the logic of the totality of the *truth* of every word as written in the Bible. As I read the Biblical assignments for my "Life of Christ" class, many references became more and more questionable. I couldn't see how it all related to life, as we knew of it in 20th century America. I doubted quite a bit and could not believe everything written, stated and interpreted could be the gospel of truth. Thus as time passed and my personal life went on, I became a convenient Christian; attending services mostly on Christmas and Easter or whenever someone could drag or coax me into going.

I believed and could accept the existence of Christ, His miracles and purpose but I came to believe in only as much as I felt was necessary... *just in case it was, all true.* To be safe, I pretty much lived my life according to the "golden rule," because I did not wish to enter the "gates of hell," if there really was such a place in an afterlife.

In my years with my wife Claricé, organized religion was not a priority for us. She was a Kamaiura Indian, and her mother was from a small village in the rainforest of northern Brazil. Her spiritual beliefs were somewhat different, but, at the same time, similar to mine. Her belief primarily consisted of God as a supernatural being or force that created all that is; a belief common to her heritage and to the tribe her mother was born into. When her mother died while she was still a child, Claricé was raised in a Catholic orphanage in Rio de Janeiro until she was 16 and then began working. She finished high school and went on to college, receiving degrees in both Fine Art and Journalism.

Not only did Claricé lose her mother when she was 6, her only son was killed in an automobile accident when he was only 7. She could not reconcile these tragedies and in her sadness this left her distant from the Catholic Church. The faith she had developed was lost in her grief, sorrow and lack of understanding. As a result of this, her employer, TV Globo, Brazil's National television station gave her an assignment as a foreign correspondent covering arts and humanities; her territory was in Western Europe, North Africa and the British Isles. She lived in London for about 12 years.

It was only in the last few years of her life, after we had married and when our children became "born again" Christians, that we began to attend religious services on a regular basis. When we did, it was primarily for family harmony, being together more often, and sharing what our children enjoyed.

It was exactly two months to the day following her gift of Conversation with God - Book One, that we first discovered Claricé was seriously ill. We began searching for the cause and chasing miracles only to find that she was terminally ill with her death coming just 40 days later. *It was five months after she had bought me Conversations with God - Book One.* Before we discovered her illness I had picked up the book a few times. I read it through quickly, scanned the content and began to get somewhat interested in the manner of Neale Walsch's communications with God; but it was still from my somewhat doubtful and skeptical mind-set.

As Claricé's condition quickly worsened and I was told she was terminal, my anger toward God and the doctors was almost beyond comprehension. Several times I almost tossed the book and companion workbook into the trash. I wanted no part of God's conversation with Mr. Walsch. Only Claricé's beautiful words, in her own handwriting of the inscription to me, caused me to keep the book.

I didn't know what they would later mean to me, or their true purpose in my life. I had literally come to hate GOD with every breath I took and I couldn't even consider thoughts of a loving, caring *"merciful"* entity that would allow the cruelty of her death... at the young age of only 53 years and truly at the peak of her artistic career. Her death from metastasis breast cancer was seemingly unnecessary.

Angels in My Life

The diagnosis should have come early enough for her to beat the disease. Twenty-one months earlier, when we first discovered a mass in her breast, she had a lumpectomy to remove it and was told, "It was not cancerous." When the symptoms returned, over and over again, *she was told not to worry.* Eventually in referrals to other doctors, she was given as many different opinions and diagnosis as there were doctors. I was devastated by her death, as were my children and grandchildren, who adored her.

After the first holiday season without her I was virtually on a suicidal path and it was only because I could not put my children through additional pain, that I survived. (Synchronicity 2 & 3) On January 5th 2000, the fifth month after her death, I cried out in the night wanting to speak to her "just one more time." That was the beginning of my spiritual communications. Claricé answered me:

She said: *"You can, my love."*

The words "my love," were Claricé's pet name for me and I clearly heard them come through. The communications were exactly like our earlier conversations and her Brazilian accent was clearly evident. One of the principal messages she gave to me was that I still had much work to do and I was to develop my spirituality as noted in her inscription in the CWG book. (Synchronicity 4) A total of five communications with her took place between the 5th and 17th of January 2000.

While I was doubtful and thinking I must be hallucinating, (Synchronicity 5) on the 10th of January five days after her first visit with me she spiritually caused a teen-age friend of mine to also come through to me. *Chapter four.* He had committed suicide in 1963. Claricé knew of him and had met his daughters and his former wife in 1992.

I had several visits with him and, again, I recognized his voice and speech patterns from when we were best of friends. There were several visits from him over the next couple of weeks as there also were with, Sally my children's grandmother. *Chapter seven.*

Two more communications followed. *Chapter eight.* A brief but humorous message from Barry, a former client of Claricé's who gave Claricé's eulogy at her memorial service; and finally, different from the other communications, during one session, Archie paused for a moment in the middle of a dictation he was giving me and said, "ML has a message from John for you."

Following Claricé's communications and the others, I thought I might be "losing it." I truly questioned my sanity. It was then that I became an avid reader of anything related to spiritual communications, journeys of souls, souls in transition, messages from loved ones who had crossed over, after-death experiences. Finally I got up the courage to pick up and read Conversations with God - Book One again for a second time, but this time with real purpose.

In all of my reading, I had begun to get confirmation of my personal experiences and began to accept and believe in the probability of an afterlife and the reality of the spiritual communications that had come through to me. Many books I read contained references and stories, which were similar to what I had been experiencing, and I couldn't help but become a believer in what was happening with me. I was in awe and still questioning the experiences, but I finally knew that something supernatural or paranormal was happening with me.

It was during this period that I heard the mention of a CWG discussion group that was being held in Tampa, 15 minutes away from my home in St. Petersburg, Florida. I don't remember how I heard about it, but it piqued my interest and, out of curiosity I called the phone number and was invited to my first meeting a week later.

In my second or third visit to the group, a discussion came up about the group facilitator and a couple of other group members who had attended a Neale Walsch seminar in California. (Synchronicity 6) In the discussion, it was mentioned that a former group member had recently read the "Angelspeake" series of books by Barbara Mark and Trudy Griswold. She had found through the guidance of the Angelspeake books that she was able to communicate with her angels and guides. Through her communications she was being led to a new purpose in her life. That again piqued my curiosity, because I was still researching and trying to understand what had been happening in my own life.

Through my reading I was coming to terms with Clarice's passing and the acceptance that she had crossed over. For many, many months, somewhere deep within, I hoped it was all a nightmare and I was waiting to hear her voice say, "Hi hon. I'm home" and that my loved one would one day walk back in the door, coming home from shopping or some other place.

Following my second reading of Conversations with God – Book One, I came to believe that through some "miracle" of God, that my spiritual communications from my wife and the others was in the same manner as Neale Walsch had been speaking to and receiving his messages from God. However, when they abruptly ended, I had an insatiable thirst for understanding.

It was a couple of weeks after I heard about the Angelspeake books in the discussion group that I was in Miami visiting my dear friend and editor Shirley. She is a big reader of primarily non-fiction books and has a deep interest in spirituality. When I saw her, I asked if she knew anything about the Angelspeake books. She hadn't heard of them, but said she did have two books about angels she would lend me. She gave me *"Ask Your Angels"* by Alma Daniel, Timothy Wyllie, and Andrew Ramer, and also *"The Angels Within Us"* by John Randolph Price.

After my spiritual communications ended, I had begun to hear voices in my head. The noise was beyond that of the normal *monkey chatter* that seems to take place within our minds. It was nightly and continual... fragments... bits and pieces... nothing that made any sense other than disturbing my sleep. It was a cacophony of voices nightly that once again made me think I might be "losing it." I was suffering from sleep deprivation and was under a doctor's care.

As soon as I returned from Miami, I immediately read, *"Ask Your Angels."* Right away I began to get clarity of what was going on with me. I began meditating, listening and observing my thoughts. This had been suggested in some of the many books I had read. I heard nothing but the noise. I then read the *"Angels Within."* I then got a better understanding of angels, but I still wasn't getting anything when I tried to communicate with the angels or hearing anything specific. I desperately wanted more clarification and with my still somewhat skeptical and doubtful mind, I sought out the Angelspeake series and found all three at a Border's bookstore.

It was in early August of 2000. I absorbed them like a sponge that had been squeezed, dunked, and released in water. I read *"How to Talk with Your Angels"* first, *"Prayer and Healing"* second and *"The Angelspeake Storybook - How Angels Work In People's Lives"* last. Clarity almost screamed through to me and I knew that everything that had been happening with me *was a reality* and I believed if I followed the guidance in the Angelspeake series, *I would be able to communicate with angels.*

On the 19th of August 2000, the 1st anniversary of my wife's crossing over, my grief was still profound and I was still hearing the undecipherable, fragmentary voices in the night. They were keeping me awake and I was still under my doctor's care. Following the final communication with Claricé I had tried to continue communicating with her, but even though she had told me everyone has the capability of spiritual communications by using their sixth sense, I wasn't able to stay in contact with her.

In the early communications I had with her, it flowed, I had images of her, in what I now know of as the third eye, and it was *her voice* in her Brazilian accent. There was no longer a question in my mind about that. However, as I continued to try to maintain contact, I realized that I was creating the new conversations myself. They were not spiritual and I was asking questions of her and mentally saying what I wanted to hear from her. I also realized it was not healthy for me. No matter how much I may have wanted to, I could not keep her with me. I had to release her and let her go. I couldn't accept being able to talk with her and not touch her.

From the fragmented voices and bits and pieces I continued hearing, I knew it had to be something else, and with the five books I had now read on angels, (Synchronicity 7) I began to believe the voices I kept hearing were the angels trying to speak to me, and that in some way I wasn't really listening to what I was hearing. Perhaps it was because I still lacked the required faith.

On the night of the 19th, a year to the day following my wife's death, in my on-going grief and agony, I once more cried out in the night. I said aloud, "If all of you talking up there are the Angels, who are you? Talk to me, and tell me who are you?" I got nothing, and then I asked, "When is this pain going to end?" Still, there was nothing. I just heard the continued cacophony of fragments of words and voices. I had imagined that, because it was the anniversary of Claricé's death, perhaps I would hear something to ease the ongoing pain and grief.

I repeated this nightly and suddenly on the fifth night, that of August 24th/25th... I got an answer. (Synchronicity 8) I heard a voice very clearly:

"Hello Victor, I'm Archie. I'm glad you finally have asked for me. I think now, that you are ready to listen."

He then answered my questions regarding the pain and my grief. Chapter Nine details this first communication from Archie.

In the beginning of my angel communications, I was obsessive. I couldn't get enough. I wanted to absorb, know and get as much as I could. The nights were long and sleepless and each day I sat at my computer transcribing what I thought I remembered from the night

Angels in My Life

before. The writing sessions were as long as four hours in a sitting and a few times there were two in a day, four hours in the morning and another three hours in the evening.

Soon I realized the details I was writing were more than my conscious memory could account for. Also the content I wrote as I sat at the computer, I knew was more and different from what I had received in the twilight hours before sleep and/or in a daytime meditation session.

As I continued to write, I began to ask more and more questions relative to what *I thought* I was remembering. Soon, I realized there was more going on than what I was remembering. I was "auto-writing." Apparently it was much like Neale Walsch and others have done; but my communications were from angels... messengers of God.

I have now come to believe that how the communications come and what you receive is a matter of who, how, and what you believe and that it is filtered through your higher-self, based upon your individual belief system and life experience. It has been clearly said to me that the same messages from God are coming through around the world for all who will and do listen, and most of the differences in out-put can be explained by how the messages are filtered through *the receiver's* individual experience, frame of reference and intellect.

I began receiving messages from Archie and sometimes other angels during the same session. (Synchronicity 9) After a few months it seemed to have settled into <u>five</u> angels who are presently available to me any time I choose to listen and/or make contact with them and ask questions. Who they are and their individual purpose had been noted in earlier references, so I will not go into depth again here.

"Archie," however, has been identified as my dominant angel guide who has been with me for life and I speak with him most often. The "speaking" is a mental process in the twilight hours and in meditation and via the computer when I am auto-writing.

"Jules," my other life-long angel is my mentoring angel in both my written and verbal communications and is also involved in the translation process of the messages that come through from the other-side in converting the vibrational frequency levels to human understanding. Then there is "ML" is my relationship angel, and "Ali," my angel of good health who seems to like humor as well.

A bit of her humor came out one night when I had a lingering cold and bronchial infection. It had been bothering me for almost two weeks when wondering about her role, I finally called out and asked what she could do to help me get rid of the cold. I sensed a bit of laughter in her voice as she mentally said to me:

> *"I was wondering when you were going to ask for my help, but I'm afraid I'm going to disappoint you."* She replied. *"Colds, sore throats and most other common ailments of the human condition are the creation of man as the world has evolved. They have come about due to man's pollution of his environment with toxic chemicals and his obsession with satisfying the 'I want' of the ego, which has led to gluttony and greed in many forms. I really can't help you with mankind created ailments. I can only remind you to eat healthy food, exercise, keep your doctor appointments and do whatever is necessary to maintain your earthly body/vehicle as God wanted it to be."* Then, with laughter in her voice again, she added, *"Regarding your cold and bronchial infection, I would suggest that you take two aspirins and call your doctor in the morning."*

"Gosh," I wondered, "why didn't I think of that?" It was my first angel disappointment.

Lastly to date, there's "Miriam," who is my angel of miracles. Miriam has identified and described to me several times in my life when she has intervened when my life may have been in jeopardy and possibly could have been taken in various ways before God's plan for my life on Earth was complete. These are the angelic interventions we read about so often in the media, when angels involve themselves in our lives without being asked.

Although there are <u>five</u> who are presently with me, it has also been made very clear to me that if I have a question or problem I need assistance with that is outside of their ability to assist me, help is there. I have been told, "God created His angel messengers before mankind" and, to use an earthly terminology, "there are angels of every *'job description'* imaginable and for every purpose or need."

God's angel messengers were created for the express purpose of assisting mankind in their lives on earth and the learning processes we must go through. Each soul has two angels assigned to them for life and other walk-in angels and guardian angels who are available and with you as needed... if you will only learn to ask for them and then listen for guidance and believe what you get. The angels have often repeated Christ's words, "Ask and you shall receive."

My angel communications happen in many ways and the more they continue, the more and more I can recognize that it is happening. If I go to bed with a question or questions on my mind, answers begin to flow. As they do, often follow-up questions come to my mind and they too are immediately answered. It is much different than the earlier spiritual contacts where I recognized voices. With the angels it is more of a mental process; more like what I believe mental telepathy to be. Like the answers you may receive from God during your prayers, angels do not have recognizable voices.

It was quite awhile before I learned I have the control of the communications and when they can come about. It took from August to November 2000, before I realized that angel communications were entirely my choice and I can be with them or shut them off, as I choose.

In the early stages, my communications with the angels were time consuming, problematic and very tiring. However, once I learned I could control them they stopped being a problem. I also learned that early on, like dreams most of the "twilight communications" are often forgotten by morning. I'm certain I missed following up on many of the early communications because I had forgotten about them when I woke up in the morning or didn't go to the computer. However, as I am becoming more and more familiar with Archie, and how he continues to repeat things, I'm sure that he has made up anything that I may have missed or forgotten. On one occasion when I asked him why he repeats things so often, he said:

> *"Because your life on earth is a lesson, you are to learn; like going to school the information given to you is repeated, and presented in many forms to make sure you learn and understand. It is the same with angel messages."*

When reading about my angel communications, I'm sure you will see some things are repeated to me over and over so that I might truly learn and transcribe the messages, which are being given. Some of the information is repeated because it relates to the overall context of the information then being presented within the chapter. This chapter is a good example. Although some of the material has been stated before, it is necessary to show how the CWG book series has impacted my life.

At Archie's request, I learned to keep a 4" x 6" note pad by my bed to jot down notes to remind me in the morning what was said to me at night. Often I don't even turn on the light and I will reach out in the dark for the pad and write a brief note; normally just a word or two to remind me; then later, sometimes I will reach for the pad again and write another note... sometimes right on top of the first one, and then I have to try and decipher the two of them in the morning.

As the experience has blossomed, I have become aware that the angels are always with me and I can consciously recognize their presence, even when I am not listening or looking for them. For this chapter about the impact of my Conversations with God experience in my life and the purpose of it, I know that Jules is guiding my words because spreading the word as I receive it today is a part of my current purpose in life; and this is a mentoring function.

Knowing that I have a life plan and accepting that Claricé's crossing over when she did was in accordance with her life plan and that her purpose on earth was complete was the basis for my healing. It was this understanding that led me to the peace I have today.

One of the things I have learned is to look for the synchronicities in our lives. Look at those things that happen, which we think of as an accident, a coincidence, or even a tragedy. Eventually a pattern or series of one coincidence after another will emerge, which will then lead to an overall purpose which is inevitably positive in nature and therefore, a synchronicity.

Synchronicities often begin small, a few happenings thought to be an accident or a coincidence. They may not make sense at the time they occur. Many times they can include a very painful experience, which is not understood at the time they happen, as it was with Claricé's passing. But, when you study them and lay them out like building an inverted pyramid with children's lettered toy blocks on the floor, one... two... three... five... ten... or more, suddenly they will tell a story. You will see their purpose. There are no accidents. Each is a part of a synchronicity, a part of the whole, or different groups of synchronicities, which eventually come together to become the story of your life. A good example of a synchronicity follows and is part of the purpose of this chapter.

In summary, Claricé buying me Conversations with God - Book One was not a coincidence: it led me to the Conversations with God discussion group. It too was not a coincidence: the discussion group

Angels in My Life

led me to the Angelspeake series of books. This then led me to my friend who loaned me the Ask Your Angels book. This in turn led back to the Angelspeake series mentioned at the Conversations with God discussion group. And reading the Angelspeake series gave me guidance for and how to ask for my angels. Then, when I asked for the angels to speak to me, "Archie" answered and he knew that I was ready to listen. And with this, the door opened for my angel communications, which then brought me peace, healing and gave me new purpose in my life. As noted in closing out this chapter, in explaining their meaning, I do not believe the series of <u>fives</u> is a coincidence either.

All of this would not have happened if Claricé had not read and given me the Conversations with God – Book One, and its companion workbook. They were her final gift of love. I still grieve, but now I understand more about how life works on the planet Earth and within our physical body/vehicles in one of the universes God has created. And through all my past personal successes and perceived failures, I now understand many of the lessons that have been learned and have more awareness of purpose in my life and future than ever before.

I am often asked how I know what I receive is the truth. That was explained in Chapter Ten, "Archie Defines The Truth." Sometimes the information that is conveyed to me I know is beyond that of my conscious mind and intellect. Never before could I have written Chapter Fifteen, "Changing Your Perception Can Change Your Life." When this communication first came through, I had to read it over several times before I really understood what I was writing. I then asked Archie for it to be simpler and easier to understand; I needed clarification, for both my self and my readers. It was done. Now, whenever I read back what I have transcribed, what often happens is that I question the meaning or intent; clarity then immediately comes through.

Archie has said each of us may interpret and filter the information being given differently, based on our individual understanding. On a few occasions in past CWG group discussions, the topic was very similar to what I was in the process of receiving and writing myself at that particular time. There was no real disagreement, and if anything, perhaps only a slight difference in interpretation. But, of utmost importance to me is to always maintain the integrity of what I receive and write. For this reason I did not buy or read Conversations with God - Books Two, Three or Neale Walsch's other books. I didn't want to confuse what I am getting with that which Neale is getting and writing about.

I now believe the same is true with the Bible and any other theological or reference book one is reading to understand life and how it works on an individual basis. Many books are guided... and the information filtered as stated above. You must take from them what is meaningful to you and helpful in understanding your own life. As you know right from wrong in your life based upon God's Ten Commandments and the Golden Rule, so you will know right and wrong when you read it. In the same way you can learn to tell the difference between *the good* that only comes from the spirit within and your higher self, and *the negativity* that is always of the ego – lower self. *You just know it!*

I am certain that communicating about the reality and the truth regarding the afterlife, the power and strength of the mind, and ready access to Spirit of God, the angels, within the higher self is my purpose for the coming years. The biggest and most important message I get is the same as that from Christ... and other religious theologies. "Ask and you shall receive... and he who believeth in Me will have everlasting life." This comes from God. As the Hindus say, we are all climbing the same mountain, but we are just taking different paths.

My purpose in writing this is to show how reading the books will give you divine guidance. It can be Conversations with God, Ask Your Angels, the Angelspeake series, and many other books on the subject of spirituality. Many books you may not agree with or understand, but take from them what works for you in your life. They will give you understanding. Some books with evil intentions, may even attempt to steer you in the wrong direction as does the negativity within the ego lower self. If you have faith and listen to the guidance of God, his angels and the Holy Spirit of the higher self within... *you will know, because you <u>know</u> right from wrong.* Spirit within will guide you to your truth, and believing that God or his angel guides can and will speak to you can impact your life in ways that are beyond belief.

For myself, I am just an *ordinary guy* from "Motown" who has been blessed with the ability to open my mind to an acceptance of what can be, which then opened the door to a direct relationship with God. If it can happen to me, it can happen to anyone who consciously and intentionally seeks the answers with faith, peace and love in their heart. Although my experience came as a result of emotional trauma, I don't believe that it is a necessary prerequisite. All it takes is true intention and sticking with it as you would any other discipline you might undertake to change your life, such as yoga or as exercising on a regular basis to rebuild or maintain good health, or even a serious weight reduction program for the same reason. There must be a consistency in what you do and a strong belief in purpose to achieve results. In my own case, in my earlier life I didn't have that intention. I never looked for the truth until it was essential to my personal mental health and well-being.

For those who are still searching, I know that some of the books mentioned and others can be a stepping-stone to belief in eternal life and acceptance of all that is. There are many books to guide you. I have read over forty since my journey began. From some of them I got nothing and others just a little, while others were affirming and showed me the way. With God, or *your God* by whatever name you may call Him or Her in your heart and mind, and His divine guidance *anything is possible.* And this comes from one who was a skeptic until January 5, 2000... a little over two years ago as of this writing.

- - - - -

Finally, I want to point out again the **fives** or what has been called the five-ness in my life as mentioned earlier. The underlined number five appears many times between the start of my journey when my wife Claricé bought me the Conversations with God – Book One, and completing the pathway to the beginning of my spiritual journey in communicating with the angels. As well there are multiples of five in the numbers 10, 25, 40 and 2000, the year it all began.

So far, the reference books I have looked at in the science of numerology imply that multiple fives indicate, *life affirming changes, rebirth, new beginnings, and regeneration.* One book stated that *three fives* means you will have *significant life changes*, and that the more fives in the sequence, the greater the changes will be in your life. It suggests that with a string of fives, *"You should buckle your seatbelt, because a major life change is upon you."* I believe you will agree that I have gone through a major life change.

Victor K. Hosler

Chapter Twenty
Sammy and Synchronicities
Another series

In January of 1995, a former associate of mine in the advertising business who has an agency in Miami, Florida contacted me. He knew that I'd had a successful small ad agency in Miami and wanted to know if I would be interested in looking into a troubled ad agency in Cancun, Mexico. A resort owner and client of his whose firm was the majority owner of the Cancun agency couldn't understand why the company was about to go under. He was looking for someone who had a full understanding of an agency operation like his to be a trouble-shooter. The initial offer was for me to look into it for two weeks. It was financially reasonable and included all expenses, a penthouse suite at their luxury resort, and air travel for Claricé and me.

At the time Claricé was busy with her paintings of the Brazilian rainforest, and I was trying to decide what to do for myself. I had retired when we moved to St. Petersburg in the fall of 1992, and I had just completed the two-and-a-half-year project of remodeling our home. Neither of us had a *regular job,* so I thought that the offer was a great opportunity. At the time, I had no idea of what a synchronicity it might be, but I did know the intrinsic value of a two-week all expense paid vacation for two in Cancun.

At the agency, I found a host of problems that could be solved with a reorganization of the company, implementation of new production procedures and upgrading the computer systems. Following the report to the CEO after my two weeks' review, he negotiated a two-week a month, contract for me for one year. I was hired to restructure the advertising agency. The job was much bigger than I expected with over 130 employees rather than the 25 to 30 that I was initially told by my Miami associate. In addition to the ad agency, the company also was a magazine publishing company and a printing company. Not only that, they had a radio station and distribution center. After a month or two, I recommended that they sell off the print shop, close the distribution center and give the radio station to the man who had been the General Director (President) as a part of his severance package. The agency was cut to 68 employees, and by the end of November it showed its first profit in three years. I stayed on overseeing the operation through middle of February of 1996.

I didn't speak any Spanish so Claricé, who spoke and understood several languages, was an integral part of the agreement. In Cancun, when she wasn't helping me with translations, Claricé began a new series of drawings for paintings of undersea life. In our off time, she had the opportunity to learn snorkeling and spent hours on the tourist submarine discovering the beauty of the undersea world and the Great Mayan Reef. In her research and study of the aquatic world, she discovered that the coral reefs in the oceans were in as much danger environmentally as was her beloved rain forest in Brazil, where she had lived as a child in her Kamaiura Indian village. She soon developed a passion for painting the different kinds of fish, colorful coral and fauna and the aquatic life of the Caribbean Sea.

About eight months into the project, we had fallen in love with Cancun and began talking about making it our winter home. I had turned down the offer to run the agency, because I had no desire to go back to work full-time, but I had quickly determined that there was a market for her art with the thousands of tourists who visit the area each year. We decided to produce limited edition lithographs of the new work she did in the weeks we were home in St. Petersburg and also, to put the scenes on T-shirts and coffee mugs. While she was painting during our time home each month, I went into production of a half dozen different aquatic lithographs and produced samples of the mugs and T-shirts for the gift shops and tourist attractions. Included in the T-shirts and mugs were some of her animals and birds of the rainforest.

As we began to see the end of my work with the agency, over a dozen gift shops and tourist attractions were selling her new work, and her paintings were displayed in two of the Cancun seafood restaurants. There was enough of an indication that it could be a successful venture that we began looking for a place to live and planning the new business venture. Our plans grew to include the opening of a small gift shop in nearby Playa del Carmen, which was a small seaside town that catered to the cruise ship industry with several ships visiting every week. There were thousands of tourists who didn't go to visit the nearby Mayan ruins and had little to do other than browse around the small village and it's string of seaside gift shops.

Sammy was an Art Director and an employee of the ad agency in Cancun when I first went down to check everything out. He soon became my good friend. Of all of those we met while in Cancun off and on for over a year, Sam was the only one Claricé and I really became close to. Was this a coincidence, accident or synchronicity? Or was it the beginning of my unique experiences? I'll let you decide as I tell you how our friendship developed.

During our two-week a month venture with the ad agency (perhaps adventure) Sammy and I became very close friends. Along the way as Claricé and I began to talk seriously of opening a business, Claricé met Sammy and also became good friends with him. He began helping out when we started to bring in product as we went back and forth to St. Pete each month. In addition to becoming a good friend to us, we discovered we would need a Mexican partner if we were to form a company in Mexico, and we asked Sam to participate. At the time his wife and son were still living in a suburb of Mexico City, but he was planning to move them to Cancun soon. He said his wife would be able to run the gift shop when we got it together, and he would be able to service our clients.

When the agency project ended, Claricé's work was being well received and we were very excited about the new business venture. In St. Pete, as we were moving ahead with the plans and staying in contact with Sam, we ran into a hurdle we could not overcome. We found that there was a substantial duty imposed by the Mexican government for items produced in the U.S. to lessen competition for Mexican owned companies and produced goods.

The initial quantities we were taking down were not questioned as we went through customs each month, but the larger quantities we planned on bringing in would be taxed. This made our wholesale pricing schedule unprofitable and if we raised our prices, we would be uncompetitive. After a few months I decided it would be impractical to produce the products in the States, and setting up manufacturing and distribution in Mexico was more work or involvement than I wanted to do. The plan for the business fell apart around April of 1996, and we soon lost contact with Sammy. With the product we had already produced, Claricé and I decided to begin touring the national art show circuit instead. In addition to her high-priced original works, she had quick studies and other originals that fit the art show market place as well as the reproductions.

Near the end of the second season, in the fall of 1997, Claricé discovered the lump in her breast that was diagnosed as non-cancerous in her surgical lumpectomy, but over the next 20 months she had become ill with breast cancer and passed over in August of

1999. Shortly after, I was blessed to have a series of five spiritual communications with her between the 5th and 17th of January, 2000. Following the communications with her there were others, from other spiritual beings and I began to research the metaphysical world to understand my new experiences.

Moving ahead now to the end of April of 2000, I received a telephone call from my friend Sammy in Cancun. Unknown to him, Claricé had made her transition to the other side, and I was living alone in a large, empty house. Sam wanted to know if there was work for him in the St. Petersburg/Tampa area. Was this just a coincidence?

Once I had got the agency in Cancun back on track, the owners of the resort that hired me sold the advertising agency and publishing company, and soon the new owners took it down hill again. Sam had quit the new company, and he and his family were struggling to get by with whatever income he could make from selling his original paintings to the tourists at a resort in Cancun. I later found out that the call had come about because his wife, Erika, had a dream in which a "lady in white" told her that Sammy should call his friend Victor in St. Petersburg to see if there would be work for him in our area. Was this new contact a synchronicity?

I was delighted to hear from him and invited him to come to stay with me. Although I was well into researching and studying my new path in life, I was still very lonely and knew the companionship would be good for me. With his fine talent and computer skills, I was sure he would find work in advertising right away. Unfortunately, I was wrong. He had opportunities for work outside of his career field, but in the beginning I discouraged him from *just taking a job*. The trouble was that in the art and advertising business, computers have totally changed the industry. Although he was computer literate, he was in his late fifties and of the "old school," and the aggressive young creative directors were not interested in him. Finding suitable employment in advertising was next to impossible. After a couple of months I decided it would be less expensive if his wife and son would also come to St. Pete. All of them living in my home would be more practical than helping her to maintain their residence in Cancun.

Sammy was most agreeable, but said that there was something I should know before I decided to bring them to St. Pete. He said, *"My wife Erika is pregnant and is soon going to have a baby."* I told him that it didn't matter and as long as she was able to travel it would be better for her and his son to be here with us.

Angels in My Life

Now, you may recall that in my first spiritual communication with Claricé, when I first asked her why and how she had come through to me in the way she had, she told me, *"the how was through the use of your sixth sense when you cried out that you wished you could, 'speak to me just one more time,' ...and the why was because our good friends Rob and Kelly were going to have a baby."* When seconds later she told me she was in Heaven, and I wasn't sure whether or not I was hallucinating and I facetiously asked her what she does all day. She replied, *"First of all, there is no all day here. It is timeless in the spiritual realm, but what I do is I am teaching and working with new souls who are about to be born."*

The next morning when I called our friend Rob to share my sudden spiritual communication experience with Claricé, he surprised me then, by telling me that the previous Sunday he and his wife Kelly found out that Kelly was pregnant.

With that I naturally assumed Claricé had been talking about Rob and Kelly, in her communication, when she said she was teaching and working with new souls about to be born. Unfortunately, a week or so later Kelly miscarried. Because of the awkward timing of it, my friends and I all thought that perhaps Claricé had been making a prediction that turned out not to be true. This caused us confusion over my first spiritual communication.

We debated this confusion, but Claricé clarified it in her fifth and final communication with me on the night of the 17th of January 2000. She said she had come back again to clarify everything for us. She said was not predicting Kelly's pregnancy in the first communication, but that she had been with them spiritually when the pregnancy test was taken. This was in her role as of our "guardian angel." In that communication she said that if she *had looked ahead,* she would have known of the miscarriage and would not have mentioned it to me in the first place. She apologized for doing so, saying that in her time in the spiritual realm, there was still much for her to learn.

Adding to the confusion that came with her first communication was that Claricé had told me, *"You will live another 20 years and you have much work to do in developing your spirituality."* This also had sounded like a prediction, but again on the 17th Claricé clarified that she wasn't making a prediction about that either.

She said that immediately after crossing over, she had gone to what is known theologically by humankind as "the hall of records" to find out when I would join her in the spiritual realm. She used those words, because in human understanding it was the only way she could explain it to me. There is much in the spiritual realm that there are no known words for in our semantics and use of language. There is no understanding. Faith is required. She told me the hall of records is where every soul's life plan is recorded.

After Erika arrived, Sammy then told me that it was during the first week of January when they found out that Erika was pregnant... about the same time as Claricé's first communication with me. When he told me this, he still didn't know anything specific about Claricé's communications to me. Although she never mentioned Sammy and Erika by name, I now believe this is who she was referring to. Was this a coincidence or synchronicity?

In a later communication from Archie, my dominant angel guide, when he referred back to the difference between prosperity and abundance he said this, leading into his explanation of a synchronicity:

> *"Victor, getting back to abundance for a moment, consider your new 'adopted family' from Cancun, Mexico: Samuel, Erika, their sixteen-year old son Henry, and their infant daughter, Caika Claricé, born on September 9, 2000 and named for your wife, I know they have brought a smile back to your face and joy to your heart. We will get to other examples later, but when a string of coincidences, accidents, or accidental meetings take place, all coming together and directed toward a specific point in time and with meaningful intent, they are spiritual synchronicities.*
>
> *"God does work in mysterious ways. And He is delivering more abundance to you now than you would ever have imagined. When Claricé said in her first communication that she would 'bring you someone to live with and make you happy,' you thought she was going to arrange for a new romantic interest in your life. Instead, surprise... she brought you a whole new family; and with them, came the peace, joy, happiness and abundance that was missing and now has returned to your life.*
>
> *"Do you think it was a coincidence that during the year you were consulting in Cancun restructuring the failing advertising and publishing company that, although you made many friends, Sammy was the only*

good friend both you and Claricé became fond of? Then, too, is it also a coincidence that Erika and Sammy found out that Erika was pregnant the same week Claricé told you in her first communication that she was, 'working with new souls who are about to be born?' Then too, shortly afterward in April at a time when work and conditions in Cancun became difficult for Sammy's family, was it a coincidence that after not speaking to him for over three years he would call you to 'see if there were any job opportunities for him in St. Petersburg?'

"This call came at a time when you were in great mental anguish from grief and you had a home that was empty and very lonely. Sammy didn't know Clarice had passed over to this side. If she had been still with you, she would have been in need of her studio suite, and you would not have had room for the entire family. And lastly, is it just a coincidence that the rooms they are using are those that were Claricé's art studio and sitting room, and shortly after their arrival became the nursery for their daughter Caika Claricé, named in honor of your wife and her given Kamaiura Indian name? When do coincidences become more than a coincidence? Yes Victor, God does work in mysterious ways. He may not always provide financial prosperity, but he does give you the choice and opportunity for abundance when you are open to receive it and ask for His grace and guidance."

In closing out this pattern of synchronicities, there are a few additional thoughts for consideration that may be further validating.

Shortly after Sammy's wife Erika and Henry arrived, my daughter Vicki was visiting. Claricé's large walk-in closet was still filled with all of her clothes. I had asked Vicki to help Erika pack up the clothes so that the family could use the closet. After they had been working and folding clothes for an hour or so, Erika came out of the closet carrying a hanger with a fancy, lace and embroidered white on white dress. She didn't speak English, so she went to where Sammy was and explained to him that the dress she was holding in her hands was the same dress the "lady in white" was wearing in her dream, who told her that Sam should call his friend Victor in St. Petersburg. Another coincidence?

The baby, Caika Claricé was born on September 9th. My oldest daughter Kim was with Erika, assisting her in the birthing room. The entire experience of Sammy's family being with me was a blessing for my entire family, all of whom still missed Claricé deeply. They surely did bring joy back into my home again.

In the first weeks following her birth, Caika was a fussy and colicky baby. Erika would try to quiet the baby... then Sam would try to quiet her and at times, their son Henry would try also. Mostly it was frustrating and to no avail. After this had gone on for a couple of weeks, I thought I might try my hand at quieting little Caika. After all, I had quite a bit of experience in raising my own four kids.

Strangely enough, the first time I took the baby in my arms to help Erika quiet her down, the baby became silent and gazed upon my face. If she had been more than a couple of weeks old, I think it would have looked as if she was studying me. From that point on until the baby got through her colicky times, when Erika or Sam couldn't get her to quiet her down, Erika would give her to me. Every time almost immediately the baby would become still and content again looking up into my face. Erika called it "Victor's magic."

There was another time when the baby was about two months old when I was holding her to comfort her. As I stood slowly rocking her in my arms, I noticed the baby's attention was on Claricé's painting of the *Angel Of The Night,* the same one that is on the cover of this book. I just happened to be standing by the painting, but what caught my eye after a moment or two was that the baby's attention was on the painting. From having raised four children I knew that babies as young as this did not have a very long attention span. But when I was holding her by the painting, Caika's eyes were glued to the picture and they slowly scanned the entire painting up and down, studying it with what I was amazed to feel was a sense of recognition. I got a lump in my throat and a flush of emotion. Another coincidence?

A week following this Erika and the baby went back to Cancun to sell the family car and to clear up their personal affairs. Unfortunately she ran into delays that caused her to stay beyond the date on her visitor's visa. As a result, Sam learned he had to file papers for her to become a legal immigrant in the U.S. After 14 months we finally received notice the approval would be coming soon and they will hopefully be home in a short while.

Now, a final coincidence, event or synchronicity came to us in an email at Christmas time, 2001. Erika was telling us everything she could about little Caika: how much she had grown; that she had teeth and was walking; how playful she was and also said that the baby had developed a strange habit. Erika always keeps a fresh fruit basket with apples on the dining room table, and when she would give one to Caika, the baby would take one bite, set it on the corner of the table, and then would go back to playing. As the day passed, the baby would return, take another bite, set it back on the table and then return to play again... and again. All the while the white of the apple was turning brown. She said that Caika would do this repeatedly throughout the day. The apple would be brown and mushy, but it lasts the baby all day long.

Now I don't want to suggest any more than what is stated in the words but my wife, Claricé, was the only person *I have ever seen do this before*. Whether we were at home or traveling, whenever Claricé would eat an apple, pear or other piece of fruit, she would do the same thing. When traveling she would take one bite out of the fruit and then put the remainder in a napkin and put it in her purse. At home, my kids would tell you that any time you would open the refrigerator there would be an apple or pear, half brown, with one or two bites out of it on a small plate. I had questioned her and teased her about this from the first day we began living together, because I, or anyone I knew in a similar situation might set the fruit aside after a bite or two but then before biting into it again, would take a knife and cut away the discolored part.

Synchronicity or what? I don't know, but I do know that I still have a lot to learn and as time goes by nothing spiritual seems to surprise me any more.

God surely does work in mysterious ways!

Victor K. Hosler

Chapter Twenty-one
My Purpose For Being

One morning I awoke around 4:30 a.m. with thoughts about my purpose in life running through my mind. I knew immediately Archie was with me, because I couldn't drift off to sleep again as I often do when I wake up and go back to sleep several times enjoying the mini-dreams that are quickly forgotten upon waking.

"Good Morning Archie," I said aloud, as I gave in and focused on what was taking place within my mind. "Your wake up call came rather early, and from the various thoughts that have been running through my head, it seems that the real purpose in my future life and activities is about to unfold."

"Yes, Victor I accept now that you have become a believer in the communications you have been receiving and are ready to know their purpose. This came about as you listened to your spiritual friend at the Conversations with God discussion group. As you listened to her, and as she told the group that she believed her newly defined purpose was in spiritual healing, I knew you were questioning the purpose of your experience beyond that of the healing of your grief. You are meant to be going in a different direction than your friend is, and I decided it was time to show you the path you will be on over the coming months... and perhaps years.

"All that you have been doing since your first communication with Claricé in January 2000 has been directed toward this one purpose. And, in reality, it really goes back farther than that. In March of 1999 when we knew Claricé's time was short, she was directed to purchase the Conversations with God books for you. Although you were somewhat reluctant to read them at the time she gave them to you, you did pick up Book One and read it quickly. Months later, when you read it a second time your spiritual journey finally began... both for your remaining years and for this purpose.

"You were so shocked by her final diagnosis and death after you both had believed everything was being done right that you began a crusade to find the answers. When she first discovered the lump in her breast and had the lumpectomy, you both were told and believed she was cancer free, but she wasn't. I don't mean to rehash everything and bring back your pain, but it is somewhat necessary to 'set the stage' to get into your purpose for being.

"Your upset and anger, even toward God, was generated from this side. This was because there is an ongoing crisis and need in your world today to bring more attention to, and focus awareness on breast cancer treatments and survivorship. Breast cancer is a condition, which is treatable and survivable. Unfortunately, it is also a disease that has come about through evolution of mankind in the environment that he has developed and in some cases is somewhat difficult to detect. But it is diagnosable and curable even in its early stages.

"Although Claricé's time on Earth in your worldly plane was according to God's plan for her life, the cause of her demise changed when the need for more breast cancer awareness came about with the inadequate treatment she received and the lack of a proper diagnosis, when the curability of her disease was most likely. This is true with many souls presently residing in the physical form on your earthly plane. The end of one's earthly life is predetermined in God's plan, but God allows also for change when changes are necessary to focus on worldly problems. God can change things at will to bring mankind toward His divine plan when need arises. When planning the life to come with the masters prior to joining the physical vehicle, there is an agreed-upon demise for a soul to leave the earthly plane; however, it can and often will change based upon the needs of your world societies. What factored into this in Claricé's departure was the condition of your medical community today, as evidenced by the inadequate treatment she and others *receive due to the changes that have come about in recent years.*

"A part of the learning process of the world in its own evolution is to learn to heal the illnesses that are brought about by mankind in their growth and development. As stated previously, most illness that create the demise of the physical vehicles in which man's soul resides were and are created by the conditions of the environment man has created himself, often resulting from the abuse of the environment he has created as well as the many forms of self abuse. You must keep in mind that the condition of your world is a co-creation of God <u>and</u> man due to the freedom of choice given by your creator.

"Regarding Claricé's breast cancer, from the time of discovery of the lump, she visited well over a dozen doctors, and medical technicians. All of them missed the signs until you yourself insisted her condition was more serious than the two of you continually were being told. It was then 20 months from her lumpectomy to an accurate diagnosis, and then only 40 days to her death. Under normal circumstances, with a proper diagnosis of this disease, there should be no way that so many medical professionals could <u>misdiagnose</u> a condition such as hers, especially in the last six months when her condition was in a late stage and had become critical. In this period she was referred to eight different doctors and underwent several examinations and tests. Many, many mistakes are being made due to lack of proper diagnostic procedures and — as has been reported in the media — encouraged by medical groups, insurance companies and HMOs. Claricé was put on a path to focus awareness on this major problem in your society. We knew that you would search for answers. It just didn't make sense to you, and was magnified due to your disbelief, anger and logical mind.

"As stated above and earlier, a part of the equation which contributes to cancer and so many

other diseases is the contributing environmental factors. The environment is the connection to Claricé as well as her being an, 'older soul.' She had honest concerns related to the condition of your world as a result of earlier incarnations and those that stemmed from the continual destruction of the rainforests of the world and your world's changing environment. The beauty of her beloved rainforest in Brazil was depicted in of some of her paintings. Claricé was very concerned over your environment. This led her art toward showing the creatures she played with as a child living in a jungle village and the fragile undersea life she later discovered among the threatened coral reefs of the world.

"So Victor, with your disbelief and anger, unknown to you at the time we put you on a mission shortly after she crossed over which began with your quest to find out the big WHY relative to her death and the 'why me' question when the communications began. The first 'why' was because it was in God's plan for her life and the 'why me' is that of your underused communication skills which had been dormant and for the most part untapped since the time the two of you were brought together. Your communication skills are to bring awareness to the world.

"Even before she left you in your anger over what was to come we guided you to contact your lawyers, the act that put you on your mission to begin accumulating her medical records. As you did this you became more and more angry because of the discovered misdiagnosis and ongoing 'Diagnostic Farce,' as noted in the title of a chapter in your earlier LifeClouds manuscript, which gave birth to this particular story. It became so obvious to you, and you quickly realized that if this was happening to your wife, it is happening to a multitude of other women.

"God gave his children the gift of choice. When you accumulated her medical records, you determined rightly so that the two of you were not

given adequate information, which would have afforded you the opportunity to make <u>informed decisions</u> and intelligent choices. You believed as you were continually told by the doctors; for 20 months you believed she did not have cancer.

"Although bringing in lawyers so early was initially from your anger and hurt, from the beginning you wanted to get <u>media attention</u> to focus on breast cancer awareness. Unfortunately, this has been an uphill battle for you and your lawyers, because it is necessary for them to have such a strong case to prove cause to take a case into court. Also unfortunate is that due to the high cost of preparing for this type of legal battle, the law firms generally only want what they believe to be a relatively easy case with a big win. In this, too, we've helped you to persevere. You have had to dig deeply, change lawyers and firms, and prod them onward as you fought your grief. This has become a learning experience for you and knowing the doctors were wrong has been the incentive to keep you on track. It will be interesting to see the end result of this process.

"What I've shown you are all pieces that fit into the puzzle of what <u>your purpose</u> in life has come to and will be. What you are being given is no doubt the most important "marketing project" of your career and life. As I continue, you will see more of the pieces and how they are all destined toward your purpose.

"As you know and it has been clearly stated before, I have been trying to get your attention throughout your life. As has God and many of His other Angels and Spiritual Guides and departed loved ones. It finally took the grief over your devastating loss of Claricé to break through to you. You had to quit "controlling" everything in your life and give it up to God, the Almighty and the Creator of all things known and unknown in His universes.

"When Claricé spiritually spoke to you that first night, although you were in a state of disbelief, it was the power of God coming through to you, and it was

such a unique experience, you finally opened your heart and mind. For months, as you researched the medical records, becoming angrier and angrier, you began to think in terms of some kind of legacy for Claricé, so that the beautiful person she was had not died in vain. You knew there had to be a 'purpose' for such a needless tragedy.

"Think for a moment about the first night she came to you and what she said and also your response and the many coincidences, better-called synchronicities, which have followed. She said you had '20 more years to live and much work to do.' But you said you were 'looking forward to joining her fairly soon and wasn't sure you wanted another 20 years to live,' let alone understand the work she said you would have to do.

"Creating the legacy you want for your wife Claricé is a part of the work she mentioned to you and what we have in store for you. If you continue to let us guide you from this side, you will get your media attention and, in time you will be able to establish a <u>Claricé Carvalho-Hosler Scholarship</u> in her memory and a legacy for perpetuity. The purpose of the foundation would be two-fold; primarily for <u>Art Students</u> in need, either in your hometown of St. Petersburg, or one to be administered by her brother Jorge in Brazil. A second part if possible... and if you will excuse a bit of humor, but Claricé has indicated and you know she would enjoy having a <u>Starving Artist Award</u> named for her, for ecology and environmental themes in local or regional art shows that she participated in. ML said that when the two of you toured the art show circuit, you found that the words 'starving artist' to be a truth rather than a cliché.

"So Victor, if that is not enough to keep you busy for the next 20 years, I'm sure we can find something more for you to do along the same line of thought. Now, you might think that this is a mighty big task for you to accomplish, but with our help and those we are aligning you with, it is not as big an order as you may

think. You already have the ball rolling and we will help keep it going.

"Getting back to your writing was the first step. In LifeClouds, your first manuscript about Claricé and her death, two of your designated readers brought to your attention that there were three different stories being told. We have guided you to begin with <u>this</u> story about your spiritual and angelic communications, and then we will assist you as you proceed in the other directions.

"We know you have dreamed of and visualized writing a best seller for many years. We know it is not an easy thing to do, but hopefully, Victor, you can find the way and if so, it will lead to more than you ever dreamed possible. You might ask, 'couldn't we make it happen?' No, all we can do is guide your writing, and your need to stick with it and persevere. Remember, agents, publishers and your anticipated audience of readers also have freedom of choice. Writing about your belief in the spiritual and angelic communications may well be met with as much doubt as some of those you have talked to about your experiences.

"There are however a lot of opportunities ahead of you. As an example, there is much interest today in spirituality and curiosity about life after death of the physical body. This is the reason we guided you to write this story first.

"Lastly, I want to mention once again, that things don't just happen by accident. There is a purpose to everything in God's plan to bring harmony to the world and universe He created. Before I end my discussion of your work assignment for the next 20 years, I want to mention that, friends of the past, your friends in the present and those yet to come will be there for you to support the work you have to do. The list is endless, but they will become more and more important and meaningful to you as you move ahead and begin to understand how the puzzle will come together. They are all part of your life for a purpose. We have brought them to you, there will be more to

come to assist you in the work you have to do. There are your attending angels including myself, Jules, Miriam, ALI and ML who are with you daily; also, the entities who have crossed over who have contacted you spiritually and other guardian angels who will be there to assist you. Each of them has already been supportive in your cause and instrumental in assisting you toward your goal, as well as aiding you through your grieving. More will surely follow. It is a long path, but with our help and the assistance of your support group, you will achieve the unexpected. Good luck, Victor.

Chapter Twenty-Two
After Death Experiences

Another morning when Archie woke me early as he had been doing off and on I was quite tired and upon realizing he was with me again at 4:30 am, I said, "Good morning, Archie. I wish you guys had to sleep occasionally so you wouldn't keep me awake as much as you have been doing lately. It seems like you only let me get a good night's sleep about every other night. Last night when we chatted about the bumpy road we often travel in life, you agreed that my word 'LIFECLOUDS' was a good metaphor for describing our walk on the planet Earth that God created in his universe. Before I drifted off to sleep you also began chatting about "After Death Experiences" (ADE's) that happen in our dreams and in other ways. You suggested I ask you about it again the next time we talked. So, all right, you have me awake again and I'm asking. What is the meaning of dreams that are ADE's and other similar experiences?"

"Great, I'm glad you remembered to ask me. Now then first, this answer is directed to your daughter Vicki and her mother Jean, your first wife, and your sister Ruth, all who have mentioned to you they have had dreams of departed loved ones. As well, this message is for all others who have had similar experiences and questioned them or wondered about this type of dream and other occurrences.

"After Death Experiences with loved ones and others who have crossed over are real spiritual contacts or connections. Dreams are the most frequent ADE's people have and question most often, yet they are inclined to believe in them. They don't understand them, but for the most part they accept them because they want to believe...that they have had a visit from a loved one. Very often upon awakening they wish the dream would continue and they try to go back to sleep. Or they hope it will continue the next night, and they

will go to sleep with that thought in the forefront of their minds. It sometimes works for them.

"The reason dreams are the most frequent occurring ADE's is because of their clarity. They generally happen just after a person has gone past the initial twilight of sleep but before reaching a deep sleep... or in the morning, just prior to awakening. The early morning dreams are the ones most often remembered, because they are of shorter duration and seem clearer than the normal state of dreaming. Although regular dreams are meaningful, they often are strange, seeming disjointed and nonsensical and are more quickly forgotten.

"Another reason for the ADE's frequency in dreams is that at this level of sleep, a person is most receptive to opening up and letting their loved ones in, or they may let the angels come through or even, on occasion, have direct spiritual communications such as you have been experiencing. Those who do have this direct spiritual contact however, generally dismiss it as a dream. What you called a cacophony of noise often is just the chatter of your angels. If you had kept doubting, your experiences and did not begin making notes to remind you in the morning, you probably would not be writing our dictations at this moment. At that point in the twilight before sleep and the moment before completely waking from the dream-state, the higher conscious, or super conscious as it is called, is open for reception without the blockage of the conscious mind that normally is in control during waking hours. The conscious mind sometimes referred to as the 'ego,' has both positive and negative attributes. It questions, often blocks, and filters out that which it doesn't or can't control. The higher consciousness of the mind is the pure state of mind where "sixth sense" resides and through which God, his angels, spirit guides and souls/spirits of loved ones can make contact.

"Lifelong conditioning of that which is beyond the simple understanding of verbal communications among mankind is what makes spiritual contact so *difficult to accept and comprehend. From mankind's earliest days, societal leaders in almost all religious persuasions have conditioned their followers to believe that only they have the power and ability to contact God, or their Gods. Many leaders have convinced their peoples that 'I am your God.'*

"Mortal beings like yourself have been told and/or convinced by religious or Biblical doctrine that they cannot communicate or have a two-way dialogue with spiritual entities. Parents too often inhibit and discourage their children from talking to their 'invisible' friends by telling them it is their imagination. Because of this pre-conditioning, they develop the idea that they cannot communicate with the 'other side,' as it is called. Therefore generally speaking they do not believe they can, even when in reality it is possible if they listen and truly believe in their ability. After all, loved ones can choose to become guardian angels and many allow for angel communications, so why discount a communication from a loved one by calling it 'an evil spirit masquerading' as your loved one?

"Sounds a little like a word game, doesn't it? Remember what I've said about semantics. Well, communication is a game of words, a game of interpretation, perception, belief and disbelief. The problem is you are playing the game by the rules of your cultural leaders, theological or religious leaders, and parental teaching during your formative years. Therefore, you shut it out. If you were not taught otherwise, you would follow your instincts and you could play the game by your own rules. If you all did this you would find the game to be more fun as well as spiritually enlightening.

"Most mortal beings only believe in prayer... prayer to God, and whomever their personal belief or conception of God is. Mortals 'only hope' their prayers, to their God, will be heard. <u>There is only one God</u>, by whatever 'label' one's teaching or culture happens to use as a designation of His being, power or presence. When God answers them, many believe they

are creating the answers with their own 'wishful thinking' to satisfy the need or wish of their ego-self when in fact they are answers from God or His angels.

"In many cases, especially when their specific prayers are not answered, God's power is then denied because he didn't fulfill their expectation that God answers all prayers. What they fail to realize is that there is a reason for all things and God is fulfilling a prayer request according to His plan for your life in the universe. Your prayer request, wish or intention is not always God's plan or intention. What may be a negative experience for you, in retrospect very well may be that of a positive and necessary learning experience for you or those around you.

"You and all of mankind and the world are here to learn, Victor. As you had to learn how to deal with the death of family members or friends in the past and most recently what you thought to be the insidious loss of your wife. They are learning experiences, not for only yourself, but for those around you who have never experienced the pain or a loss of such magnitude and who are learning from your experience.

"When God does not answer prayer, in less meaningful situations or perhaps in a selfish request they may be making, they brush it off and respond in an 'oh, shucks' manner. They then take the attitude that there _really_ is no God, or that prayer _really_ doesn't work. Denied prayers like your own for Clarice's healing, often lead to a denial or a hatred of God. This is because you do not understand that God's reason for not answering your prayer or His calling a soul back into His arms is a part of His plan for that life and these are lessons to be learned from the experience for those left behind.

"The same reasoning applies to many tragedies of your world, as I have mentioned. Most of your social programs, such as MADD, 'Mother's Against Drunk Drivers, Just Say No,' and others have come about for this reason. For those who experience this type of tragic loss, they justifiably have a lack of understanding when one of their loved ones has been *killed or maimed by a drunk driver. Yet it is still a lesson to be learned by society at large. You must remember that your world is learning as it evolves, and the end result of many tragedies is that those who have experienced the loss become activists for a cause of learning in your world. Through the creation of the MADD organization many lives have been saved. Acute awareness of the problem was brought about by the organization: laws were changed regarding lowering the allowable percentage of alcohol in a driver's system; the age limit for consuming alcohol was raised in many states; and other measures have been taken on a national level in the U.S. In many cases, responsibility has been put on the places where alcohol is consumed and this has made the servers more careful. These have been lessons well learned and it is all a part of God's Divine Plan for your world. Unfortunately for those who suffer the loss, the <u>why me</u> is an endless question which probably will never be understood by any one individual within your earthly consciousness.*

"*Victor, this is one of the bigger reasons that people on your earthly plane of existence need to come to God: for the understanding that will help them continue their personal and spiritual growth. Look in the mirror, Victor. Your reflected image may still show your sadness and loneliness, but within your eyes, there has come an understanding that has brought you to God, to learning and to the purpose in life that Claricé's departure has given you.*

"*It bears repeating that prayers of a more serious nature relative to a perceived, real need or asking God for a cure to one of life's many illnesses or for him to save the life of a loved one often do go unanswered. After experiencing many of these unanswered prayers, disbelief is paramount and a hatred for God and life often follows, as it did for you for a short while. It is difficult for mortal man to understand, but when any situation is a direct part of or result of God's plan for an individual being or the Earth and world he created* in His universe, no amount of prayer or begging will reverse the course.

"There is <u>purpose</u> in all things, even the 'bad things' that may happen to you. Man does have free choice and can change God's plan as it relates <u>to his individual being</u> and within the framework and parameters of God's plan for his life. Overall, God alone is directing the course of the world to reach the balance of love, harmony and peace in the universe and world He created and in a manner, which still allows for the unconditional 'free will' He granted the human race on the planet Earth. It is when man goes outside of the parameters set by God that sin and bad things happen. Very often this is the greed of the ego – lower self of mankind and it can alter the course of His plan for a life when God is forsaken and forgiveness is not asked for.

"This is when God steps in with His angel messengers and guides to create the will of those who experienced loss to develop an organization like MADD or societal structure to counteract the negativity brought forth by those who reach outside of the parameters and structure of God's plan for their lives. If you look back through the eons of time, you will see where He has made corrections in the course of history and has kept mankind on track toward achieving His purpose. Your world is moving toward love, peace and harmony and will continue to do so at a more rapid pace in this the new millennium.

"As I usually do, I've rambled on and gotten off track so to speak in explaining dreams that include ADE's with loved ones. In an ADE dream normally you will experience the visual imagery of those you knew and loved as you knew them in their most perfect human physical form. Dreams of youthful loved ones who have made the transition are your most frequent visitors because their crossing over was so unexpected and so hurtful. The higher consciousness of your minds crave for the contact to ease the emptiness and your aching heart. The same applies to those victims of what you consider mindless tragedies, accidents, *killings and unexpected deaths; again, this includes situations like your loss of Claricé.*

"Other ADE experiences are those similar to what you have experienced and we have talked about previously: your touch experience with Claricé and the dancing candle flames at the church services. Others might be sudden positive thoughts that come to mind or seeing the fleeting image of a lost loved one in your peripheral vision, the thought of a loved one when you see a butterfly...or a dove. There are many ways a loved one will try to get your attention to let you know they are all right. Often they will try any way possible, and if you are open to believe, they will find the way. It may take some time, as it did with you, but when you believe, all things are possible.

"Although there is a purpose to everything, you cannot know the purpose of coming negativity in advance, because you would not understand the reasoning and you would attempt to change the plan for your life. You most certainly would do all you could to avoid such an occurrence. The true purpose and understanding will only come sometime after the fact or upon your own crossover to the spiritual realm. The simple logic of an explanation for this is: <u>everything</u> is a part of God's plan and He doesn't explain His reasons.

"Claricé's breast cancer illness is a perfect example of this. Your complaint was that if you had received the proper diagnosis and all the information available early on when her lump was first discovered, you would have taken a different course of action and perhaps she would have been cured. However, because it was her time to leave according to God's plan for both of your lives, she still would not have been cured. In your research into her health records and getting expert opinions, one forensic pathologist told you that, '...in my opinion, there was a 95% chance Claricé would have died regardless of what had been done to try and extend her life.' It wasn't meant to be.

"If you had foreknowledge or had looked at the medical information you later received, the two of you would have tried any method of treatment available to you: you would have tried chemotherapy, radiation, a major mastectomy and perhaps breast reconstruction. And in God's plan for her life, her leaving would have come about regardless of what was done.

"As it turned out, your wife had a good quality of life up until the last two months of her illness. You were able to enjoy each other almost until the end. How would it have been if you had fought a futile battle and still lost her? It would have been even more devastating. Sometimes, Victor, mistakes are a silent blessing; you and others must realize this. It was only through your acceptance of spiritual and angel communications that you were able to come to this understanding. Without it, you would still be hating and denying God.

"The 'ripple effect,' to use an earthly an term, would come into being if a change could be made: if it were possible to change a God-created event, it would certainly alter the course of your destiny, the future, and God's plan for your life and His world. This cannot be!

"As Claricé told you, this is one reason why your angels or spiritual communications cannot and will not give you personal information that would specifically foretell your future. To do so could affect the course of humanity in the world. It would change the pre-planned God-created synchronicities of your life — those things that appear to be but are never accidents, both in the things you do and the people you meet. Predicting the future is only possible in what might be called non-events. These are things that are already within the parameters of God's plan for your life and even if changed, would be a non-event.

"For a spiritualist to tell you that you are going to meet a 'tall, slender, beautiful, stranger with big blue eyes' is what would be called a non-event. Remember, beauty is in the eyes of the beholder. Victor, as you have proceeded through life, you have met many of *such a description, and you will again. That you might find the right chemistry and 'fall in love' again is a part of God's plan for your life. God wants you to be with those to whom you might develop a close bond with and soul mates are always crossing your pathway.*

"Angels, spirit guides and others cannot predict anything that would or could change the outcome of God's plans. This happens to be a problem with some of the messages from false psychics, fortune tellers and charlatans, those who are driven by greed and have learned all of the trickery available in the magical field of deception. They feed off lonely, troubled souls who are trying to find 'easy answers' to overcome their life's sad experiences. They will prey upon those unfortunates who believe that they have mystical powers that can help them overcome their misery or can lead them to untold riches. And they take advantage of the grief of heartbroken souls who are looking for any kind of contact or communications with loved ones who have crossed over.

"As much as I dislike giving credit to those who do feed their riches from troubled souls or those of many needs, I have to say that right or wrong, some do fulfill an emotional need. It is not my place to judge their value in the universe. God has a plan for their lives also, and when they stay within the parameters of God's plan, they too are fulfilling His purpose for their being. Many of you on the earthly plane need to believe and to have some sense of knowing that a departed loved one is okay, and these troubled souls need to have hope for the future, which they may receive.

"I will say, however, that none of you need to use the services of a spiritualist, intuitive or psychic, if you would only take the time and effort for learning how to get in touch with the higher power within <u>your own higher self</u>. If everyone would take the time to learn, all of you would have the capability of being able to get your own answers without seeking the assistance of others. After two years of communications, Victor, you have found this to be true. It didn't happen overnight.

You faced doubt for several months, and it wasn't until I finally got through to you that you truly believed. The trouble is that most beings on your planet Earth are always looking for the fast and easy way. Timelessness on the spiritual plane does have its advantages. We are not 'rushed' over here.

"Your people have created such a fast-paced environment on your planet that you don't have enough time, in earthly hours, to give to and satisfy your basic and personal needs. Victor, you see people every day who are 'caught up in the treadmill lifestyle' and are so busy they cannot even find their true selves. It doesn't matter if it is a need to exercise for the better caring of your earthly vehicle bodies, which you, Victor are very guilty of, or eating properly balanced diets, or whatever it takes for self-improvement. It is a vicious cycle many cannot get away from.

"Getting in touch with your spirituality is no different than exercising to maintain a good cardiovascular system for the engine that keeps your physical body running. It takes time! You must find time for yourselves, and this is a large part of your purpose in writing this manuscript. It is not necessary for everyone to spend hours and hours with their spiritual and angel guides as you have had to do to reach this stage of your writing. For you, this has become your purpose. For all others, to satisfy their spiritual needs, it only takes the time required to look inside themselves, to determine what their real needs are and to learn to listen to the voice of the higher self within and to question the voice of the ego.

"It depends completely on what each of you really wants from your remaining years on the planet Earth in your earthly bodies. Once again, like exercise, those who want to 'look good' and others who are determined to remain healthy and stay within God's plan for their lives will do what ever is necessary to accomplish their goals. The most you need to do is to be able to slow down long enough to look within: a simple schedule of quiet meditation may be enough for some. For others, who may want to get in touch with

their angelic and spiritual guides, it may take a while longer and more practice and determination. Once again, determination - - as you were those first four nights when you cried aloud in the night to let me know you were ready to listen. You didn't give up. Through your research and reading you came to believe angel communications were probable. Many resist out of their theological understanding and teaching. But there is plenty of middle ground within the realm of one's own religious and/or theological persuasion and within the bounds of logical reality for one who wants to move into the understanding of their spirituality within their higher self.

"*To repeat an explanation of the process, I want to tell you, if you are willing to breath deeply to relax in meditation or to just let your mind look within for a few quiet moments, pray, listen and trust your inner knowing; accept and believe what comes through to you. <u>It will happen</u>. The necessary factor for remembering however is to make a note of it. The communications you may receive whether they are those of an ADE or some other spiritual or angelic format will occur in your dreams, in a meditation or in the twilight moments just before sleep or immediately upon awakening, and they will soon dissipate. Like dreams, you must make a record of what you experience and in some way write down a couple of words that will trigger a later recall of the event, or they will be quickly forgotten. Spiritual communications come through as perceived voices, in mental impressions or vibrations of a telepathic nature and occur within your higher level of consciousness, where the God within resides.*

"*For you, Victor, the earlier spiritual communications although silent were still in recognizable voices and speech patterns as they came to you. Later, when I came through as well as your other angels, they are silent voices in the night. Like the voice of God, there is nothing, which is recognizable in an auditory way of remembering, but you do hear a silent voice in words, thoughts and ideas. You, too, quickly found you forgot. You forgot all but the essence of the communication until you began to write it down on the note pads or when you were guided to go directly to the computer and we began dictating to you.*

*"But the most critical element is that you have to <u>believe</u> in God and that communicating with him, his angels or other spiritual entities truly can occur. Because yourself, we in the spiritual realm, and all creations of God's universe **<u>exist</u>** — it is within your consciousness — and therefore, 'if you will believe, anything is possible,' as it is stated in the Bible. I ask you then, why should it not be? The one fact alone in accepting that <u>you are</u>: accepting that you are a living, breathing, thinking, feeling, tasting, smelling, and seeing spark of life or being should be all the proof you need.*

"Unfortunately, some religious leaders and false prophets have cast a negative energy, connotation and disbelief in situations such as the one you are now experiencing in communicating with me today, yesterday and all of your tomorrows. There is an ominous cloud of doubt connected with any earthly being that remotely suggests he or she has the ability to communicate with spiritual entities. You have a difficult road of disbelief ahead and you have only begun to experience the negativity you will face in the future. You must be strong, tolerant and understanding. Those who have not had your experience will continue to listen with a doubtful mind. You yourself did this in the past and even today you still have a shadow of doubt in yourself and questions in your mind about what are called 'psychic experiences,' such as those you have witnessed in person, seen in the television media or that you have read about or have heard of.

"What a person does not experience for him or herself is difficult to understand and accept the reality of. When an earthling child first puts his finger into a flame, it quickly learns it will burn. Anything other than direct experience of one's self, immediately will

lead to questionability. Through science, mankind has developed a need for empirical evidence to prove something can be. Although recent studies on your planet have shown that measuring brain waves proves that something unusual is taking place, there is no way to prove 'beyond a shadow of a doubt' that communicating with the spiritual realm can take place. Faith and belief in powers of God in the universe He created is all you have to rely on. For those like yourself the proof has come from the words you write, such as these that are outside the scope of your past communication experiences.

"One last thing about ADE's is the dreams that include those who are still in their physical form. Often they appear in the company a loved one who has crossed over, or are dreams in which a 'goodbye' message is received from a loved one who resided in a different geographic location than your own. The latter example is exactly what it implies: it is a goodbye from a loved one you are not in daily contact with or perhaps from a soul mate you have not heard from in a long while. It is a simple goodbye and their purpose is generally only that they want you to know they are crossing over and that they are all right.

"When an ADE dream includes those who are still in their physical bodies, it is an example of what earthlings have called 'astral projection.' In the higher or super conscious state of mind, a loved one who has crossed over can create an 'out of body' experience and take you on a journey. Many have experienced these ADE dreams that after they awake, they remember having gone to a 'place' they have never been to before or have never experienced in their consciousness. When this happens, your loved one is just taking your soul on a journey to be with you once again and sometimes to share their experience of the 'other side' with you.

"Other times, an ADE may have the specific purpose of showing you that other loved ones have accepted their crossover and they are all right with

where they have gone and to present you with a broader understanding of the afterlife.

"What more can I tell you? ADE's happen in various forms from direct communications like the ones you have had with Claricé and the others, in visual imagery across the room of many kinds, and in full form as who they were. They may be in wispy colors, partial imagery, a cool breeze of air where it should not be, things being moved in a room. It can be a slight feeling like the touch of a feather and much, much more. Spiritual entities are always trying to find a way for you to understand that they have contacted you and that they are very content in their new state of being. They miss you and are waiting for you in the timelessness of the spiritual plane called heaven that is a part of God's universe.

Chapter Twenty-Three
Archie's Answers To Friend's Questions

Soon after I began communicating with the other side, friends who did have belief in the spiritual realm began to ask me to ask questions: ask Archie this or ask Archie that, they said. Because I still had my own doubts and was not sure I wanted the responsibility of screwing with someone else's mind or life, I quickly determined I didn't want to become a medium. With no psychological training and little personal understanding, I didn't think it was my place to tell them that the angels said this or that. I knew I didn't have enough experience or belief that what I was receiving was the truth. The spiritual communications I did share with others were met with doubt by some and even said to be the work of the devil or evil spirits. Although communicating with angels might be Biblically acceptable, I just didn't feel it was right for me to be a middleman, and I said as much to those who asked.

However what I quickly found is that the angels are listening all of the time and as soon as my mind would quiet down after I had been asked a question, Archie would begin to put in his two-cents worth. Following is just a couple of examples that, because there was nothing of a negative consequence, I did pass along. But I still have no intention to become a medium because I do not want the responsibility.

- - - - -

One Example

Shirley, my good friend of almost forty years in Miami, Florida is the one who loaned me the first book on angelic communications. She has edited my writing in the past and, as much as anyone, is responsible for me developing and following my passion for writing. I phoned her and talked to her just before I went to bed the day I completed my first session of transcribing Archie's communication in late August 2000. At the time, she was reading and editing an early draft of the "LifeClouds" manuscript that I had begun in April. I wanted to know how she was doing on the edit, and because we have been so close throughout the years, I wanted to share my new experience with her. She was not doing well on the edit, she told me, because she was bogged down in her own work and projects. She became excited about my new angel communications and after hearing about Archie she said she wanted me to ask him what she should do about her heavy work schedule.

Shirley is a professional Coach; meaning she helps people achieve the goals they set in their lives. She knew she was "spreading herself out too much" and perhaps wasn't being fair to herself or her clients. She wanted me to ask him about it. I was quick to tell her I wasn't interested in becoming a medium, but she said she still wanted me to ask him the next time I spoke with him. I believe I said I would think about it because she had always been so supportive of my personal endeavors.

I want to point out, that throughout this manuscript, much of the information I initially receive comes in bits and pieces, as in Chapter 18. Throughout most of the communications I have received, they seem to happen two or more times and flow in a logical manner only when I am at the computer and in an auto-writing mode. This accounts for some of the redundancy. Generally when Archie repeats something, it is because it is pertinent at that particular moment and relative to the discussion that is taking place. Once again, the communications go on sometime during the night, either when I have first gone to bed and I am in the twilight state, or when he wakes me during the night or in a meditation session. Archie usually does this, sometime between 2:30 and 4:30 a.m. with the sessions lasting from a few minutes to a couple of hours. By morning, I am generally left with only the essence of what took place and the questions to ask him. Like a dream, the details are forgotten. But when I sit at the computer the information begins to flow into my mind and out through my fingers with no preconceived thought or active mental reconstruction of the previous night's experience. Often when I stop in mid sentence one of my hands will begin to shake, like someone with Parkinson's disease until my fingers return to the keyboard to continue. Very often, as soon as I have totally relaxed after going to bed, I sense his presence with the fragments of sentences and words that come into my mind as they did prior to his first communication with me. That is the way it was when I went to bed the night after I spoke to Shirley on the telephone. Hearing the fragments of words and thoughts I knew Archie was with me, so I began.:

"Good evening, Archie. Are you with me this evening?"

"Yes Victor, I have been waiting for you to begin. We have a lot of ground to cover. A lot of questions were coming to your mind when you tried to rest last night.

"Yes, I was thinking about Shirley's question just before she hung up the phone… but you began talking to me before I even thought of questions to ask. I was hesitating because I don't want to be a medium. I don't want that kind of personal responsibility.

"Also I was thinking about 'prosperity vs. abundance,' another question that is lingering from the night."

"First things first. You are still just learning to accept that you can communicate with your angels. Don't worry about whether or not you are or can be a medium… and don't worry about whether or not you will choose to function in this way. You are still in a state of disbelief. That is why I picked the Shirley communication to work with. Belief is the key word right now. Ask. Listen. And Believe.

"Shirley's final question had to do with her worrying about the decisions she's struggling with regarding her present work situation. Do you see the clue?

"I think so, but I'm not sure I understand. Why don't you explain it to me so I can get a better handle on everything? It's still moving pretty fast for me.

"Yes, I do think you see it. Before I spoke to you about her worries over her responsibilities relating to her clients, you didn't even know she was thinking about changing the direction of her business. Did you? No, of course not.

"First let's go over what we talked about relative to her question. I said she was worried over the responsibility she felt toward her effect on her client's courses of action being taken to reach the goals that she is coaching them on and working toward. I think she agreed that it was 'partly true' but she said there was more to it than that.

"I'm glad she sees it as that and that she accepts what is on the surface of her consciousness. But it

does go a little deeper than that. I think she tries to pretend that the responsibility does not worry her. The reason for this is because her success is a validation of who she really is and she worries about it, even though she doesn't like to admit it.

"Shirley is a facilitator. It is a part of who she is and she gives herself fully to whomever she is assisting and into whatever she does. Victor, you may have been one of her early coaching assignments. Do you think you would ever have completed the 'Love-40' manuscript without her? And if you had not developed your writing skills by writing and re-writing that story over and over, you probably wouldn't be in the middle of the writing projects you now have underway and yet to do. It is all a part of His plan, God's plan for your life.

"Shirley is a classic example of being her own person, and she marches to her own tune. She is also... wait... Yes... what I was looking for is that Shirley has been, and remains her best client. She has coached herself every step of the way. She has had many goals in her life and did not reach them all. However, more important is that she did reach many of them and when some of the goals did not meet her expectations, she was able to make course corrections along the way, steering herself to where she is at this moment in time, and I believe she is truly satisfied with what she has accomplished and her contributions to her fellow man.

"Life is not easy; it's about making choices that will satisfy your basic desires. That is to be happy within your self. As I said last night, at different times along the way, she could have chose a traditional family life style, but this was not what she chose for herself when her life was planned in the beginning. She could not have become the facilitator she is with all that a family life entails. Her life is to help others... all others, even her family of loving animals. You Victor also know the work she has done over the years in the juvenile justice program. Facilitating those who *don't want the facilitation is an admirable and difficult task.*

"Getting to Shirley's question about the planned changes in her business is a 'no brain answer'. You know, not being able to see the forest for the trees! If one of her client's was asked by a friend if they knew someone who could coach them toward achieving their goal, they would probably refer them to Shirley. Right?

"So, Shirley, must trust in herself as others trust in her is the answer to her question. She should set the new goal, and then analyze it to see if it will give her what she thinks she wants and to see if it will serve her objectives. She must do this in the same way she would work with and serve her clients. She trusts her instincts when she is working with clients, so she must trust them for herself now also.

"Let me refer once again that one must think in terms of 'abundance' rather than 'prosperity'. Abundance brings joy into your life and heart. Abundance is earning or having enough money to serve your basic needs and purposes, but it also includes having time to serve both your personal enjoyment and physical pleasure. When Shirley is taking care of the lost pets of the world, it is a 'pro-bono' gift she gives to the animal kingdom. And it brings her happiness.

"All of mankind should <u>make more time</u> for happiness and choose that which will increase the abundance in your life. Too many people focus on prosperity, and all that does is give you purchasing power. Primal and intermittent pleasure may be for sale, but you can't buy happiness or abundance.

"Unfortunately in the busy lives you all have today, friendships have to be cultivated more than was ever needed in the past. Personal friendships contribute to the abundance in your life. As all should do, Shirley should arrange her priorities so that Shirley comes first. I'll close by twisting biblical phrase (the lower case "b" is intentional)...Do Unto Yourself... AS You Do Unto Others. Be kind to yourself and you can be

kind to others. When you love yourself, you can love others.

"Shirley is a very learned soul who has given much over many, many years and yet she still has much to give. My information for her comes from Rudy, who is one of her walk-in angel guides, and who is assisted by seven other angels who help her to fulfill the many different needs in her daily endeavors.

"Victor, thank Shirley for asking the question and for believing in the work you have been given. I know the answer to her question will also assist you in the work you have to do. May the Love of God comfort you, encourage your expectations and bring you peace."

A Second Example

Another good friend named Cathy, upon learning of my new experiences sent me an email with questions about dealing with 'fear'. I sent her a note back explaining that I didn't want to be a middleman in my communications. Later that evening, before I went to sleep, without my asking for him, Archie began to ramble on with answers regarding her question, and told me to go to the computer in the morning and ask him again about it and I could pass it along if I felt it was appropriate. Reluctantly, I did as I was instructed to do by him.

"Good morning Archie." I began. It had been awhile since I had been with him at the computer and his reply initially had a touch of sarcasm in it.

"Well good morning yourself, Victor.

"It's been a couple of weeks since you've taken the time to sit at your computer and take down my answers to your questions about life on your planet Earth that God created for you and your fellow man to work through your spiritual problems. I know you have been busy with your manuscript, and I have quietly been helping you through your dilemma in dealing with the sharp, but necessary, criticism you have received in talking to people about your recent

experiences. You will find though that criticism can be beneficial to the path you are now on, because it makes you take a second look at that which you are receiving.

"Today, however, I know you want to get some clarity and understanding relating to FEAR as your good friend Cathy mentioned yesterday in an email communication to you. I will deal with that question the best I can, but I suggest you go back to some of my earlier discussions with you and include them when you pass this information along to her. I am sure it will give her a clearer understanding, added to what I will say to you now. First, let's look at what she said and asked of me."

"Yes, in her email Cathy asked, 'What does Archie say about the reasons for the crazies in the Far East being on this planet with their greed and quest for power?' She said, 'I tend to believe it's due to one BIG reason and that being the one of FEAR. They have fear, fear of their neighbor taking control of what they have or own, fear of losing control, fear of not having enough for themselves when they may already have more than they need, (which I guess could also be construed as greed). Fear... Fear... Fear...' She said, 'I think it's one of the most horrendous of emotions that God did NOT create, but that mankind him/herself invented. Once we can rid ourselves of fear and instead merely become <u>aware</u>, then and only then I feel can we learn the one and only lesson that God has bestowed upon us to learn in our lifetimes, that of <u>loving unconditionally</u>. And not just between a man and a woman, but among all. That is the key to true bliss. Ask Archie if he would or would not agree with me.'"

" Victor, please have her read the earlier discussion on 'greed and power' and also on the problem with 'semantics' throughout the development of humankind. What she says about 'fear of not having enough' is quite true as it relates to those who are the greedy power seekers, and that which feeds their drive for more and more, but it is also true of those with lack, who may wonder where their next meal may

come from in your world of abundance. And in a more benevolent way, it is also an emotion that relates to survival for those beneath the control of those 'crazies,' as she stated.

"Where semantics comes in to play is in the many definitions and meanings of the word FEAR as understood by mankind. FEAR is only a word created by mankind to describe an emotion and is used in various contexts in all worldly languages. She is right God did not create FEAR the word, and certainly is not pleased with the application as she referenced it. Like many words created by man, FEAR is an overused word and often used badly.

"However the word FEAR and all of its synonyms describe an emotion God did create within man as one element of his survival instinct. Unfortunately, it is often used inappropriately. This was clearly pointed out in a story the two of you read about the Dead Sea Scrolls. The story indicated that a mistranslation had taken place by the early theological scholars. It said that the original writings that referred to 'reverence or fear of God,' in the new studies, now show it should have been translated to 'love of God.'

"The <u>emotion,</u> whether you label it FEAR, fright, horror, trepidation or something else, is a personal control mechanism. This is something the Spirit within uses to control the conscious mind or ego of humankind. Take a few simple examples: the little boy who thinks he can be Superman and jumps off a roof. To the boy's despair and pain, he should have listened to the 'fear' warning of the inner-mind that certainly was there. Most beings do listen to this warning and are rightly afraid. The FEAR of getting hurt does play an important role in protecting the physical vehicle in which your soul temporarily resides. Beside the laws of mankind, what keeps people from driving too fast in their motor vehicles? Once a certain speed is attained or suddenly surpassed, FEAR takes over and slows them back down to what they consider to be reasonable.

"Consider your own fears, Victor, when you initially considered the possibility of finding a new mate. Your first thought about this was <u>the fear</u> of loving and losing another partner in your life. Why? Because you didn't want to experience and have to go through the extreme pain you experienced with Claricé's passing over. And at the same time, assuming you would cross over first, you did not want to put the possibility of that kind of pain on a new partner who might be younger than you. Remember, we went over that at the time. When I talked to you about it, I reminded you of earlier times in your life when you recognized this same kind of FEAR in lady friends you dated, who had been hurt so deeply in a past relationship, they would not allow themselves to love again or to be hurt again.

"This reminder changed your attitude. You then realized that if you maintained this type of fear — because of your earlier failed relationships during what I jokingly call your fifteen-year mid-life crisis — you would have missed the beauty of the ten wonderful years you had with your wife Claricé. Also I pointed out very clearly to you that throughout eternity, you have had and will have many soul mates, and that you will find love again.

"Although you and Claricé will be together again, so also will you be with other soul mates that you have had in other lifetimes on the earthly plain and during this current period in your physical vehicle named Victor. In the spiritual realm, you will only experience love. Emotions of jealousy, hatred and other emotions that 'run' your physical vehicles is absent in the spiritual realm. Remember, I told you that your time on the earthly plain is but the snap of the fingers or a blink of an eye in the eternal life of your soul. Whether you have one year, the ten years you had with Claricé or sixty-two years together as your friend Bill and his wife have had or even longer together, it is wonderful.

*"When it **is unconditional love** as mentioned by your friend Cathy, it is a beautiful experience that you should never hesitate to share, because love as well as*

peace, harmony and abundance is what God wants for the world, the Earth, the land of learning he created in His universe. Never FEAR LOVE. Love is to be cherished.

"I believe this will answer Cathy's question, but unfortunately it will not solve the problems in the mideast or 'the crazies' around your world until meaningful communication brings about an understanding that all neighbors can live and love together. Remember, God realizes there will never be a 'perfect world' and this is a part of His plan. He only wants harmony and a place for the souls of mankind to learn their spiritual lessons in life, which will bring them to the God-like state and perfection for your eternal life with God as chosen Angels to carry on God's work in the universes he has created."

Chapter Twenty-Four
Healing and a Return to Joy

"Good morning, Victor. You had a busy and fruitful day yesterday, didn't you? This last few weeks, it has been nice to see the happy-go-lucky Victor back again... the way you were during your life with Claricé."

"Yes, it was a good day Archie... and I am happy to feel truly alive again."

- - - - -

Yes, Archie was back again. It was a Monday afternoon. Archie had awakened me just before 8:30 in the morning to clarify a discussion I'd had the day before with my good friends Rob and Kelly.

Along the way of and during my spiritual experiences over the past couple of years, I have talked on a regular basis about them with my friend Rob, but not with Kelly. Rob, a born again Christian and I have had some interesting discussions, because of our differences in beliefs. With Kelly however, I've been reluctant to speak much about it because of her earlier questioning regarding whether or not Claricé was making a prediction in her first visitation with me when she told me that, "Rob and Kelly are going to have a baby." Then later after Kelly's subsequent miscarriage, I chose not to discuss with her what was happening to me. I knew she didn't fully understand it and that she had to go through her own grieving and healing process.

Yesterday, Sunday, was a nice day. It began with services at the First Unity Church I now attend and lunch afterward with my daughter and son-in-law, Kim and Mark. The day before Kim had invited me to go to the movies with her after lunch, so we went to see the movie *Dragonfly,* with Kevin Costner. Kim earlier had seen the preview on television. The movie was about a husband whose wife had been killed in an accident and was spiritually trying to contact him. She thought I would enjoy a movie that, although different in context, was experientially similar to my own. I thought the film was excellent. When Kevin Costner was hearing his name called out, beckoning him in his wife's voice, and then later when he saw her in a wispy vision, for me it was almost a déjà-vu experience.

After the movie I went over to visit my friends Rob and Kelly and spent the evening with them. We had an enjoyable visit and we talked about several aspects of my recent experiences and even laughed about some differences in our belief systems. Both of them recognized that I was once again in a very good frame of mind. I told them that I attributed how much better I was feeling to having been in therapy for several months and how it had been better working things through with a therapist than trying to talk it out with family. Whenever I would speak of Claricé with our kids or very close friends, I had difficulty controlling my emotions. I told Kelly I didn't think most of the family or our close friends truly understood my grief, and that I think one really has to have experienced grief of losing a very close loved one, themselves to truly understand how painful and traumatic it can be. Although it was quite some time ago, Kelly had always expressed more understanding than others, because she had lost her mother as a young teenager and she acknowledged that Claricé had become somewhat of a mother figure to her and they had been very close.

Regarding my grief and hearing of my enthusiasm about the angels and my therapy sessions, Kelly asked me, "What about the angels? Why did you have to go into therapy, if the angels were helping you so much?" And then, "Wasn't it the therapy that helped you, rather than the angels?" Her questions expressed her doubt.

Her willingness to discuss the subject surprised me, and I struggled to find the proper words to answer her. Where the therapy fit into my healing process, I had not thought through before. Instead, I alluded back to the first visit from Archie, described in Chapter Nine, where I wrote about how the angels *"took my pain away."* I told her I believed I had been doing well in moving through my grief with my writing and communicating with the angels, all of which I thought had been cathartic. I knew I was improving daily, but somehow around the time of the tragic 9/11 event I slipped into another bout of deep depression.

I thought it had been going well for me until the terrorist incidents and the aftermath. With so much reporting in the media of death and devastation, it brought my painful loss back to the surface. It was immediately afterward that I fell into a profound depression. I didn't quite understand how or why the 9/11 event triggered it, but I quickly lost all incentive, meaning and purpose in my life again. For weeks I spent my days emotionally upset, staying in bed for hours on end, crying over my thoughts, sleeping and watching mundane daytime television that I wasn't even able to focus upon.

Although I lacked awareness at the moment, I was sure the angels took control on the night I took my newly purchased prescription bottle of Valium into my hand, stared at it, and wondered, "How many will it take?"

My silent question, I'm sure was answered by the angels. The answer wasn't what I had asked for, but it was the right answer. Almost immediately I was guided to pick up the telephone directory and to call the local Crisis Hot Line. Before that moment, in my worst state of depression during the first Holiday season following Claricé's passing and just prior to her first spiritual visit with me, I had thought about taking my own life, but I had never reached the point where I took the first step or gotten as close as I was at that moment.

The counselor who answered the crisis hotline talked to me about the reasons for my depression, my family relationships and pointed out to me the many things I still had to live for and how much it would disrupt and bring tragedy and grief to my entire family. "Do you really want that to be your legacy to those you leave behind?" he asked. He then asked questions about my kids and grandchildren and talked to me until he felt certain I was okay and he was convinced I would make an appointment with a therapist for my condition to be evaluated. At an early point in his counseling me on the telephone, he used the word *"choice."* That word triggered a response in me and reminded me of what I had been learning from the angels over the past couple years and had been reminding others about. I thought about my good friend Marti and the words I had spoken to him to encourage him to think positive, even when the outlook was bleak.

The "choice" was mine I realized. I recalled what Claricé had said in her first visit when she told me I had, "*20 more years to live and much work to do.*" I had replied to her, "No, I don't think I want to live another 20 years." And then, "I was hoping to join you soon." As the counselor was talking I had a mental flashback to the visual imagery that had come with her words. There was a smile on her face and I could hear it in her voice. With that thought as the counselor spoke I knew Claricé would not want me to change the plan she said God had for my life.

Interestingly enough, however, I remembered that she also said, "That is only the plan." And then she explained that if I chose to do something destructive in my life, I could *change the plan.* When I told her about wanting to join her soon she gave another example, such as drinking and driving and perhaps having an accident that could kill me... and change the plan. I knew she was only using that as an example, because I very seldom drank anything other than a glass of wine or an occasional Rusty Nail, my favorite sipping drink.

When my treatment with my therapist Linda, began several months earlier, she was quite concerned over my well being and the depth of my depression. She strongly urged me to become more active in my daily life. She said that it was critical for me to do something positive in my waking hours to get my mind off the negativity related to my wife's passing over and my grief relative to the *absence of her physical presence* in my life (my words). She encouraged me to check out the newspapers for availability of activities taking place in town that I might be interested in and to begin exercising. She suggested that walking would be good for me and, although I try to maintain some semblance of a schedule for doing so, I am inherently lazy when it comes to exercise and it is still something I often *conveniently* forget.

As I entered this state of depression, I wasn't doing anything. I had stopped writing and wasn't even communicating with Archie and his friends or going to the movies. Although the movies had always been a favorite weekend pastime of mine, as well as for Claricé and I throughout our time together, I disliked going alone and instead avoided them.

In the first couple visits with Linda, I thought I might have to change therapists. I quickly found she had a fundamentalist Christian background. Like some of my family members and others, with a similar spiritual belief system, I expected her to react negatively as some of the others had done, when I first began to speak of my new-found spiritual experiences.

I was quite surprised how non-judgmental Linda was upon hearing about the spiritual and angel communications I'd been having. At that time they had been going on for almost two years and I thought she might relate to them as a reason for my depression and/or my *almost losing it*. She didn't. She listened with compassion and understanding. I believe when she evaluated what was going on with me, she determined my spiritual experiences were not of an immediate relevance or a major part of the problems I was having.

Initially just being able to share my experiences with someone who really listened without judgment or disbelief relieved the pressure that had been building within. I began exercising by walking around the small lake in back of my home on a semi-regular basis, took in a couple of movies and returned to the Conversations with

God discussion group that I had earlier quit attending. Little else beyond my church and family was of interest to me. I checked the papers, but like the movies, I don't like to go to museums or other similar activities alone.

Along with this, Linda had said I would have to look for a way to make conscious decisions to do something new and different. She said I had to break the *"depression cycle"* (Again these are my words based upon my understanding of her guidance.).

In thinking this through during the period I was still having difficulty functioning, the most recent *Nike Company* advertising slogan came to my mind. It was, *"Do It!"* I began thinking these words, and they became a trigger in my mind any time I found myself back on the *pity pot*. When I would lie in the bed some mornings and not want to get up and face the world, I would focus on something I needed or wanted to do. With the awareness that Linda said I had to "do something" to heal, I would say the words aloud, *"Do It!"* And then I would consciously *force myself* to act upon the words and do something... anything but stay in bed and grieve. Soon improvements in my life began to occur.

After about two or three weeks of therapy, I had an unexpected setback. My lawyer's office called and told me that I was scheduled for a sworn statement by opposing counsel in the negligence lawsuit I had begun prior even to Claricé's death. It had bounced around to different legal firms until it now had become a reality. In five or six weeks I would have to relive the details, answering questions step by step and why I believed there was negligence from the beginning of her illness to learning her condition was terminal and facing her unexpected death.

As the date with the lawyers approached, I forced myself to review her medical records and write another detailed time-line with every questionable treatment and the referrals to a dozen or more physicians. It all came back to haunt me. As I recalled each and every appointment and every detail I remembered more and more. This point-by-point recall became like a tape recorder. It played over and over again in my mind. It played in my quiet moments of the day as well as in the silence of the nighttime — every night for several months.

When the meeting with the lawyers approached, at Linda's suggestion I asked my daughter Kim go with me for moral support. I thought it would be upsetting and was surprised that I handled their questions without problems. Kim cried off and on throughout the session, but I believe I got some sense of relief from just being able to tell our side of the story. The relief was momentary however. The "tape" never stopped playing in my head.

Even still I thought I was on a healing path. A few weeks after entering therapy, one of the things I did to stay active was that I went back writing this manuscript. At first I thought getting back to it might upset me, but instead as soon as I began I found it cathartic once again. And the angels were still with me. As soon as I started thinking about writing, Archie was answering my questions and I was back in an auto-writing mode. I still didn't fully understand it all, but as long as I felt good doing it I stayed with it and continued chatting with the angels and keeping my therapy visits with Linda.

Now, Linda is a very lovely lady. She is beautiful and kind and has the personality of a lady I would like to have in my life again. Early on in our professional relationship, I began to tease her about my attraction toward her. Although it may not have been the right thing to do, I found it served two purposes for me. First in the beginning when the therapy sessions were very emotional, it lightened the mood and covered my awkwardness at crying in front of a lady who was still a stranger to me. My joking about being attracted to her would add a touch of humor and take my mind off my upset. Secondly, it gave me a sense of clarity that perhaps I might be ready to have a new relationship in my life, and we did talk about the possibilities of a new lady a few times.

Linda showed a little concern over what is called "transference." That happens sometimes when a patient falls in love with the doctor or therapist due to the intimacy of their relationship. I had to assure her that although I was very much attracted to her, my head was on straight and I had a good sense of reality and was aware that she was a bit too young for me. At the same time in reaching clarity of purpose I was able to discuss with her my thinking that I believed the strong, close, loving bond I had with Claricé would enhance my next relationship. I don't believe that one love necessarily overshadows another, but that the love and learning experiences gained in one relationship can be beneficial to another.

As the weeks turned into months I was able to push the legal matters to the back of my mind, but the "tape" continued to play. It seemed like the tape had been playing every night since Claricé's passing over. In the still of the night, it was like a sad song that often comes to mind and a melody that never ends, one where you keep humming it over and over and over until it almost drives you bonkers.

But this "tape" was much more unsettling. I couldn't get the details, the neglect, the doctors or the legal maneuvering out of my mind.

Finally in March or April of 2002 I brought the problem to Linda's attention and once again, she truly came through for me. She told me of an experience of another patient with a similar problem and suggested I would have to find a word or phrase that would trigger a response which would move my thought pattern from the negativity of the "tape" to a positive thought process; I had to think of something good or productive in my life. I followed her advice and suddenly my healing — and what I believe to be a miraculous recovery — began. It was even better than the *"Do It!"* exercise.

That night after my session, when the "tape" began to play, I thought about what could I think of or say that would *erase the tape*. As often happens simple is the best way to go so I just said aloud, "Get out of here," when the tape began to play. Then I said, "I'm going to take a walk around the lake." As I did this, I mentally began to visualize myself taking my walk around the lake, looking at each house on my way as I did in reality. This was my lazy, *easy way to exercise*, visualize it. Three times on the first night I had to say, "Get out of here."… then I would begin the walk again. On the second and third night I said it only once each night and began my walk. The tape has not played since, and I have found that now whenever my mind wanders into negativity, if I think, "Get out of here." my mind will quickly go to something positive. Friday of that week I left Linda a BIG thank you message on her answering machine. I couldn't believe what a relief it was.

Strangely enough this was a reality that Archie had given me months earlier when he told me the story about, "Changing your perception can change your life." Linda's guidance helped me to turn most of my negative thought patterns into a positive. Changing my perception is surely changing my life.

On the Sunday a few weeks later when I was visiting my friends Rob and Kelly and she asked me about why the therapy helped and not my angels, I wasn't able to come up with a good answer. I fully believed in my angel communications and I knew they had been beneficial in my life and were guiding me on the path God wants for me; but I couldn't find a simple way to explain it to Kelly. Two days later I discussed my visit with Rob and Kelly with Linda in my therapy session and still couldn't quite figure it out.

Because I wanted those close to me to at least believe my experiences were not some form of hallucinations and understand what I have been going through, I went to bed with a troubled mind. Everyone is entitled to his or her own belief and I don't really expect everyone to believe exactly as I do. For one to totally believe the truth of what I have gone through, they would have to experience it in the same way for themselves.

I know that if **I** had heard my story, prior to Claricé's first communication with me, I would have been quite skeptical. Throughout my life I had that attitude about all things spiritual or metaphysical.

The "tape" has not played again, but it troubled me that I couldn't express in a simple way or explain why I suddenly began feeling better and enjoying life again. I was a happy soul once more but even though I knew it was connected to the angels and my therapy with Linda, I could not really say how it had come about so suddenly.

The next morning clarity came through loud and clear. As often happens when my mind is troubled, Archie woke me. It was at about 8:30 am Wednesday of the same week. He was with me until about 10:00 am before I finally got up and had coffee and a bowl of cereal for breakfast. Afterward I still wasn't clear about his answers and felt a need for more information, so at 11:00 am I began meditating off and on as information kept coming through. At about 2:00 pm I thought I had enough and ended the meditations.

Although this communication originally came in fragments over three or four sessions, this is what Archie said when I went to the computer about an hour later. I mentally asked him to go over it again, and I began to take his dictation. As always it flowed through my mind and out my fingertips.

"Good afternoon, Victor. Thanks for asking for me. I'll try to simplify things for you a little further. In your discussion with your good friends Rob and Kelly on Sunday and with Linda yesterday, it appears you need clarity in how your angel guides really work in your life.

"Your breakthrough to learn of your ability to have spiritual communications came with your visit from Claricé the first time you were considering taking your own life, and before it was your time in the plan God has set for you. As I have told you before, I have been with you for life and so has Jules.

"I'll try to explain it to you a little differently this time. As God does for all souls, we were both assigned

to your soul's energy force or aura just prior to your birth. The essence of it is that we are and always have been a part of your soul energy or spiritual self. We are a part of your being, existing with your soul energy within the physical vehicle that your mother named Victor. My direct role has always been as your dominant angel guide and is that of assisting and guiding all of your thought processes or processing within the higher self of your mind. Jules is your mentoring angel, the <u>word</u> he chose for your understanding of his role in human terminology, that is in guiding and assisting your higher self in written and verbal expression of the total available knowledge within from God and that which is there for you to use as you choose. As stated many times, we guide you and assist with your verbal or silent requests, but we do not come with your awareness until you ask for us and mentally listen for our response. It is no different from your prayers asked specifically of God. He too does not come into your awareness until you pray and listen for his answer."

I interrupted him. "If this is so, Archie, why are you the one with me when we communicate or when I am at the computer auto-writing?"

"It's more complex than you realize. However, simply put, it is in working with and developing your thought processes. I locate and translate the vibrational frequencies of God's word into thought patterns within your higher self and as well bring you the walk-in angels as you need them or request them to guide you through your daily activities in your walk through life on the earthly plane. Jules takes these processed thought patterns and turns them into words of human understanding.

"As I know you have realized, from the beginning when Claricé first came through to you, there are occurrences, or things, to use your terminology within the spiritual realm in which there are no words of human understanding to explain them. Jules does the best he can with what I and other angels bring to him and in a way that you will understand them and be

able to express them. The <u>voice</u>, if I can use that word without confusing you and which you acknowledge by name, can be that of any of your angels based upon the guidance requested or given. You are with me most often because I am your dominant angel guide and give you the most guidance in your every day experience of living in your physical vehicle.

"Once again, in your physical vehicles, different souls come to believe through different means in a way that works for each of them. Some get words as you have come to accept as your truth, others may get symbols, which they can translate and still others, images or what they believe they hear. In the beginning for you it was hearing and seeing until the realization came about you that there was no sound and the words just entered into your mind. Eventually you reached a point of knowing; this is where you were finally able to reach the greatest level of your higher self, also known as your super consciousness. In human terminology as mentioned to you previously, it is called 'claircognizant,' an all-knowing state of mind that is there for you when you accept it, want it and let it be so.

"Shortly after your first Holidays without Claricé, you were at a crisis in determining what to do without your wife in your life. This thinking was of the 'I want' of your conscious mind and was coming from that of your ego and what you now understand to be of your lower self.

"Due to the active, busy and satisfying life you have had, the ego of your lower self and conscious mind was saying to you, 'What's the use? I have enjoyed my life and I am tired. I would rather be with Claricé than continue on without her. I probably only have a few years left anyway.' These and other negative thoughts were permeating your mind to the point of being self-destructive.

"As a part of your higher self and higher consciousness and what is sometimes called the 'super conscious state of mind,' I became concerned over where it was leading and I called upon Miriam, your

walk-in angel of miracles and ML your angel of relationships to assist us in keeping you on God's plan for your life. When you called out in the night to speak to Claricé, 'just one more time,' Miriam was able to open the door to your belief in your higher self just a crack. She then was able to bring Claricé through to you. As Claricé told you that night it was your sixth sense that you were using. After her second visit, when you needed validation for understanding the experience and changing your belief system, she began to bring each of the other four spiritual visitors that came through to you. She brought them in ways and with words that would give you a true belief in your experience and the manner in which it was happening to you. She knew that it would help to heal your grief and to develop a relationship with God in you and for you. She ended the spiritual visits when she was certain you truly believed in that which had been brought through to you.

"A couple of months later when our chattering voices in the night troubled you and began depriving you of sleep, you cried out again in the night. Because you had read the books on angels and had some understanding of them, or us, I believed then that you were ready to listen. You learned from the books you read that what you were hearing might be angels, and you asked aloud if the voices you were hearing really could be the voices of angels. When I heard this repeated nightly, I decided to come through to you in a way that you would acknowledge our truth as the angels in your life.

"As difficult as it was for you to believe in the spiritual visits, I waited until I believed that you were truly ready to go beyond the earlier experiences you had been encountering.

"I knew then that you had developed a sense of understanding that your higher self had made the spiritual visits possible. It was then time to show you that there are two guiding forces within the energy field of your soul, as has been earlier noted: your higher self and your lower self. Now you need to

understand more clearly that the ego is of the lower self, and that it too has two forces within that the soul and you Victor, your physical vehicle, the body answering to your name, must reckon with it as well.

"More specifically they are the forces of good and evil, which became your gift from God when the freedom of choice was given to all His creations of the human species. You've had somewhat of an understanding of this but you need more.

"When communicating with others about your experiences and in your writing, you have suggested that you thought the ego influences, in a souls life were about 50-50, in terms of good and bad intentions. You were almost right with the exception that the percentages you applied vary as the pendulum of life swings back and forth. The ratio is variable: it could be 60-40... 30-70 or anywhere in between. The percentage arc can change from <u>near</u> 100 percent good to <u>almost</u> zero percent bad for those who truly have accepted God, or Christ as their savior and live their lives accordingly... to the extreme opposite for those who are termed atheists with a disbelief in God and Christ's words or purpose and those of whom evil deeds permeate their lives. The latter group are those with predominantly evil intentions who feed off their greed and quest for power, like dictators who seize control through barbaric means. I used the words 'near' and 'almost' because perfection could never be achieved in one's life on Earth, and even with those driven by evil intentions, there is some good to be found.

"Other negative factors of the ego are those mentioned to you several times earlier... hatred, greed, jealousy, fear, avarice, envy, etc., on and on; any negative thought is of the ego – lower self. When souls are lost within the forces of the ego's negativity with little or no good resulting, you have the evil doers of your world society. Those who kill, rob, steal, rape, cheat and take advantage of those who are weak.

"On a personal individual basis, for those who become confused over their individual purpose and/or

identity due to the circumstances of their life, often there is an internal fight within the lower self of the mind and it thereby shows itself as an illness or mental illness. This is when one gives total control over to ego and sometimes happens even when they may seem to be functioning normally in your world, as what is called a functioning alcoholic or other addictive behaviors. Although they know right from wrong, they are not always able to control, who or what they are or what they are doing; they are obsessively compulsive in their behavior patterns. When one lets the LOUD voice of the ego's negativity take control, the pendulum of their ego-self can swing widely and erratically beyond their self-control and thereby the lower self will block most of the good available to them from spirit and the higher self within. Sometimes this negativity has the label of psychosis in your human understanding and when multiple moods or faces are shown it is sometimes labeled as being schizophrenic or perhaps delusional.

"If you will recall, in one of your early sessions with Linda, because of your speaking with or communicating with spiritual beings and so many angels, you asked her if she thought that you might be delusional. You didn't think so yourself and she agreed with you. This is because there is nothing of a negative nature in what you have experienced. Actually, through your higher self, the 'real you' is more in control of your life than you have been throughout your many years occupying the physical being of your existence. Your experiences may be unusual by most standards known to your fellow humankind souls, but it is not unheard of. Are your communications with the angels any different than say, 'a man of the cloth,' using a theological metaphor? No, of course not. A man of the cloth might prepare a Sunday sermon for his parishioners and pray to God for guidance. The next day he may say I asked God for 'this or that' guidance and then he says, 'God <u>said</u> this to me.' Was the man of the cloth delusional? No. His experience was the same as yours. Others throughout

the Christian Bible it is written have spoken with angels. Were they delusional? No. Victor, you are an ordinary man who has had an extraordinary experience. Do not let your ego worry yourself about it; we will be with you always."

"When you use the words 'speaking or talking to spiritual beings or angels,' because of your unique experience it is often misleading for you and misunderstood by others, but it is really your only word choices for human understanding. When Claricé and the others came through to you, you thought you were hearing their voices and you answered aloud until you realized it was all taking place within your mind. In human understanding for communications of your kind of experience the expression of speaking or talking is the only thing that makes sense to others. However, what actually takes place is happening in what is understood to be your super consciousness... or higher self. Our thoughts are placed there vibrationally, as I have repeatedly told you. In the higher self of your mind I then process the vibrations into thought patterns, and Jules then turns it into words for self expression based on your known English language and usage. In the case of spiritual visitations — or voices with mannerisms you will recognize for your belief and understanding — we use this process, as it is necessary to build and develop your belief in what you need to experience.

"Voice recognition is not true of your angels. As you found out when I came through to you, your angels or God do not have a recognizable voice and therefore your understanding comes from the vibrational messages converted to cognitive word recognition or acknowledgement when they appear in your mind rather than sound. When some souls refer to 'hearing the voice of God,' as with a man of the cloth, in reality they are only receiving and mentally processing the messages or words that silently enter their higher self minds cognitively, which is a sense of knowing. Some beings, for their individual belief they need to hear a voice and, when necessary, we can make this so as we

did with you when Claricé first came through to you. It was the spiritual energy of Claricé's soul, but we knew you would need to hear her voice in order for you to believe.

*"Victor, you still were not sure how all of what you were experiencing fit together in your life. So I will throw a new word out to you. You have heard it before, but not from me, and I don't think you understand how it works. The word is **alter ego,** as I understand the word is used in your human terminology and understanding.*

"There are times in a soul's life when the emotional pain they are suffering in their physical body/vehicle is far too much for them to bear in their conscious lower self reality or awareness. Victor, you were in pain. This was where your personal ego - lower self and emotions had fallen to in the months following Claricé's transition to the spiritual realm, known as Heaven to most mortal beings. Bringing Claricé and the others through to you began to put you on a recovery path where you also looked for understanding in your reading, research and writing, but it wasn't enough.

"It was at that point, a year and a few days following her leaving you that I had to create for you an acknowledgement of my presence in your life.

"Victor, I am of your alter ego and as it is with most souls, when their dominant angel guide does become apparent in their lives, it comes through what has been called the alter ego...in mankind's understanding. In that sense, any angel present in your consciousness or that you request are of your 'other self' commonly understood as your alter ego, and while with you resides in the higher self – super consciousness of your mind, where the spirit of the God within also resides. Myself and Jules are always with you... and we are your direct conduit to God and self-understanding and realization. This is true with all souls, but I don't want you to get into a debate with another's belief system. Each soul or being has the God-given right to believe as they choose to believe,

and it is not your place in life to convince them one way or another. All beings learn only from the direct experience of their own experience in whatever they choose to learn or way and manner in which it happens for them. This is true of all learning processes and is the purpose of being, for all souls of mankind.

"The only question is in the understanding and/or the acknowledgement of what is. And, what is for most souls... is the lack of awareness that two of God's messenger angels are always with you and others, which are available to you as needs or requests arise. The acknowledgement of your God, a God, a Supreme Being, The Creator, Allah or what ever name or description happens to suit their particular societal structure is accepted throughout most of your world, even though there are many different theological belief systems. Are there 'false' theological belief systems in your world? Of course, like the power mongers that try to control a country or a segment of their particular society. There are also demigods who control different theological cultures espousing belief systems, which are opposed God's plan and what He wants for the earthly world He has created.

"Those who are not consciously aware of the assigned angels or of the walk-in angels' functions in their lives, pray to their God and they receive His answers; but the essence of it is, is that the process doesn't matter. It is the same process and the prayers all go to the same place: even if it is to a Saint, to an Archangel or to the Virgin Mary. Having a belief in a giving and loving God, Who is the Supreme Power of the universe is what is important. 'Ask and you shall receive,' says the Lord. That is the truth. If it is God's will and when it is within His plan for a soul's life all prayers will be answered.

"Your friend Kelly said to you, 'If the angels are present and active in your life, why did you have to go into therapy? Why couldn't the angels take care of your healing?'

"The simple answer is, the EGO HAS A VERY LOUD AND CONTROLLING VOICE, as it does for those who do have an addictive illness or mental illness as noted above. You had been communicating with me and with your other angels for just over a year and you had become less depressed and were making progress. Then in September the 9/11 terrorist incident came about. Like many throughout your country and your world, the massive death and destruction was upsetting and depressing. That event filled most minds with anger and the want for revenge. The last words are why you had to seek out Linda, your therapist. Your own deep-seated want for revenge resurfaced. Remember what you learned earlier, the 'I want' state of mind is always of the ego, as is negativity.

"Your, Victor's, EGO - lower self was still crying out with anger and want for revenge over the many doctors who had cared for your wife. No matter how much I explained to you how and why it was her time to return to your Heavenly Father, your EGO self was not able to process the idea or let go its anger and desire for revenge. In your higher self, consciousness, you could intellectually accept and understand it, but your ego consciousness could not process it emotionally. Why? Because you were still carrying deep seated guilt over all of the 'what ifs?' regarding your lives together and your wife's health care. Your ego driven fear of the 'what ifs,' and possible guilt over the 'what could have been or might have been' regarding her health and your personal relationship was preventing the completion of your healing. Then a couple of weeks following the 9/11 incident came the call from your lawyer's office notifying you of the need for you to come in for a sworn statement. You were going to have to give the details of what you believed to be neglect in your wife's care during her illness that you determined was the cause of her death.

"When you began to relive each and every moment, and your own personal anger and revenge and guilt related to Claricé's passing, compounded

with the depression, anger and desired revenge of the 9/11 incident you hit bottom again and this time it was much more severe.

"With the assistance of Ali, your angel of good health, you were guided to seek the help which led you to your therapist Linda. With Linda's help you were then able to bring forth some of the normal (if there is a normal) problems that appeared in your relationship with Claricé. As it is, between any two people most problems result from misunderstood communications and lead to the negativity that comes about. You were burying those thoughts with the 'what ifs' without realizing that there could be a positive purpose resulting from whatever problems you may have had in your lives.

"All things do happen for a reason. With Linda's guidance, and with my words that expressed that it was Claricé's time and there was nothing the doctors could have done which would have changed God's plan for her life, you were able to put together a better understanding of your relationship.

"The example which led to your final healing was the disagreement the two of you had just before her illness was determined that led to her reading Conversations with God – Book One and then to buy it for you. When discussing that particular situation with Linda, a cloud and heavy burden lifted and freed you of your guilt: the 'what ifs,' as well as your anger and desire for revenge began to dissipate. You realized then that Claricé buying you that particular book was the first synchronicity in the series of synchronicities that led you to be on the spiritual path with the purpose in life that you have today.

"There was nothing you could have done to change the outcome, and you now see that some of what you thought may have been problems in your lives were really a necessary part of both of your lives for each of you and for you to become the person you are today. This reality and awareness that all things good or bad have a positive purpose has brought peace back into your life and with it joy and happiness once again.

With the angel's guidance you have been shown your future purpose in life and through it you have rediscovered your passion for the written word. As time goes on you will better understand the visual image we have shown you of how God, His angel messengers, walk-in angels, guardian angels and souls reside and work within the environment He created. Ultimately it will clarify the oneness of God and that God is love and that someday peace, love, abundance and harmony will prevail in all of His universes.

"Victor, to have a communication directed toward another or a two-way dialogue for creating an understanding of what is, it is also necessary to have a name for who you are talking to or what you are talking about, be it any person, place or thing. In mankind's way of life or communicating with God or his angels on a spiritual level semantics, as has been mentioned many times earlier is mankind's way and method of communication among and between one another. That is why human beings have names and it is the same with angels or in fact, God. Names are no more than labels for understanding of what is. In all souls the alter ego is <u>of</u> divine purpose and <u>of</u> the higher self. This is where all intelligence of the universe is available to you and this is where the spirit of God resides in your being. Just because angels come through what is called your alter ego, does not imply you are talking to your self or your 'other self;' it is a means for understanding what is being experienced. It is more like your alter ego is the conduit through which to reach God or your angels, as your angels are your direct conduits to reach out to the spiritual realm. Often there are times when souls are in a religious or theological atmosphere in which when talking to God they will take on a different persona...as in their 'other self.'

"The alter ego, can also be defined as your conscience, because it comes forth from your higher self when the evil force of your Ego – lower self is trying to push you off of God's path for your life.

"When Claricé first came through to you, she told you that you were using 'your sixth sense.' This is a truth and all souls have the capability of reaching into and using their sixth sense for understanding and communicating with God or their angels for guiding their being. Unfortunately, most souls within their physical body/vehicles do not have an understanding of this capability that has now come to you. Although it is available to all who believe, have faith and will listen for the words that come from God and through His angel messengers, most do not realize it is directly available to them. Awareness often only comes about in the face of a tragic circumstance, desperation or the pain and grief that comes with the losing of a loved one, as it did with the loss of your beloved Claricé.

"Victor, as you continue to write the words of the angels, your belief will grow and strengthen to give you more and more clarity in your purpose for being. Stay with us and we will stay with you, always and ever you will be of God.

Epilogue
Final Thoughts and Clarification

Upon completion of the manuscript for this book, I had a half-dozen copies printed and eagerly put them out to close friends, relatives and new acquaintances that have fast become dear friends. I selected a cross section of friends with different religious, professional and personal backgrounds so that I would get diverse and objective feedback. To date, there have been ten readers and the overall response has been quite positive and satisfying to myself after two-years of working on the story. In addition to the readers, I have also been talking about the story with others and explaining some of the content that has given me a new understanding and that which has brought about my newfound close relationship with God that had previously been lacking in my life prior to the overall experience that began on 5 January 2000.

Because some negativity has come about due to the content that is inconsistent with current translations of the Christian Bible from devout Christians, I would like to repeat the open "disclaimer" and add a few words to further explain my personal view. The disclaimer reads as follows:

This manuscript shows examples of spiritual and angel communications between myself, Victor the writer with my late-wife Claricé and others, Archie my dominant angel guide, Jules my mentoring angel and other walk-in angels. These experiences began happening for me on the night of 5 January 2000. Much of the content is "auto writing" which just flows in and out of my mind and will be of a somewhat personal nature. It was presented in a dialogue format and shows examples of what it can be for a reader's communication with his or her own angels.

The communications take place in the "higher self" of my mind and I believe the process is available to all who acknowledge our God, as a supreme being. It is only necessary for you to ask for them, have faith, believe and listen.

In all cases, the content is strictly of my mind and/or resulting from my communications of a spiritual nature and not intended to portray a "universal truth" regarding any of the subjects discussed. As to the truth, it is mine, and my truth alone. It is being presented so that you, the reader may be able to relate to your own personal experiences and belief system and thereby discover your own truth.

To this, and at Archie's direction, I would like to add that myself, and the angels truly honor every persons religious and/or theological belief system, and their right to believe as they choose. If your belief and spirituality brings you peace, joy, happiness and harmony in your life, that is exactly what God, our Supreme Being wants for each of his children. As I have found, when the Spirit that lives within each of us, gives you this peace it is a beautiful experience.

As there are many millions throughout the world who have found this peace through their individual belief in their religion of choice, there are many more millions who continue to search for the elusive "something" that is missing from their lives. There are many millions also who have attempted to find their peace in a variety of the hundreds of different theological options available to them in Christianity as well as Judaism, Mohammedanism, Hinduism, Buddhism and a host of other choices. All religions have their devout believers as well as those looking for the missing, elusive "something" in their lives.

God, the Supreme Being and the Holy Spirit that lives within our hearts spoke to mankind in the early days of the world, in Christ's time and He is speaking today to all of His children who have faith and will listen to His "Word."

There are and have been many of what has often been termed "New Thought" and/or "New Age" authors who have been publishing what they have been hearing from the Spirit within or have been guided to write by God or His angel messengers today and over the past 50-years of the second millennium. We could go back through earlier years and create an anthology of past writers and thinkers who have published their own words, and perhaps guided words that at the time they were written were met with as much doubt and skepticism as have been today's writers.

I wrote the word "skepticism" in the last sentence intentionally to remind the reader of the skeptic I had been throughout my life until this experience began. I tell you now, that I have written this manuscript from a position of great humility and a "why me?" attitude. I am just an ordinary guy from "Motown" and still in awe of every word that comes through my fingertips.

In my brief hiatus from taking dictation from Archie and his angelic friends due to a brief health problem, he came to me often, eagerly putting words into my head. I had a mild heart attack about the time I began to finalize the editing process. Interestingly enough, my symptoms were so mild, in the past I would have ignored them and went on about my day. However, as I mentally questioned whether or not I should do anything about it, Ali, my angel of good health came through to me and said for me to call my doctor. Due to my cardiac history, my doctor sent me to the emergency room. Strangely, I was at peace throughout the testing without a worry on my mind. God was with me and I clearly remembered that Claricé had told me I had 20 more years to live and both she and Ali had told me I have much spiritual work to do. Although there was a minor problem, I was told it was a warning and with a change of medications and getting back on a regular exercise program, I would be fine. My only concern was when I thought, "This can't be serious. I have to live the balance of my 20-years to prove that Claricé was right." At that thought, I clearly heard her words once more. In her style of speaking, she said, *"Hi baby. I'm happy you are listening to your body as I taught you to do. It's better to be safe than sorry, isn't it?"*... And she was gone again.

After all the testing, I was released from the hospital 48 hours following my admission to the E.R. Throughout, I was happy, joyful and playfully chatted with my nurses and roommates. Fear of death never entered my mind as it had on other occasions since the beginning of my heart problems in the early 1980's. My peace and joy stayed with me as I returned home to rest for a week and then continue my normal routine. As in the title of Chapter 24, "Healing and a Return To Joy" the week following my release, everyone commented that I was still like the new person I'd become a few months earlier and I was like my "old self.". The person they saw was of the joy and bliss that resulted from my relationship with God and the transformation that had come about over the past couple of years.

Going back to personal belief systems, I'm now asking Archie to elaborate on what he has been bringing me in the last two weeks regarding some of the feedback I've received from readers of the manuscript.

- - - - -

"Good afternoon Victor. I've been waiting for you to ask what I think. First I want to go back to what you have just said about the 'New Thought' and 'New Age' writers and some of the negativity they receive and as you now know, that which you have received and will continue to receive. I might be a little repetitive here because I have said it before. One of the biggest

problems writers have faced since time began is doubt whenever they write something 'new', as you stated in new thought and new age. This is especially true if it is inconsistent with that which is in their spiritual references or what they have been taught is the word of God. It really doesn't matter if it is the Christian Bible or any other theological reference book. That is why you should not be troubled by negativity and let the doubts flow in one ear and out the other. In the human condition, if a person has not had an identical experience, they will doubt yours. The majority of humankind does not listen to the voice of the Holy Spirit within, angels or spiritual entities. They don't believe they are capable.

"You are probably a good example to relate to. You have questioned why it is that God is the one who talks to Neale Donald Walsch, the author of the <u>'Conversations With God'</u> series of books that put you on your spiritual path and which is different from your experience. The truth for you is that God has been trying to get through to you for many years as he has most others, but you didn't listen any better than the rest of the skeptics in the world.

"It was only after Claricé made her transition to the spiritual realm and you became so depressed that we had to find a way to get through to you. We did, and as I have heard you say many times, 'If God wanted to get your attention and bring you into his service, He certainly found the right way to do it by bringing Claricé through to you after her death.'

"I have said in earlier chapters, when it is truly necessary for God to get your attention, He creates a means for it to happen, a means, which will be acceptable and believable. Most humans, mainly those with devout religious belief systems, when their prayers or spiritual questions are answered, attribute the words or voices in their heads to God. This is fine, regardless if it is their angels or the Holy Spirit because it is coming from the same source. Where many miss out however is in not listening to the guidance for their walk through life that can be

*brought to them by their angel guides or guardian angels. Instead, they often go astray. They are instead led by the **louder voice**, the 'I want' of the ego, and the evil intentions, which also can come through.*

"Each individual must become his or her own understanding relative to their personal belief system. It is with great hope that in whatever theological manner they are accepting God in their lives it will lead them to the peace, love, joy, harmony and happiness He wants for all of His children. True acceptance of God and 'what is' in their lives brings freedom from your worldly fears, worry, pain and doubt. 'What is,' is your personal belief that brings you to God and what he desires for each of you.

"One of the controversies that has lingered since the time of Christ and probably will continue for another two thousand years or more is the debate over reincarnation. This you have found out since writing Chapter 7, about 'A Spiritual Communications With Sally' and Chapter 16, 'Reincarnation vs. Only Living Once.' This is where most of the negativity in your manuscript has come about. Other terminology for reincarnation would be rebirth, born again, metempsychosis, palingenesis, transmigration, and re-embodiment. Although some have distinctive meanings, the terms can be used interchangeably. I point this out just to add to the confusion of semantics and lexicon of words. As stated previously reincarnation is only a word, as are the others, created by mankind to label an unexplainable phenomenon.

"Again, the difficulty comes about because of semantics and the total lack of provability beyond doubt. The truth for or gainst an afterlife all of mankind will only come about when each makes their individual transition to the spiritual realm that man has labeled Heaven.

"As it says in the Christian Bible, 'If you believe, all things are possible.' As well, simple logic would tell you, <u>because you breath</u>, anything is possible. The controversy over reincarnation did not begin with

Christ or the Bible. In your own research you found that it began as early as 510 B.C. and perhaps earlier.

"Whatever way any person of the human species believes is fine and there should not be controversy or negativity attached. As stated above each individual must become his or her own authority relative to their personal belief system.

"In a brief survey you did among Christian family, friends and acquaintances, you found that about one-third disbelieve and two thirds believe in the probability of reincarnation. Again the truth is, in your individual lives it doesn't matter until you have made your transition. To question the 'word' in the Bible would be pointless because whoever reads the words makes up their mind based upon their own interpretation and belief system or what they may have learned through their religion or theology.

"Where some like yourself Victor have a strong desire to have another incarnation due to your satisfaction with your present life and wanting to have another career, family and everything that comes with it, others feel differently. Many perhaps have not had quite as positive of outlook on their present life experience and others want the peace, love and beauty described in Biblical terminology. Many accept the view of their eternal life as blessed spirits meandering through heaven in a beautiful, flower-filled meadow. They believe they will live an infinite existence walking happily, hand in hand with loved ones past with nowhere to go and nothing to do. Be it tomorrow, a hundred earth years or thousands of thousands of earth years they will be in a place of peace and beauty until what the Bible calls judgment day arrives.

"In closing, it is your 'choice' and each of God's children's choice to believe as they choose. God wants, the angels want, and your spiritual loved ones want <u>what you want</u> – peace, joy, happiness, love and abundance in your lives.

# # #

Reincarnation (An East West Anthology) – Head & Cranston – Aeon Books
Sai Baba, Man of Miracles –Howard Murphet – Samuel Weiser, Inc
Signals (Life After Life) – Joel Rothschild – New World Library
Still Here (Embracing Aging, Changing and Dying.)
 – Ram Dass – Riverhead Books
The Angels Within Us – John Randolph Price – Fawcett Columbine
The Divine Purpose in Us – F. Henry Edwards – Herald Publishing House
The Lightworker's Way – Doreen Virtue, PhD – Hay House, Inc
The Purpose of Life –Sadguru Sant Keshavadas – Vantage Press
The Seat Of The Soul – Gary Zukav – A Fireside Book
The Second Coming of Lucas Brokaw - Matthew Braun – Dell/Bernard Gets
The Wisdom of Letting Go (The Path of the Wounded Soul.)
 – Father Leo Booth – SCP, Ltd.
The World's Religions – Huston Smith - HarperSanFrancisco
Through Time Into Healing – Brian L. Weiss, MD – A Fireside Book
Unlock Your Psychic Powers – Dr. Richard Lawrence – St Martin's Paperbacks
We Don't Die (George Anderson's Conversations With The Other Side)
 – Joel Martin & Patricia Romanowski – Berkley Books
Where Is God When It Hurts? –Philip Yancey - Zondervan
You Will Survive After Death – Sherwood Eddy – Clark Publishing
Your Sacred Self (Making the Decision to be Free.)
 – Dr. Wayne Dyer – Harper Paperbacks
Your Sixth Sense – Belleruth Naparstek – HarperSanFrancisco

About the Author

Victor, an ordinary guy from "Motown" had a career in advertising as a Creative Director and Copy Writer. In the late-seventies he began writing fictional supernatural and reincarnation stories. Research taught him hypnotism and doing past life regressions and brought forth unexplainable responses and gave him a curious new outlook. When his business blossomed, the writing and the manuscripts had to be pushed aside.

A skeptic about most things spiritual, his attitude changed on January 5th 2000. His wife, Claricé, who died the previous August, began to spiritually communicate with him... not once, but five times... then others... and then the angels!

Retired, Victor began writing again... about the experiences he'd been having. Soon, he realized he was auto-writing dictations from the "other side," and his life took a 180-degree turn. The experiences gave him a new understanding of the spiritual realm and a "relationship" with God, the creator of all.

Made in the USA
Lexington, KY
16 March 2011